Praise for Rhonda B. Saunders and *Whisper of Fear*

"No one knows stalkers better than prosecutor Rhonda Saunders. She and Stephen Michaud have given us a fascinating and authoritative inside look at the legal and psychological aspects of this frightening phenomenon."
—*New York Times* bestselling author Vincent Bugliosi

"Prosecutor Saunders is an authority on her subject . . . She engrossingly explores the menacing crime of stalking as she relates the story of her more than two decades of work in the courtroom . . . Readers will be intrigued and sobered by this illuminating guide." —*Publishers Weekly*

"Rhonda Saunders changed the law on criminal stalking, and we can all sleep better knowing it."
—Roy Hazelwood, retired FBI profiler and coauthor of *The Evil That Men Do*

"Rhonda Saunders is without question one of the leading figures in the fight against targeted violence . . . No one who is serious about preventing targeted violence should miss what she has to say."
—Charles Friend, special agent in charge, Office of Protective Research, U.S. Secret Service (Ret.)

"Unsettling, thought-provoking . . . The special talents of Saunders and Michaud have resulted in a fascinating and illuminating look into the dark terrors of stalking."
—Carlton Stowers, two-time Edgar® Award winner for Best Fact Crime book

"Rhonda Saunders is known by both law enforcement and the private security sector as the go-to person in the field of stalking. *Whisper of Fear* provides valuable insight into the often misunderstood and underestimated crime of stalking. Anyone working in the field of stalking prevention or who is touched by the crime of stalking should read this book."
—John Stilo, director, corporate security, NBC-Universal

D0423905

WHISPER OF FEAR

THE TRUE STORY OF
THE PROSECUTOR WHO
STALKS THE STALKERS

Rhonda B. Saunders
and Stephen G. Michaud

BERKLEY BOOKS, NEW YORK

THE BERKLEY PUBLISHING GROUP
Published by the Penguin Group
Penguin Group (USA) Inc.
375 Hudson Street, New York, New York 10014, USA
Penguin Group (Canada), 90 Eglinton Avenue East, Suite 700, Toronto, Ontario M4P 2Y3, Canada
(a division of Pearson Penguin Canada Inc.)
Penguin Books Ltd., 80 Strand, London WC2R 0RL, England
Penguin Group Ireland, 25 St. Stephen's Green, Dublin 2, Ireland (a division of Penguin Books Ltd.)
Penguin Group (Australia), 250 Camberwell Road, Camberwell, Victoria 3124, Australia
(a division of Pearson Australia Group Pty. Ltd.)
Penguin Books India Pvt. Ltd., 11 Community Centre, Panchsheel Park, New Delhi—110 017, India
Penguin Group (NZ), 67 Apollo Drive, Rosedale, North Shore 0632, New Zealand
(a division of Pearson New Zealand Ltd.)
Penguin Books (South Africa) (Pty.) Ltd., 24 Sturdee Avenue, Rosebank, Johannesburg 2196,
South Africa

Penguin Books Ltd., Registered Offices: 80 Strand, London WC2R 0RL, England

PUBLISHER'S NOTE: The content of this book does not reflect the opinions of the Los Angeles
County District Attorney's Office, or of any other law enforcement agency. The book is not intended
to provide legal advice. If you believe you are being stalked, you should contact your local law
enforcement agency immediately.

While the authors have made every effort to provide accurate telephone numbers and Internet
addresses at the time of publication, neither the publisher nor the authors assume any responsibility
for errors or changes that occur after publication. Further, the publisher does not have any control
over and does not assume any responsibility for author or third-party websites or their content.

WHISPER OF FEAR

A Berkley Book / published by arrangement with the authors

PRINTING HISTORY
Berkley hardcover edition / November 2008
Berkley mass-market edition / October 2009

Copyright © 2008 by Rhonda B. Saunders and Stephen G. Michaud.
The Edgar® name is a registered service mark of Mystery Writers of America, Inc.
Cover design by Judith Lagerman.
Cover photograph © Arcangel / Punchstock.
Interior text design by Tiffany Estreicher.

ISBN: 978-0-425-23110-4

BERKLEY®
Berkley Books are published by The Berkley Publishing Group,
a division of Penguin Group (USA) Inc.,
375 Hudson Street, New York, New York 10014.
BERKLEY® is a registered trademark of Penguin Group (USA) Inc.
The "B" design is a trademark of Penguin Group (USA) Inc.

PRINTED IN THE UNITED STATES OF AMERICA

10 9 8 7 6 5 4 3 2 1

···
Penguin is committed to publishing works of quality and integrity.
In that spirit, we are proud to offer this book to our readers;
however, the story, the experiences, and the words
are the authors' alone.

In Memoriam
Marie McGowan Poynton

ACKNOWLEDGMENTS

I would like to thank the following people, who have helped give birth to this book:

Theresia, Elisabeth, and Marianne Martin, for their encouragement and organizational skills in keeping an archive on my life and career since 1997;

My agent, Elizabeth Kaplan, for her belief in the value of this project;

My editor, Shannon Jamieson Vazquez, for her patience and many extraordinary ideas and contributions;

Marie Johnson, my friend and assistant, whose hard work and amazing research skills have helped put the pieces of this book together; and finally,

My family, for giving me the strength, through their love and encouragement, to overcome all obstacles.

—Rhonda

FOREWORD

Three months after Mark David Chapman shot and killed John Lennon, he told a psychologist, "I always knew in the future that this was going to happen...I always knew the whole world would know who I was. I always felt different and felt special and felt odd and peculiar." This is the mentality of the violent public-figure stalker, clearly articulated by a disturbed, socially adrift, personality-disordered young man whose solitary act of murder jolted a generation.

Stalking is a crime composed of three elements: an unwanted pursuit, a threat, and a fearful victim. It has been in the public consciousness for barely twenty years—although there are references to it that date back centuries—making its way into the penal code of California in 1990 following two high-profile celebrity attacks and several killings of women by disgruntled ex-lovers in Orange County, California. Deputy District Attorney Rhonda Saunders stepped into this vortex almost right from the beginning, and made her mark. She played an instrumental role in shaping the evolving criminal law of stalking, and at the same time successfully prosecuted some of the most notorious celebrity stalking cases of our time: those against the stalkers of Madonna, Steven Spielberg, and Gwyneth Paltrow. There are now stalking laws throughout the United States, Canada, Australia, New Zealand, Britain, and many European countries, many of them modeled after California's statute.

I have known Rhonda for more than a decade, and have had the pleasure of working with her as a forensic psychologist on several of these cases. Not only did she impress me as a hard-boiled LA prosecutor, but she also curiously understood something that prosecutors often dismiss: Many of those who stalk are not only dangerous but severely mentally ill. They live in the often murky netherworld of the mad *and* the bad, in need of both incarceration and mental health care. In my experience, this is a very unusual stance for a prosecutor to embrace, one quality that has made Rhonda Saunders both an extraordinary person and a formidable prosecutor. I hope she will forgive me for writing this, but it probably has to do with her artistic side—most artists appreciate that everyone has an internal life and a story to tell, even criminals.

What do we know about those who stalk? The state of the science tells us that stalkers typically fall into four groups: those who pursue prior sexual intimates, acquaintances, public figures, and private strangers. We refer to this as a *typology*, and call it RECON, an acronym for two important parameters: the RElationship between the stalker and his object, and the CONtext in which the stalking occurs. Rhonda Saunders paints disturbing and colorful portraits of all four of these types, with a particular emphasis on ex-intimate and public-figure stalkers. Both of these groups have some distinctive characteristics.

The stalkers of ex-intimates make up the most malevolent and dangerous group. They also represent *half* of those who stalk. They are typically males who have been rejected by a wife or girlfriend, and furiously yearn for a reconnection. This seems like a bit of an oxymoron—how can someone be so angry and yet desperately seek to be with the one who has spurned them?—but that is exactly the point. These combined emotions escalate the prior intimate's danger. I have worked several cases in which such a stalker has killed his love object, and as he stands over her body, tells the police (or the 911 dispatcher) how much he loved her. Shakespeare, through the lips of Othello, put it well: "I will kill thee, and love thee after...this sorrow's heavenly; it strikes where it doth love." *More than 80 percent of men who kill their ex-spouses or girlfriends stalk them beforehand.*

These men typically have criminal histories, drug or alcohol abuse problems, and psychiatric disorders. What is unusual, however, is that most are not psychotic. In other words, they show none of the symptoms of someone who has lost contact with consensual reality, such as delusions (fixed and false beliefs) and hallucinations (false sensations, such as hearing voices that no one else hears). Yet they are exceedingly dangerous and persistent. The majority of these stalkers will assault their object of fixation sometime during the stalking, and will pursue for almost two years.

The public-figure stalkers are quite different. The public has a skewed perspective on these particular stalkers because the high-profile cases, such as John Hinckley, Mark Chapman, and Robert Bardo—young violent males who attacked with a handgun—are assumed to represent all such pursuers. They do not. Most public-figure stalkers are well into their fourth generation of life, and their fantasies of fame are supported by the hope that the celebrity figure will bring them romance, or at least goodwill.

Like the stalkers of prior sexual intimates, most are men, but the pursuers of the famous *are* often psychotic, and have severe mental disorders such as schizophrenia or bipolar disorder—what we used to call manic depression. While such individuals also abuse alcohol or street drugs, medications to treat their mental disorders are often necessary, and they do best when the heavy fist of the law is accompanied by the velvet glove of treatment. In one large study of Hollywood celebrity stalkers—Rhonda's bailiwick—we found that only 2 percent were violent, and none of the attacks resulted in serious injury. Such characters live on the margins of society, among "all the lonely people," in the Beatles' words, yet they are infected with a desire for fame, hoping to capture it in the reflected light of the famous.

There are also women who stalk. Little research has been

done to understand who these women are, but we do know some things. Unlike the male stalkers, women do not typically stalk a prior sexual intimate, but instead prefer to stalk male acquaintances, often slightly older ones. They are usually divorced or single women in their midthirties, and desperately pursue their object to establish a relationship with him. About one in four will be violent, not a significant departure from the average frequency of violence for all stalkers. Glenn Close actually got it right in her portrayal of the female stalker in the movie *Fatal Attraction*. Although the ending was a bit dramatic—most female stalkers do not come to life out of a bathtub—Ms. Close portrayed a disorder common to female stalkers called borderline personality, the "stably unstable" character.

But what motivates a stalker? Although the answer to this remains elusive, there seem to be seven necessary ingredients: loneliness, social isolation, poor social skills, pathological narcissism, obsessional thinking, attachment pathology, and aggression. The first three of these need little elaboration, but the narcissism, obsessions, attachment difficulties, and aggression deserve comment.

Stalkers are not genuinely confident, but have an inflated, often fantasy-based view of who they are to deny the failures and misfires of their own lives. We call this *pathological narcissism*. Unfortunately, the more severe this problem, the more other people's needs and desires are ignored. Stalkers also think *constantly* about the object of their pursuit. They write volumes. They telephone, fax, text, and e-mail. They physically chase. This is *obsession*.

Attachment is a bit trickier. We typically form a bond, or an attachment, to people who take care of us and like us. If our parents loved us when we were little, and did not abandon us, either emotionally or physically, we will seek such relationships when we grow up. This is healthy, secure attachment. Unfortunately, some are not so lucky, and such children are stuck with parents who neglect, abuse, abandon, or are just indifferent to them. Such *pathological attachments* become familiar to children and are paradoxically sought after when the child grows up. Seeking proximity to someone who doesn't want you around is, on the surface, quite bizarre. But this is the core of stalking. In one study, we found that the majority of imprisoned male stalkers had lost a primary caretaker as a child, and also had had a significant loss in the year preceding the onset of stalking.

Finally there is aggression. All the preceding ingredients would not create a stalker unless the individual had the boldness, tenacity, and *energy* to pursue in the face of often insurmountable odds. Stalking is a labor-intensive crime.

Rhonda Saunders takes us on a journey that is disturbing, perplexing, and often dark. But you are in the hands of a master prosecutor and, above all, a thoughtful human being. She is fully aware, as St. Augustine was, that the line between good and evil runs through the heart of everyone.

J. Reid Meloy, Ph.D.
Clinical Professor of Psychiatry
University of California, San Diego
President, Forensis, Inc.
www.forensis.org

ONE

THE TRANSFORMING CASE of my career landed randomly in my lap on the two-to-ten night court shift. It was 1992. I already had eight years of experience prosecuting rapists, thieves, murderers, drug dealers, and most every other type of felon. The Jane Smith* case, however, was something completely different. I remember looking at the file and thinking, *Oh-oh. This is stalking.*

Stalking is ancient behavior, but in 1992 it was a brand-new crime. Only two years before, California had enacted the world's first stalking law, which at the time had seemed far-sighted of the state legislature, and was politically popular. However, from a prosecutor's standpoint, the new statute was generally useless.

Then I met my first stalking victim.

Jane came to see me with Detective Doug Raymond, a member of the Los Angeles Police Department's newly formed Threat Management Unit (TMU), the first police unit anywhere dedicated exclusively to stalking investigations.

---

*Denotes pseudonym

She was a well-spoken, tall (although because I'm very short, *everyone* looks tall to me), attractive, tastefully dressed, professional woman in her forties, with blonde hair kept stylishly short. Smith was also an emotional train wreck; the term "human damage" came to mind as I gazed at her. Her fear and mistrust of everyone were palpable, and for good reason. Jane had sustained a horrendous psychic battering.

Slowly, hesitantly, she revealed to us the source of her terror— Susan Dyer, a cunning, resourceful, and highly dangerous woman. Susan's obsessions consumed her. In time, the sly and demented Ms. Dyer even came after me. My first stalking prosecution would easily be the strangest, longest, and scariest stalking case of my career.

The convoluted tale had begun in the early 1980s when Jane was working as a graphic artist at a trendy design firm owned by Susan's father. She met Susan just once, and spoke with her briefly, so when Smith later moved on to a new job, she was surprised to learn that Dyer had asked several people if they knew how to find Jane.

Seven or eight years later, in November of 1990, Jane and her boyfriend, Scott, were at a movie theater in Century City when they chanced upon Susan and her father. It was a dreadful time for the Dyers. Susan's eighteen-year-old sister, Teak, had recently been brutally beaten and murdered, one day before her high school graduation, by Darnell Garmanian, a security guard. The sensational crime was a front-page story.

Jane and Scott did not linger with the Dyers. They spoke briefly with Susan and her father, then moved on. Suddenly, and somewhat to Jane's surprise, Susan ran up behind them to ask Jane if they could get together at some point. Smith said, "Fine," and thought little more of it.

The next day Dyer called Smith's unlisted home number. Only later would Jane realize that she had not given Susan the number and wonder how she got it.

Susan was highly agitated. She said she thought she was suffering a nervous breakdown over her little sister's murder. She added that she felt comfortable with Smith and looked forward to the chance to talk together.

Although Smith hardly knew Dyer, she was sympathetic. They met in a city park near Susan's house, where Jane bought herself some lunch at a taco stand, then sat and chatted with Dyer on a bench. They got along well.

Sometime soon after this meeting, Dyer offered to drive Smith to the lumber store in her pickup truck. Jane needed to purchase some lath to build a latticework fence in her backyard. Smith enjoyed doing such projects around the house and yard. She owned a cozy 1924 Sears Craftsman house on South Harvard Boulevard in Los Angeles, with a pair of towering palms in front, near the curb, and Tropicana roses she had trained onto a trellis framing the front porch and door. After the trip to the store, Susan hung around to help with the fence-building.

"After we went into the house," Jane later testified, "I believe she said she was attracted to me and wanted to kiss me. And I said that made me very nervous and I was uncomfortable with that. But as well I was kind of intrigued by it, I must say."

Smith's history with men had been uneven and often painful. As an eight-year-old girl, her stepfather, Albert, had sexually abused her. She had recently begun group therapy, and was keeping a personal journal of reflections to try to come to grips with that memory. Jane had been married three times; one husband—the father of her only child, an adult daughter then living in northern California—had been violently abusive and had committed suicide in the middle of their divorce proceedings.

Dyer gave Smith a kiss as they sat on the couch, and they caressed each other. "It was kind of silly and giddy," Jane recalled on the witness stand. "It wasn't overt or scary or threatening."

Smith had had one brief and unfulfilling lesbian relationship in the past, but her attraction to Susan Dyer was different, more certain, in the beginning. Jane felt she could build an emotional bond with Susan. They saw more of each other, and began to exchange some deep confidences. Susan, for example, revealed to Jane that she had been adopted at age three, and also disclosed that her birth mother was a schizophrenic who required hospitalizations.

The attraction between the two women seemed odd on the surface. Susan was twenty-eight, fully twenty years younger than Jane, and not nearly as well educated or refined in her tastes. She worked as a train engineer, and spent little time on her clothes or appearance. She also had a moustache and a heavy unibrow.

My impression upon later meeting Susan was that she reminded me of one of Charles Manson's women, with her long, lanky hair and crazy eyes. Although a native Californian, Dyer often affected a Southern country drawl, which we'd come to refer to as her "Elvis" voice. Other times, she would suddenly switch to speaking in a tiny, waifish voice, sort of like Little Orphan Annie.

Nevertheless, by early December of 1990, Jane and Susan were lovers. But the romance soon went sour, and by the end of the month Jane realized that she had made a major mistake. Susan proved both jealous and possessive. She seemed determined to take over Jane's life. Dyer also liked rough sex— "simulating male sex in a very rough manner," as Smith put it in court—which Jane herself emphatically did not.

Disenchanted, and also increasingly concerned for her personal safety, Jane tried to break it off, suggesting to Susan that they just be friends. Dyer responded obsessively, as if she needed to *own* Jane and didn't care how she did it.

She called night and day, leaving gifts such as theater tickets and letters at Jane's house, on her windshield, and at her job. The notes begged for them to resume their affair. Smith discarded the early ones; then she starting saving the letters in a shoe box, which she hid under the paper bags in a kitchen utility drawer. She left the presents in an open box on the front porch, hoping that Dyer would take them back and desist.

She didn't.

Susan began leaving angry, violent, vulgar messages on Jane's answering machine, sometimes on an hourly basis. Changing her unlisted number did no good. Dyer soon had the new one.

She showed up at Jane's job and exploded into obscenities in front of Jane's coworkers. Susan was escorted from the premises. Jane's boss asked her to look for work elsewhere.

Smith resumed her relationship with Scott, who consequently became a target as well. One night in April of 1991, as Jane and Scott slept at Smith's house, Dyer startled them awake at two or three in the morning by pounding on the front door. Then she started screaming, demanding to see Jane.

"You have got to get out of here!" Scott called back to her.

"Leave us alone!" When she wouldn't leave, Jane and Scott called the police, who escorted Susan off Smith's property.

Peculiar scratching and banging sounds began welling up from the crawl space beneath Jane's house, sometimes so loud she couldn't sleep. So she hired an exterminator, who assumed the problem was a squirrel or opossum, and put out poisoned bait. Still, the noises did not stop.

Neither did Susan's pursuit of Jane. If Smith went to a restaurant with a friend, Dyer always had her own table nearby. When Jane went to the movies, Susan would be waiting inside the theater. Not until later did Smith figure out how Susan always knew where she was going, and when.

"You are never going to get rid of me," Dyer vowed at one point. "It is not going to end."

Meanwhile, she kept escalating the stress. Jane told us of several occasions when she would be in her bathtub and Susan would approach the house from outside, climb up on a box, open the bathroom window, and peer in to say, "I'm here watching! I'm here!"

Another time while Jane was in the shower, she heard the sound of breaking glass in her living room. Wrapping herself in a towel, she cautiously walked out to find that Dyer had broken the glass pane on a French door, and was sticking her head through the jagged hole, yelling obscenities at her. Again, Smith called the police. Susan was gone before they arrived.

Shortly afterward, a neighbor approached Jane to say she had seen her roommate and her gardener sitting on her porch recently, sharing a cup of coffee. The "roommate," of course, was Susan. Jane later discovered that Dyer often appeared at her house during the day while she was at work, posing as her roommate if anyone asked. She used the shower and would rest in Jane's bed.

Robert Studenny, an old friend of Jane's, house-sat for her in June 1991 while she was away for the weekend. When Studenny made a quick trip to the food market that Saturday evening—he remembers being gone fifteen minutes or less—he returned to find Dyer in one of the back rooms. Aware that she'd been harassing Smith, Studenny was not happy to find her there, and said so.

"I was quite angry," he testified. "I basically said, 'What

are you doing here?' leaving out the obscene words I was using." He recalled that Dyer was very nervous and muttered something about coming in the back way.

"I would love to beat the shit out of you," he told her. "You can't do these things. What are you doing?"

"Did you stay around the house after that?" I asked.

"Yes," he replied.

"Did you hear anything unusual in the house?"

"Yeah, I heard rustling under the house. I kept waking up, going, 'I don't know if I can stay here anymore.' It was quite noisy, like opposums or something."

He also remembered that Smith's dog, usually a quiet animal, barked throughout the night. In retrospect, Studenny would have two regrets over that Saturday night: that he didn't call the police at once, and that he waited two weeks to tell Jane of the intrusion. He had hoped to spare her the added anxiety.

Dyer, it turned out, had broken into the house that night with a purpose. She had found and retrieved her letters from the kitchen utility drawer, helped herself to some of Jane's family photos, and stole Jane's Rolodex—her master file of family and friends' names, phone numbers, and addresses.

Within a few days, several of these people, complete strangers to Dyer, began receiving rambling, handwritten letters entitled "The Saga of Jane and Susan."

They were treated to long disquisitions on Dyer's relationship with Smith, including intimate physical details of their time together. Susan also included a sheaf of Jane's reflections from her incest journal, pages she had also apparently ripped from the notebook on that night in June.

Dyer alleged in her "saga" that Jane had seduced and victimized her in "a game of seek and conquer," and that Smith had carried on simultaneous affairs with both her and Scott. "At strange times, three–four in the A.M.," she wrote, "she would leave my bed, claiming insomnia. Months later, after I figured out where Scott lived, I began to realize that after we had our dates and made love she would go over to his place, which is so close to mine. She would call him on my phone and I would have to go for a walk so she could make her stories..."

Susan also enclosed with the "saga" pages of her letters addressed to Jane. "You are acting like a paranoid child," read one passage. "You are not scared of me, just of the way you think I might act because of the pitiful way you have treated me and I let you treat me. I am not your violent ex-husband reincarnated or ex-boyfriend. Your lies are really destructive to yourself and the people that love you."

On another page, she wrote, "You've manipulated everyone into feeling sorry for you with your lies, and it is working as usual. That's a part you play so well, 'the innocent victim.' You can't relate to me honestly or argue or even talk."

Susan was capable of exceptional cruelty. In early July, she met with Jane's elderly mother, who had never known that her ex-husband, now deceased, had sexually abused her daughter. Dyer filled her in: "I know how Albert was fucking your daughter," she said.

Jane by now was "hysterical," as she described herself. She'd gone to the police, who told her they could do nothing unless Susan actually attacked her. Otherwise, she could forget it. She had tried, with Scott's help, to fill out the paperwork for a restraining order, but never completed the documents. She feared angering Susan any further.

But the discovery that Susan had violated, and then maliciously exposed, her most personal secrets galvanized Smith. She was still scared, but now she was angry, too. In late July, Jane filed a burglary complaint against Dyer. A few weeks later, her case was referred to the TMU, and Detective Raymond entered the story.

A new, bizarre, and violent chapter in the saga of Jane and Susan was about to erupt.

RAYMOND'S INITIAL INVESTIGATION persuaded him that there was sufficient evidence to charge Dyer with burglarizing Jane's house on the night that Robert Studeny discovered her there. He swore out an arrest warrant, and drove to Susan Dyer's house on October 3 to personally serve it. When he arrived, Raymond discovered Susan in the act of addressing one of her poison "saga" missives to Scott's parents. The detective also found a makeshift altar she had built and dedicated to Jane. Photographs of Smith were arranged around it, lit by candles.

Susan was arrested, but her father posted her $20,000 bail on Saturday, October 5. Jane Smith, who had assumed that after her arrest Dyer would be locked up indefinitely—and that she was therefore safe—had invited two friends, Alice Brown* and Martha Johnson*, to lunch at her house the following day. Brown and Johnson arrived together at about one that afternoon.

As they sat down to eat, Susan Dyer sneaked into the back of Smith's house, carrying a loaded handgun that belonged to her father. She knew that Jane kept a .22 in her bedside drawer, and grabbed it as well. Then she waited.

Midway through the meal, Smith excused herself from the table. As she walked down her back hallway, Susan popped out, holding a gun in each hand. One she pointed at her head, the other at Jane.

"Oh my God!" Smith's scream filled the house. "How did you get in here?!!"

Susan glared. "I want you to see this," she said icily. "I can always get in."

Jane screamed once more and dashed to call 911. A neighbor, hearing the commotion, came running to the house and hurried Jane to her own home, where a frightened Smith locked herself in the bathroom, and the neighbor called 911 also.

Brown and Johnson, meanwhile, were left to deal with Susan Dyer, who still had one of the guns pointed at her temple. "She seemed to be getting more worked up and angry and scared," Alice later testified. Martha stood in a doorway, shouting, "Why are you here?" at Susan. "What are you doing? What is the matter with you?"

Brown watched Dyer walk into a room off the hallway, where she backed up against a wall. "Why don't you sit down?" Alice asked her. "You look very upset. You look very scared."

When she took a step forward, Dyer pointed one of the guns at her. "Go back!" she said. "Go back. I don't want to hurt you."

Brown did not require further encouragement; she bolted out of the house with Johnson. A few minutes later, the first LAPD black-and-whites arrived, followed closely by thirteen members of the SWAT—Special Weapons and Tactics—squad. It was two o'clock in the afternoon.

Susan Dyer's ensuing standoff with the SWAT team would feature marathon telephone conversations with their negotiators, who put Jane Smith on the line with her, too. Dyer told Smith that she knew they would never be together in this life, but they would be in the next.

The long siege was also punctuated by three tense encounters between Dyer and Officer Jimmy Clark of the SWAT squad.

Soon after the SWAT team members had taken their assigned posts encircling the house, Dyer appeared at the back, carrying a gun at waist level in her right hand. She pushed open the wrought-iron door onto the patio and then took two steps down a small staircase before she saw Clark, watching her from cover in the next-door neighbor's backyard, about forty feet away.

Dyer pointed the gun at the SWAT officer—it looked like an auto pistol to Clark. "I know you are the police," she said. "I want you to leave. I am going to hurt you, or I am going to hurt somebody else."

Clark identified himself and asked her to put down the weapon. She refused and returned inside.

A few minutes later, Dyer emerged once again through the wrought-iron door, and descended the stairs to the grass. "She looked directly at me," Clark testified, "and then again said the same thing. I said, 'Susan, I am here to help you. We are not here to hurt you. Please put the gun down and be directed by me or someone else.' She said some profanities directed toward me and then she went back into the residence again."

Fifteen minutes later, Dyer walked down to the grass one more time. "Hey, Cop," she called to Clark again. "I know you're still here. I am not leaving."

"Susan," he answered, "I am not leaving either. We are not here to hurt you."

She disappeared inside once more. It was about four o'clock.

Six hours later, the SWAT negotiators finally persuaded her to bring both handguns out and place them on the front porch. She retreated inside, then emerged again for the last time and tried to make a run for it. SWAT officer Michael Odle tackled Dyer in the front yard. She was handcuffed and taken to the police station.

We charged her with threatening Officer Clark and assault with a deadly weapon on the luncheon guests, on top of the earlier burglary charge. Of course, Jane Smith had been her main victim; for many months Dyer had stalked and terrorized her. But because of deficiencies in the statute, there was no way I could charge her with those crimes. Bail was set at $500,000.

The next day, Jane called a security company to install an alarm system in her house; she was done with surprise visitors. No sooner had the installer, David Stanwood, begun work in the three-foot-high crawl space under Jane's house than she heard him shout from below, "Oh my God! There's been someone living down here!"

Stanwood had discovered a pillow, a blanket, and a pair of red Adidas sneakers that Jane recognized as Susan's. The installer also found a makeshift bed, dried food scattered around the crawl space, and marks on the telephone switch box that suggested Jane's telephone had been tapped. Suddenly it was clear to Smith how for months Dyer had known her phone number no matter how often she changed it, and how she knew practically every move Jane would make in advance.

WE WENT TO trial in March of 1992. Prior to jury selection, Dyer's attorney, Bea Ingram, unsuccessfully tried to persuade her client to shave her facial hair in order to appear more sympathetic and vulnerable to the jury. I remember one day when Bea was out sick and another public defender stood in for her. This lawyer asked me if I thought Dyer would talk to her. I said it depended on which Susan was there that day. The lawyer returned from the lockup a few minutes later with a strange look, and came up to me. "I talked to both of them," she said.

Jane was a very effective witness, poised and responsive even when Ingram probed deeply into physical details of her sex life with Susan. She told the defense attorney, as she had told Officer Raymond and me earlier, that she was not embarrassed to admit she'd had a lesbian affair. In light of her experience, however, she *was* embarrassed to say her partner had been Susan Dyer.

Dyer, who did not testify, sat at the defense table smirking throughout the four days of testimony.

The jury convicted on the assault and threat charges, but hung 11–1 for guilt on the burglary charge. To prove the crime of burglary, we needed to prove that Susan had entered the house for the purpose of committing theft or a felony, and I was later told that the jury had had difficulty determining whether Susan's sole purpose on June 21 was to steal the Rolodex, or if the theft was an afterthought.

Prior to her sentencing, Dyer wrote irate letters to her father, threatening to kill him because he was not able to help get her out of trouble, as he had done in the past. Afraid of his adoptive daughter, her father forwarded the letters to our Superior Court Judge, J. D. Smith, who was so outraged by Susan's behavior that he sentenced her to the maximum term of nine years in state prison. He also ordered that the California Department of Corrections place her in a prison with psychiatric facilities, where she could receive treatment for her obvious mental problems.

When I called Jane to tell her that this meant Susan would be off the streets for at least six to seven years, she tearfully answered, "Thank you for giving me back my life."

I wish I could say that it was the end of everyone's ordeal.

TWO

STALKING IS AMONG the most common and widely discussed of all antisocial behavior, yet the crime is incompletely understood outside professional circles—and inside some as well—and widely underappreciated as a problem for our justice system. The fact that I couldn't adequately prosecute Susan Dyer in 1992, even under California's famous first-in-the-world stalking statute, underscores that dilemma for law enforcement.

Since then, every state and a number of foreign countries have passed their own stalking laws—I helped Germany write theirs—but these statutes vary widely in their value as prosecutorial tools. The U.S. federal law, for example, is as useless as the original California statute.

The full extent of the stalking problem is difficult to gauge, except to say it is large and complex. In my experience, stalking is at least as common as DUIs. As of January 2009, the U.S. Department of Justice Office on Violence Against Women asserted that, "During a twelve-month period, an estimated 3.4 million persons age eighteen or older were victims of stalking." Approximately 60 percent do not report victimization to the police.

Unlike most other predatory offenses, such as homicide or rape, stalking is an ongoing crime; it unfolds over time. And although celebrity stalking grabs the headlines, stalking by current or former intimate partners (of either sex) is by far the more widespread and serious problem. In these cases, the stalking tends to go on much longer—I know of one case in which the stalker persisted all over the United States for a quarter century—and the victims are much more likely to suffer injury or death. According to one survey, 81 percent of the women stalked by a current or former husband, or cohabiting partner, also suffered physical assaults. For all she endured, Jane Smith was actually an exception.

The victims of domestic stalkers also frequently lack the knowledge of the law, or a celebrity's resources, to effectively protect themselves.

I think of stalkers as mental terrorists. They are generally male, and their victims are usually women, but anyone can become a stalker, and anyone can be a victim. These criminals tend to be intelligent and narcissistic. Compared to other types of criminals, particularly aberrant offenders such as serial killers, they typically make little or no effort to mask their identities.

Many of those I've convicted have been sentenced to therapy as well as confinement. In my experience, psychiatrists and psychologists make very little therapeutic headway with them. The reason: Stalkers, whether they are sane or insane, see nothing wrong with their behavior. They feel entitled.

IT'S COMMONLY BELIEVED that the original California law was passed in response to the 1982 stabbing attack by stalker Arthur Richard Jackson on actress Theresa Saldana, and then the 1989 murder of actress Rebecca Schaeffer by her stalker, Robert John Bardo. That's only partially correct.

During the 1980s, Ed Royce, a state representative from Fullerton, in Orange County, was the first lawmaker to come up with the idea of a stalking statute in California. After a six-month period in which four of Royce's female constituents were murdered by their ex-husbands and ex-boyfriends—despite the fact that all four had restraining orders—Royce introduced his legislation, though it got nowhere until Schaeffer's murder. Yet even then the resulting law was toothless. As Ed (now a congressman) personally explained to me later, by the time his bill got through all the legislative committees, the only thing left was the title "Stalking."

My experience with Susan Dyer and Jane Smith convinced me that immediate changes in the law were essential.

"We need to do something!" I argued to our legislative deputy. "We need to make changes!"

At the time, I naively thought that it would be the legislative deputy's job to craft the necessary legislation and send it on its way to a sympathetic legislator who'd shepherd it through the system to passage and eventual enactment as law. Fat chance.

Instead, he said, "Really great idea. Go ahead and write it."

"You've got to be kidding me," I said.

He wasn't.

And so I tried. I had some very definite ideas.

To begin with, under the law of the time, the Dyer prosecution was a first-time stalking case in which no restraining order was violated. In 1992, it could only be prosecuted as a misdemeanor. Nobody in the justice system pays attention to a misdemeanor. It's a low-grade crime.

Susan, however, was not a low-grade criminal. She had inflicted devastating psychological damage on her victim. It deeply bothered me to see how a person's life could be totally, permanently damaged, as Jane's had been, without the offender paying for the crime. Even if she had obtained a restraining order—which Jane, like many stalking victims, was reasonably too frightened to do—the stalking might only have risen to what we call a "wobbler," which means it could be filed either as a felony or as a misdemeanor.

That needed to be corrected. First-time stalking had to be a felony offense, period, whether or not a restraining order was in place. Furthermore, if *any* type of court order was in effect, then I wanted its breach to be an *aggravated* felony, meaning a longer sentence if the defendant was convicted. Also, if the defendant had any prior stalking convictions—then a near-impossibility given the difficulty of a conviction in the first place—any subsequent cases should also be automatically filed as aggravated felonies.

Another of the original California stalking law's major deficiencies was its definition of a credible threat as "a threat of death or great bodily injury" to a victim. Judges were interpreting that language to mean a stalker had to be standing in front of the victim with a gun or knife in his hand. Additionally, it did not cover a threat of sexual assault or rape because during the late 1970s, the California Supreme Court, led by Chief Justice Rose Bird, handed down a decision that rape and sexual assault were not examples of great bodily injury. This absurd decision had never been overturned.

Since a good percentage of stalking cases do involve threats of a sexual nature—threats that keep terrified women cowering behind locked doors for fear they'll be raped if they step outside—it was essential that we alter the law to extend its protection to cover them.

My answer was to redefine "credible threat" in the law from "threat of death or great bodily injury" to "a threat against the victim's safety, or the safety of the victim's immediate family," with "safety" understood in its common meaning to encompass threats of rape and sexual assault, and all the other types of threats that stalking victims typically receive. The threat could be direct or implied. This seemingly insignificant change in the language of the law would later allow me to successfully prosecute the men who stalked film director Steven Spielberg and actress Gwyneth Paltrow.

WHEN I ARRIVED in Sacramento in late 1992, all my changes ready to go, our legislative aide in the state capital explained to me that my very first presentation would be before the State Senate Judiciary Committee, the most important legislative hurdle of all. That's like opening an opera with the heroine's big aria. Not a great idea.

They awaited me in a cavernous room filled with people, where I was prepared to lay out my argument, based on the Dyer case, on why we needed these changes. I had barely begun to speak, however, when the Democratic committee chair, Bill Lockyer (who later became California Attorney General), began screaming at me. He actually yelled that he was offended at my suggestions, that he saw no reason for sending mere "pests" to prison.

I was dumbfounded, and then even more amazed when Senator (and now Congresswoman) Diane Watson, also a Democrat, stood up at her chair and lit into Lockyer. No one else made a peep as Watson yelled at the committee chairman, telling him that he didn't get it, that he didn't understand. Then they began yelling at each other. At least I wasn't getting yelled at anymore.

I sat at the witness table thinking, *Go, Diane, go!* Her argument was magnificent, but it did no good. Lockyer killed my bill, and I went back to Los Angeles to regroup.

Somewhat savvier than before, I went back to work, drumming up support for my changes among police agencies and victims' groups, most of whom were concerned with domestic violence issues. I told them that they needed to start writing and calling their legislators to create some pressure for passage. That's exactly what they did, and it worked.

In the meantime, stalking came to Sacramento. A secretary who worked for the state senate was shot and wounded in a parking lot by an ex-boyfriend who'd been following her. When I returned to the state capital the following year, the legislative mood was quite different. Also, I would now be privileged to work with our new legislative aide, James Provenza, one of the smartest and most politically astute people I've ever known.

Provenza persuaded Assemblyman Bob Epple, a Democrat from Downey, to sponsor my law, styled AB1178. The cosponsors were Mickey Conroy, a Republican from Orange County, and Tom Umberg, a Democrat from Santa Ana, who later served in the second Clinton administration as deputy director of the Office of National Drug Policy.

Jim also made sure I personally visited all the key legislators and their top aides. Unlike the year before, I had the advantage of being able to explain my bill directly to them, show them the statistics, and answer all their questions.

Jim told me that we had two groups opposing us—the American Civil Liberties Union (ACLU) and the California defense bar, which automatically opposes any legislation that toughens laws. This is natural. Stricter statutes only make a defense lawyer's work more difficult.

It was very important to hear what the ACLU had to say, because we wanted our bill to be both strong and able to pass constitutional challenges if they arose. Provenza therefore arranged for a sit-down with ACLU representatives in his Sacramento office, a few blocks from the capitol. He knew the ACLU lawyers very well. It was apparent he'd worked together with them in the past, and that there was strong mutual respect among them all.

We met for three hours, jointly scrutinizing the bill closely for constitutional issues. One of the most important provisions within the law was the requirement that an accused stalker have the specific intent to place a victim in fear for his or her safety, or the safety of the victim's immediate family. Just as the constitutional right to freedom of speech does not include the right to yell "fire!" in a crowded theater, stalkers cross that constitutional line when they purposefully and maliciously try to destroy someone's life, emotionally or physically. Clearly, it wasn't pests we were after, but vicious criminals.

The only change the ACLU lawyers wanted was a provision that upon conviction a court could consider sending the defendant to a locked-down state hospital for treatment. That was fine with us.

In front of the first legislative committee to consider my bill the next day, the ACLU representative rose to announce, "We're withdrawing our opposition," and the deal was sealed. The legislation passed through every committee without a single "no" vote. Even Bill Lockyer voted for it. Governor Pete Wilson signed AB1178 on September 29, 1993, and it became law on the first day of January in 1994.

THE CHANGES WE made in 1993 later allowed me to bring justice to a sweet girl named Maria Noel Sulgatti. Her stalker might not have been the most dangerous one I ever prosecuted, but he was one of the cruelest.

As Glendale police detective Randy Osborne put it, Jose and Elsa Sulgatti's lovely daughter was "everyone's perfect child. You couldn't ask for a better kid. No bad habits."

A 1997 honor graduate of Glendale High School, as well as an active civic volunteer, Maria Noel was a sheltered child with an angelic voice, hopeful for a career in professional opera.

Each Saturday morning, the pretty teenager sang hymns at her Community Adventist Fellowship Church's worship service in the sanctuary of Glendale's United Community Church on Colorado Boulevard. These appearances were taped and later broadcast on the *Carter Report*, a Christian cable program.

In the summer of 1998, when Maria Noel's ordeal began, she was about to start her second year at Glendale Community College. Eighteen years old, Maria Noel had never had a boyfriend, or yet been on a date.

"I grew up in a bubble," she says of her close-knit family.

Some time in June or July, the Sulgatti household began to receive a number of hang-up calls. Neither Maria Noel nor her parents nor her younger brother thought much of the calls at first.

Then came the first two letters, together with several pages of disturbingly graphic pornographic photos, in an envelope mailed August 6. There was no return address. The notes were produced with a word-processing program, printed in italic, and contained numerous grammatical errors, misspellings (including the victim's name), and elisions, as if English was not the writer's first language.

"Dear Noelle," read the first one. *"My apologies for these crude pictures, I am aware you will MIND A LOT. I have been admiring you for quite a while and all I could think is you every night when I go to sleep, making love to you, performing the things and more, such that in the pictures. I am madly (you might say sickly) in love with you but all I could do is these things for I am older than you and you have a very bright and promising future ahead of you. I think of you when I masturbate, and I cum and you are all in my (lustful) thoughts. I dreamed of sucking your clitoris, masturbating you and pleasing yourself until you reach your orgasm many time. Please forgive me for being lewd…"*

He insisted, *"I am not a stalker, NO WAY, nor could I be able to consider raping to fulfil my carnal mind, UH_UH."*

Then he added a postscript. *"Noelle, I LOVE YOU AND WILL ALWAYS HAVE A PART IN MY LIFE. I AM SORRY. I HOPE YOU WILL FIND IT, SOMEHOW, IN YOUR HEART TO ACCEPT MY APOLOGY."* The second note in the envelope, he said, was for her to share with her family.

"I have a big crush on you but I am older than you I do not want to hinder your plans in life. I would like you to take care of yourself. I know your parents never failed to counsel you. But please (why am I pleading, huh?) take care of yourself. You are a very gorgeous, beautiful smart lady, every man would want to be with you and want to sleep with you (sorry for being so hard toward my own gender). BELIEVE ME, MEN ARE DOGS AND THEY LIKE ONE THING. Don't submit to their sweet talks. Hormones will race one day and you may not be able to handle it, but with your faith, I am sure you will intelligently do the right thing…"

Suddenly, the Sulgattis realized that the weeks of hang-up calls were only a prelude, the stalker's first, tentative foray. Now he'd become increasingly insistent and self-assured. Soon, when Maria Noel answered one of his calls, he'd breathe deeply and suggestively into the receiver. And though he still didn't speak, he played X-rated videos over the phone, and sometimes created a strange noise by rubbing together what Sulgatti believed were two pieces of rubber.

The letters and pictures were even more troubling. "I just didn't know what to think," Maria Noel recalls. "It was disgusting. I felt violated. I felt dirty and gross and hurt."

And worried. The anonymous phone calls could have been random. She'd received similar calls at her receptionist job at the church, and nothing had come of them. But the stalker obviously now had her name and address. Moreover, the second note strongly suggested he was aware of how tightly knit the Sulgatti family was, and of their deep Adventist faith.

He *knew* things.

But who could he be? Maria Noel had male acquaintances, but no boyfriends, and no one she knew at school or in church—the two poles of her life outside the household—seemed even remotely capable of such behavior. Confused and fearful, whenever she left the house (which soon became rare) she found herself scanning faces, searching for some furtive, telltale clue that this man or that was her tormentor. When she sang in church on Saturday mornings, she looked for anything unusual in the male parishioners' eyes, any hint that her stalker was out there in the pews, watching.

In fact, he was.

There were no more letters until September 12, three days after Maria Noel's nineteenth birthday, when her mother came home at midday to find two envelopes on their front porch. The first contained a single sheet of paper with a picture of roses in a vase—a "virtual flower bouquet" copied off the Internet—plus this note: *"Dear Maria Noelle, Just to let you know that you are always in my thoughts. I love you and please take care of yourself. Extend my regards to your family. Bye."*

The second envelope contained more explicit pornography, including one picture of a blonde female performing oral sex on a seated male. *"Maria Noelle and me"* was typed across the top. Beneath the photo, he added, *"This is my favorite because she looks EXACTLY LIKE YOU. I always look at this picture transforms this into a reality…"*

In an accompanying letter, he wrote of seeing her back in school every day and alluded to her virginity. The new letter's explicit references, the mention of school and her sexual innocence—and the fact that these letters hadn't been mailed but were personally delivered—frightened Maria Noel into withdrawing from Glendale Community College. They also persuaded her family that it was time to contact the authorities.

As Officer Wynkoop of the Glendale police noted in a summary of his first meeting with the victim, "She didn't report the earlier incident because she felt the threat of the suspect was minimal. However, now that she is receiving more phone calls with the caller breathing heavy and the recent envelopes being dropped off at her door, she feels that the suspect might try to hurt her or her family."

On September 21, Pacific Bell, at police request, placed a trap on the Sulgatti family phone. Maria Noel had stopped answering the phone but was now asked to resume taking calls—distasteful and scary as the experience was—in order for the phone company to trace, if possible, where the calls originated. The cops had had no luck dusting the various letters, envelopes, and photos she'd received for fingerprints. The Sulgattis had repeatedly handled the documents, and it appeared that the stalker was taking special care not to touch anything himself.

Detective (now Sergeant) Randy Osborne, who became the investigating officer on the 22nd, was baffled by the total lack of leads or suspects in the case. "Stalking is not unusual," Osborne notes, "but the lack of any connections was." Not only was there no person of interest among Marie Noel's circle of friends and acquaintances, but the MO did not fit any of the so-called 290s—persons convicted of past sex crimes under Section 290 of the California penal code—who were living in the vicinity.

In early October, Osborne got what at first looked like a break when the telephone trap produced a number from which the stalker had placed at least two calls. The detective's optimism immediately cooled, however, when he learned that the number was listed to Mary Connor*, an elderly shut-in who lived fifteen miles away in West Los Angeles.

The Glendale police set up surveillance on Connor's residence and interviewed the woman. When Osborne asked if she had any male relatives or friends who visited her regularly, Connor said no. The only family member who came by was a niece. Nothing about the Connor connection made sense, and the detective wondered if the telephone company had made a mistake.

At about this time I entered the case at the request of Sergeant Kim Lardie, Osborne's supervisor. The previous year, Lardie and I had worked on a case in which a Glendale woman awoke in the middle of the night to find a male neighbor standing over her bed, staring at her. She screamed, and he jumped out the window.

Under the applicable law, this was a simple trespass, which could earn the offender a six-month term in the county jail, meaning he might be back on the street within a week due to the chronic problem of jail overcrowding. The sheriff's early-release program (meant to address jail overcrowding)

---

*Denotes pseudonym

can result in a very short stay at the county's expense, as was later seen in the well-publicized case of Paris Hilton.

So Kim and I went to Sacramento and drafted an *aggravated* trespass statute for cases in which the victim is at home at the time of the trespass, thereby raising the level of danger. Henceforth, committing aggravated trespass in California would earn the perpetrator up to a year behind bars, plus an added provision for a lengthy restraining order.

"We've got another really bizarre case," Kim told me over the telephone. "Can we brainstorm it?" I spoke with both her and Detective Osborne, and came away from the conversations with a deep respect for Osborne's single-minded determination to catch this stalker. He gave me hope that there really are police officers out there who actually care about victims, who will not give up until they see that the right thing is done. Randy was one of those people. So was Kim.

There wasn't much of investigative value for me to add; the Glendale police were doing everything in the book and beyond to catch the stalker, whom we all agreed was a sophisticated pervert who clearly led an active fantasy life. I did reassure Kim that this conduct fell under the revised stalking law, and that I was itching to file this case. I just needed a name.

Meanwhile, Maria Noel was descending into a personal hell of terror and isolation. The stalker had by now left several envelopes and packages—including one containing a porn video that Maria Noel discovered lying on the lawn—and was boldly telephoning at all hours. In one call he offered her tips on masturbation. Her only confidants were her mother and Detective Osborne.

"He went so out of his way for me," she recalls of the detective. "I could call him at any time."

Maria Noel couldn't call her friends—secrecy was imperative—and she feared discussing the situation with her father, lest it made matters even worse. "I prayed that the police could find the stalker first," she remembers. "One of my fears was of my father going to jail for killing some guy who was scaring me."

She tried to envision her tormentor, but couldn't. Her only mental images were of friends. Inevitably, she started questioning her own behavior. "It made me doubt myself in a lot of ways," Maria Noel says. "How had I provoked it? Was there a logical reason for it? It was very, very easy to slip and think, *What did I do?*"

The months-long ordeal ended at last on the afternoon of October 15. At about 4:30, Osborne telephoned Maria Noel. As they spoke, her phone's call-waiting feature beeped that a second call was coming in. She answered. It was the stalker. "It's him again! He's calling me right now!" she told the detective, and described how the stalker again had placed the receiver next to a television so she could hear the pornographic video he was playing before she hung up.

Maria Noel and Detective Osborne then spoke a few more moments before the stalker called back again. "Please help me!" she tearfully pleaded to the policeman. "This stuff is really scaring me!"

The detective told her to put the phone down and wait for him to call back. Then he quickly conferred with Sergeant Lardie, who authorized an emergency trace on the two recent calls. At 4:45, Pacific Bell reported back that the trace had been successful. The calls had come from an apartment at 133 South Chevy Chase in Glendale, less than a mile from the Sulgatti house. The number was listed to a male with the unlikely name of Jolly Jett-Nanez Alsaybar, who was thirty-one years old and worked as a visiting nurse.

"We got him!" Osborne informed me by telephone on his way to arrest Alsaybar with members of the Glendale PD's assaults detail. I was elated. "How?" I wondered, and learned briefly about the successful trace. I was impressed that they had tracked the call so swiftly.

Within fifteen minutes of receiving his suspect's name and address, Osborne was standing with his team at Alsaybar's door. He knocked, and Alsaybar—a slender, slightly built Filipino—timidly answered. His wife, who was unaware of his criminal activities, was at home as well. The cops noted that a XXX video was playing on the television—no doubt the same tape he'd played for Maria Noel a half hour before. Various pornographic videotapes and publications were strewn around the living room. A consent search of Alsaybar's personal computer in the apartment's single bedroom netted more explicit sexual material.

"I explained to the suspect, Alsaybar, that I was investigating a case where rude and threatening phone calls were being made to a residence in Glendale," Osborne wrote in his report. But Alsaybar quickly short-circuited the interview. "Before I could ask a question," the detective reported, "he made the statement, 'It's me. I'm sick.' I asked Alsaybar what he meant and he said, 'I did it all to her. I have a sick problem.' I asked Alsaybar what he meant by 'all' and he replied, 'The letters, the calls. I did it and I'm sorry.' I asked Alsaybar if he had made any prank calls in the past hour and he replied, 'Only a few.' "

Osborne cuffed and arrested Alsaybar, took him to the police station, booked him, then at 5:45 sat him down for a chat in an interview room. Osborne could barely control his contempt.

He asked his suspect—who had no police record and denied any history of similar stalking behavior—how the stalking had begun. Alsaybar explained that he was an Adventist, too, and had first seen Maria Noel at church a couple of months before. Her choice as his victim was "random," he said, and his single goal was to see how she coped with the letters and phone calls.

Alsaybar was particularly interested in whether she betrayed fear or stress when she appeared on Saturday mornings to sing. He said he sat in the back of the church, week after week, and watched her deteriorate. Similarly, he played the porno tape over the telephone just to see what her reaction would be.

When Osborne pressed him on the point of the terror, Alsaybar answered simply, "I am a student of human nature."

He also cleared up one mystery. He *had* called Maria Noel from Mary Connor's residence. She was one of the patients he called on regularly as a visiting nurse. In retrospect, it appears we failed to flag the connection because we automatically assumed that Connor's nurse had to be a female. Nobody thought to simply ask Connor, "Is a male using your telephone?"

Alsaybar added that he was an avid fan of TV talk shows, particularly those whose guests were forced to cope with stressful moments. Jerry Springer and Maury Povich were two of his favorite television hosts. He found fear and pain stimulating, particularly Maria Noel's, his "experiment."

"He was despicable," the policeman recalls. "He was lucky that law enforcement personnel in this country are professional."

Alsaybar—his parents apparently named him Jolly Jett-Nanez as a result of some sort of contest in his native Philippines—later denied that he had any overt sexual designs on Maria Noel. Before his recent marriage to a woman he'd met on the Internet, his sole sexual experience had been one encounter at age twenty-one with a prostitute. He claimed his devout Adventist beliefs prevented him from considering violence.

In an interview, he exhibited signs of deep inhibition, personal inadequacy, and hypersensitivity to criticism. He also harbored intense sexual fantasies that involved the suffering of a nonconsenting partner—Maria Noel.

From my perspective, now that Jolly Jett-Nanez Alsaybar had confessed his crime, the two considerations were whether he deserved to do serious time, and whether he was a threat to reoffend, perhaps to commit outright violence against Maria Noel, or some other victim. My answer to both questions was an unhesitant yes, and I think I surprised both the defendant and the private defense attorney he hired when I refused to discuss a plea bargain.

"The guy doesn't have any record," the lawyer argued. "This is misdemeanor conduct. What's the big deal?" Before we changed the law in 1994, that sort of thinking would have carried the day. His client might well have been cut loose with time served. But not this time.

I waited until the day of the preliminary hearing. "Hey, do you want to see the victim who is ready to testify against your client?" I asked Alsaybar's attorney. Maria Noel and her mother were sitting in the court together. "And her mom? Take a look in the fourth row." The attorney had obviously hoped that the victim would be too embarrassed or scared to show up, which was sometimes the case.

Maria Noel wasn't crying, but she was clearly upset. She looked so vulnerable, and her mother looked so concerned. The attorney got a look on his face that said his client did not stand a chance. So he pled Alsaybar "open"—that is, without a plea bargain. The judge could give him anything from probation up to three years in state prison. He was taking the chance that the judge would take the early plea and Alsaybar's lack of a prior record into consideration as mitigating circumstances.

But the judge had also seen Maria Noel and her mother sitting there in his courtroom. He was familiar with the facts of the case from my sentencing memo. Alsaybar was sentenced to sixteen months in state prison, heavy time for someone with no prior record. The judge also exercised his option to order Alsaybar to register as a sex offender—a 290—when he got out, a feature of the stalking statute for which I am also proudly responsible.

Jolly Jett-Nanez did the crime, and the time, but upon his release he failed to register as a 290 sex offender, and so a warrant was issued for his arrest. His current whereabouts are unknown, but we do know he made it back to the Philippines. A year or so ago, we found on the Internet a story in a British paper about a group of visiting Filipinos who had gone all the way to London to compete in a flapjack flipping competition. Standing there among the contestants was our very own Jolly Jett-Nanez Alsaybar, smiling broadly.

I doubt he'll be bringing the act to the United States. If he does, however, we'll be eagerly waiting for him.

REDEFINING "CREDIBLE THREAT" to include "conduct implied by a course of conduct" gave California prosecutors an effective new tool with which to pursue stalking cases. We no longer had to show that the stalker was standing in front of the victim with a knife or gun, saying, "I'm going to kill you now." Nor did we have to prove that the threat was one of death or great bodily injury.

However, persistent biases in the justice system, as well as misunderstanding or ignorance of the revised statute, still complicated the work of making sure that the law was applied equally to everyone. A case in point was Brian Austin.*

In February of 1994, Austin, twenty-four, a security guard at one of the swank hotels in Century City, met Lamont

Mitchell, twenty-one, at a club in West Hollywood. A romance developed. Mitchell, who was a student at the time, moved in with Austin.

At first, Austin didn't mind that Mitchell had no income. "Don't worry about it," he assured his new roommate. But after a couple of months, Brian grew impatient. "Okay now," he told Lamont. "It's time to get a job."

Lamont reluctantly found work as a salesman at Barbeques Galore, but almost immediately began complaining about his fellow employees. Brian tried to be understanding. "Go ahead and quit," he said. "Find yourself another job." But it was becoming clear that Mitchell was no self-starter.

He also was unusually dependent and possessive, according to Austin. No matter how often Brian encouraged him to get a job, and a life, too, Lamont seemed unwilling or unable to think or act for himself. He had no other friends. His constant calls to Austin at work were an embarrassment.

They began to bicker about Mitchell's lack of ambition and his possessiveness. A couple of times the arguments got physical. Finally, Brian told Lamont that he needed to go. He still felt affection for Lamont, and tried to make their parting amicable. "I will always be your friend," he said. "If you need me, call me."

Mitchell seemed to accept that their relationship was over, and left without further incident to go live with his mother and father. It was by now October of 1994. Austin thought his former partner's obsession with him was a thing of the past, but he soon discovered it was only the beginning.

First came the telephone calls, hundreds and hundreds of them. Mitchell left messages at both Austin's home and work numbers, pleading his love and begging to be allowed back. He also began appearing unexpectedly at Brian's door.

"Lamont," Austin explained to Mitchell about his surprise visits, trying to be civil, "you have to call first." It didn't do any good. He showed up more and more frequently, and was getting more and more difficult to send away. "I can't tell you how many times he came over," Austin remembers. "It was insane. One day he showed up when I had company and pushed the door open. That started a fistfight."

He also repeatedly appeared at the hotel where Brian

worked, interfering with his duties. He seemed intent on getting Austin fired. Fortunately, Brian's superiors and coworkers knew about the situation and were very supportive.

Austin reported Mitchell to the police, who suggested he get a restraining order, which he did in March of 1995. Lamont was ordered not to come within 100 yards of Brian or his workplace, and not to telephone his old boyfriend. But the restraining order was no help; Mitchell simply ignored it, and no matter how many time times Austin called the police—the number of reports in his police file eventually grew into the dozens—he was usually told they couldn't help him unless Lamont actually hurt him.

The sad reality was that the system didn't take Austin seriously because he was a gay male. He was doing everything we counsel stalking victims to do, but until someone looked beyond his sexual orientation and gender, he was not going to get the help he deserved.

"The police just chalked it up to men having a love spat," says TMU detective Alex Vargas, who eventually took over the case and brought it to me. "They'd think, 'How can that be dangerous?' When I looked at this case, I saw crime report after crime report in which the issues were not resolved."

Prosecutors and judges were no more helpful to Austin. Time after time, charges of misdemeanor battery or violation of the restraining order were filed, when the charge should've been felony stalking. Mitchell was allowed to plead for a sentence of merely a day or two in county jail. Even worse, on occasion the court would summarily dismiss the charges.

Austin remembers a moment in front of a judge in Beverly Hills. "Please hold him," he'd said, gesturing toward Mitchell. "Look at the history." According to Austin, the judge regarded him impassively, looked over at Lamont, and said, "Dismissed."

Less than an hour later, back at the supposedly secure apartment building he'd moved into, Austin was checking his mail when his landlord walked up to him. "Hey, Brian," he said, "that guy behind you, is he your friend?" Austin turned to see Mitchell standing at the building's glass doors, holding his hands together as in prayer, pleading with him.

In May of 1995, Mitchell accosted Austin at his job and handed him a note that read, "Watch your back." Again a police report was taken, but nothing happened.

In June, Lamont approached Brian at a West Hollywood club. Austin bolted out the door in fear, and ran down the street to a local sheriff's station, where Mitchell caught him, putting Austin in a headlock and pummeling him. A passerby summoned deputies, who arrested Mitchell. Lamont was charged with misdemeanor battery. He pled guilty to the charge and served a very short sentence in Men's County Jail. Two months later, Lamont attacked Brian in a similar way in front of a coffeehouse in West Hollywood, and was arrested by deputies once more. Again, misdemeanor charges were filed.

Austin moved again, and took an unlisted telephone number. Mitchell found him again. Austin started dating another person. Mitchell found out where Austin's new boyfriend worked—a coffee shop—and applied for a job there.

He also applied for a job at the hotel where Austin worked. One of Austin's coworkers alerted Brian. When Mitchell returned to the hotel, supposedly to follow up on his job application, Austin confronted him. He reminded Lamont that he was under a restraining order to stay away from his workplace. Lamont's excuse was a desperate need for work, an urge that had never overcome him in the past. On another occasion he falsely informed one of Austin's coworkers by telephone that Brian had AIDS.

Austin's irritation deepened into angry desperation. He began asking LAPD detectives under what circumstances he'd be legally justified in killing Lamont.

The case did not come to the attention of Alex Vargas until 1997. The TMU detective's first priority was to pull together the voluminous file, arrange the reports in chronological order, and then go visit Austin.

Brian remembers opening his door to see a police detective standing there with an enormous file under his arm. After years of being ignored, or worse, he was skeptical of this cop who claimed to be there to help him.

"It took a while to convince him," Detective Vargas recalls. His next step was to bring Austin to me. Fortunately for Brian, my long campaign to establish a specialized Stalking and Threat Assessment Team (STAT) within my office had finally succeeded. His case would be STAT's first, meaning that Austin would have the benefit of both a detective and a prosecutor who understood the stalking laws, knew how to utilize them, and would treat all stalking victims with understanding and compassion. After several hellish years, his case would get the time and professional attention it had always deserved.

Alex Vargas and I interviewed Austin in August of 1997. Although I'd read all the arrest reports, I asked him to recount his horror story.

He burst into tears when he told us of the night that he'd been forced into giving Lamont a ride home. Once they arrived, Mitchell started to choke Austin in the front seat. Fearing for his life, Brian went limp until Lamont took his hands away. This was yet another instance that should have been charged as felony stalking but wasn't.

Several of the previous prosecutors who'd reviewed his case had erroneously told Austin that they couldn't file felony stalking charges against Mitchell because he had never actually threatened Austin with physical harm. The fact that such a threat need only be implied apparently did not occur to any of them, even though the new stalking law had been in effect for more than three years.

Lamont's lawyer would later argue that there was no specific intent to place the victim in fear; hence, no crime. I thought otherwise. Under the old law, we could not have done anything for Austin. But under the new one, I knew that I could easily convict Mitchell of stalking. His "course of conduct," as defined in the new stalking law, easily established that Lamont had the intent to place Austin in fear for his safety. Despite some skepticism among my colleagues, I charged Lamont with felony stalking and several violations of the restraining order.

In court, I asked Austin to describe how many times he had moved and changed his phone number, trying to escape Lamont's relentless attentions. The answer was that he'd moved at least three times and had changed his phone number on half a dozen occasions. How many times had he begged Lamont to leave him alone? Countless.

Establishing that Austin was in fear was simple. I asked him on the witness stand, "Are you afraid for your physical safety?" He answered, "Yes."

I asked how Lamont had affected his daily life. Brian told the court of having to look over his shoulder constantly, the sick feeling in his stomach whenever the phone rang, and his total despair that Lamont would never stop stalking him. As for Mitchell's *intent* to place Austin in fear, I pointed out that the defendant had repeatedly been put on notice, including Austin's repeated reports to the police and his direct and unequivocal demands that Lamont leave him alone.

The defense attorney portrayed his client as just a poor, lovesick guy, desperate to get back with the object of his affections. Lamont Mitchell wasn't a stalker, he argued. He was a lover.

But Brian and his coworkers portrayed a very different Lamont, an obsessed and violent stalker whose clear intent was to do Austin harm. Several hotel security employees testified to Austin's fear and disgust whenever Mitchell called, which was constantly. They remembered Brian on the phone, yelling at Lamont to stop bothering him, and how he'd slammed the receiver down in anger and frustration.

One coworker testified that on several occasions he had seen Mitchell skulking around the employees' entrance, waiting for Austin to leave work. He'd quickly alerted Brian, who had escaped out another door.

The jury deliberated for less than an hour, and convicted Lamont of all charges. Because of our overwhelmingly persuasive case against Mitchell, as well as his lengthy misdemeanor conviction record, the judge followed my recommendation and sentenced him to the maximum of four years in state prison.

For Brian Austin, Lamont Mitchell's verdict and stiff sentence were both a relief and a vindication. "To be honest, it was gratifying," he says. "I didn't want revenge. I just wanted to put an end to it, and to let him know that you can't get away with this behavior anymore."

Lamont had always laughed at the ineffectiveness of the justice system. He would leave messages for Austin saying, "Get all the restraining orders and detectives you want!" It worked for a while, but then he met Detective Vargas and me. Justice finally caught up to Lamont Mitchell.

THREE

IF THERE IS a typical path toward becoming a prosecutor, I most definitely did not take it.

My first address in life was New York City—the Bronx. I lived two blocks from Yankee Stadium with my parents, Irving and Sylvia, until I was five, when our little family moved to a one-bedroom apartment in northern New Jersey.

My father, a World War II veteran, worked as a professional fund-raiser when he could; the rest of the time his severely compromised cardiovascular system kept him in bed, and in and out of Veterans Affairs hospitals. My dominant girlhood memory was of watching him leave and return on stretchers.

His health problems apparently stemmed from something that had happened to him during the war, but he would never talk about it to me or my mother. Whatever its cause, I knew from my earliest recollections that my father's poor health was a serious concern for us, that he was under an imminent death sentence. In fact, when I was only six or seven years old, I overheard the doctors telling my mother that he had only six months to a year to live. Absent the excellent care he received at VA hospitals, I have no doubt their prognosis would have been accurate.

Since he couldn't work steadily, and received only a modest military pension, we were chronically cash-strapped. My mother, who had considerable experience as an executive secretary and had once held a senior position with a travel agency, might have found work to help support us, but my father forbade it. That experience was apparently burned into my psyche. Ever since, I have stubbornly (and often irritatingly) resisted taking orders from anyone. Our only other source of income was the money my parents won in the summertime playing gin each day at the Pine Brook Country Club, near Montclair.

In the midst of this grimness, my sole refuge was music. I loved to sing, and regularly retreated into show tunes, anything that could be sung at the top of my voice to temporarily, at least, drown out our troubles.

The one other spark of hope in my young life was my maternal grandfather, an Austrian-born deaf-mute who'd immigrated as a teenager to the United States. He'd taught himself to read, write, and lip-read English. He seemed indomitable to me. He never thought of himself as handicapped, and never let anything stand in his way. He was the one role model in my life, the one person who gave me the love that I needed.

My father suffered his final heart attack at age forty-two while sitting on the living room couch. I, his fifteen-year-old daughter, listened to his death rattle, then watched as he was carried away for the last time. He was given a full military funeral service, with a flag-draped coffin. My mother was presented with the folded flag at the end of the ceremony, which we brought back to our empty apartment.

We were left with less than nothing, and my mother fell apart. She cried a lot. We sold his car because we needed the money and couldn't afford to drive it anyway. My mother had used a little typewriter at home to keep up her skills, but she couldn't find work without recent experience. Finally she took a job selling baby clothes in a local department store.

I stayed with my mother in that wretched apartment, watching her unravel, until at age seventeen—the start of my senior year at high school—I got pregnant and married my child's father. Marriage, I soon discovered, was not the answer to my problems.

We divorced, and our baby boy, Doug, was adopted by his paternal aunt and uncle. I was at first promised I could go to see my son from time to time. Later, however, they told me my visits were too emotionally draining for them, and so I was denied all further access to him.

I was devastated, but there was nothing I could do. I had no education. I had no money. I had no career. I had no future when I gave Doug up. There was no question of money from his father. To me, his aunt and uncle were solid people who could give him a good life. They had this nice house he could live in, and they loved him. Still, it was very, very hard.

Then came my big break. An operetta troupe called the American Savoyards, specializing in Gilbert and Sullivan, brought me into repertory with them at the Jan Hus theatre on East 74th Street in New York. My career in musical theater was officially under way.

Although I never made it to Broadway, I toured all over the country, played summer stock, worked off-Broadway, and appeared with the New York City Opera. The best part of the experience was making lifelong friends in the theater, people I still regard as members of my extended family.

My greatest stage success was touring in a three-actor drama by Norman Corwin starring Richard Kiley, a legend on Broadway as the original Don Quixote in *Man of La Mancha*. It was also my wake-up call.

As the tour neared the end of its run, and it was clear we weren't taking the show to Broadway, Kiley broke down. Distraught, he told us how scared he was. Even though he was considered a stage icon in New York, Kiley feared he'd never work in the theater again, that no one would hire him.

This hit me like a thunderbolt. I was in my twenties, having a blast. It was really fun. But did I want to spend the rest of my life worrying, for example, *If I get sick, how am I going to afford to get medicine?* And I really did like eating on a regular basis.

Not long thereafter, I moved out West with my boyfriend,

Ralph—soon to become my husband—where I'd heard that acting gigs were both more varied and abundant. We had no money, so we signed up with one of those services that arranges to move cars around the country. They provide the car; you do the driving and buy the gas. In this case, the car was a large Cadillac. Everything we owned fit into its trunk.

My mother was worried. "How are you even going to find California?" she asked. "You don't even have a map."

"When we get to the ocean," I replied, "we'll stop."

We had about $300 between us, which meant no dawdling. In fact, we stopped only once for something besides gas, restrooms, or food. We were in the Southwest, and up ahead was an exit for the Grand Canyon.

"Can we stop?" I asked. "I'd like to see it."

We pulled into the park. I got out and looked at the canyon for about five minutes.

"Okay," my future husband said impatiently, "let's go. You've seen it, and we have to get to California before our money runs out."

The Golden State did not prove to be the end of the rainbow for us. I did a show in Los Angeles, and another one in New Mexico, hoping for a call from a television or movie producer in search of a talented, singing, dancing actress. I sat there waiting for the phone to ring, but nobody ever called.

So instead of being discovered, I made a discovery. I found out that community colleges in California were free. I figured I could take some classes until my next gig came along. Fortunately, my next gig never did.

I started at Los Angeles City College, where I got straight As and for the first time attracted other people's attention for something other than my looks and talent. Two of my professors strongly urged me to get my undergraduate degree, and suggested I consider law school. They told me I was smart and motivated enough to become an attorney, and that my theatrical background made me a courtroom natural. "You'll still have your audience and you'll get *paid*!" one of them said.

This was all new. People started saying, "Wow! You're smart!" No one in my life had ever said anything like that to me. In fact, it had been sort of the opposite. When I told my mother I was going to college, she said, "What are you doing that for? Aren't you too old?"

She had grown up during the Great Depression, and dropped out of school in the eighth grade to help her family survive. Education was not a priority to her, though she was one of the most brilliant people I ever knew.

My grades at LA City College earned me a California grant that would help pay for the final two years of my undergraduate education anywhere in the state. I chose Immaculate Heart College in Hollywood because it offered a full curriculum of night classes, allowing me to work during the day.

From there I went to Southwestern Law School, where I finished in the top five of my first-year class, and promptly transferred to the far more prestigious law school at the University of Southern California. I wanted it all, including a family, so I decided it would be easier to have a child while I was still going to school, rather than after I graduated and was busy winning cases in court.

Ralph, who also wanted to start a family, thought it was a good idea. He had no doubt that I could have a baby *and* stay on top of my classes. He was right.

Our son Sean was born on the first day of spring break during my second year of law school, which meant I didn't have to miss a day of class. I even took my law books with me to the hospital. I amazed my doctor, who discovered me reading one of them in the recovery room approximately an hour after I gave birth.

My mother, who could never bring herself to fully endorse my ambitions, finally succeeded in working her way up to a good-paying position as an executive secretary in New York. She was even able to send me a little money from time to time. But just before I finally graduated in 1982, near the top of my class, she died. It was a terrible loss. All I had ever wanted to do was make her proud of me.

She would certainly have approved of my next move. Although criminal law was my first love—I won two academic awards as the top student in my criminal law and criminal procedures classes—I was seduced by the comparatively huge salaries that big LA law firms were paying new associates. So I postponed my dreams of the courtroom to make a pot of money. The downside of the deal was that I spent fourteen-hour days—weekends, too—sitting in an office, writing contracts and scanning through corporate offerings. I hated every single minute of it.

In the meantime, Ralph had decided that since I was making the big bucks, he would stay home and be "Mr. Mom" to Sean. That arrangement lasted until the evening I returned from work to find my eighteen-month-old son drinking his milk from a beer can. "Mr. Mom" couldn't understand why I was upset. He explained that Sean didn't want to drink his milk, so he had hit on the brilliant idea of serving Sean his milk in a beer can, so he could be just like Dad.

"What's the problem?" he asked. "Look, he's drinking his milk."

That did it. I told Ralph that his days as "Mr. Mom" were over. He was going back to work.

We'd need his salary, because I was terminally tired of corporate law, no matter how lucrative it was. I wanted to get into a courtroom and practice criminal law. I was fascinated with both the legal issues and the stories behind them. Criminal law was about human beings—people! At a civil firm, you have two faceless corporations fighting over money. When you're doing criminal cases, you're dealing with people's lives.

Therefore, I took a 50 percent cut in pay to go to work for the Santa Monica City Attorney's office, prosecuting misdemeanors. Within a year, I was the head of their criminal division. From there, in January of 1986, I moved to the largest prosecutorial office in the country, assigned first to more misdemeanor cases in Glendale, then to the grueling work of prosecuting felonies in Pasadena. At last I was in my element.

THE PACE WAS fast and nonstop, one case after another. As soon as you walked out of one trial, a supervisor or assistant supervisor handed you a huge file and said, "Go to Department D.

You're starting a trial in fifteen minutes." There was barely time to figure out the charges before jury selection began.

This was prosecution under fire, and boy, does it train you to think and act quickly, and to function under enormous stress. You never stop, and you are constantly on your feet in trial. I loved it.

In August of 1987 I was nine months pregnant with my daughter, Shannon, who was due in a couple of weeks. I decided to work up to the last minute, as I had in law school when I was carrying Sean.

I had just won guilty verdicts in a big trial in which we'd charged members of a motorcycle gang with threatening the founder of a rival gang, together with his son, as well as assault with a gun. Though neither the victims nor any of my witnesses were at all sympathetic figures, the jury convicted on all counts.

I was feeling pretty good until I walked out of the courtroom to find a supervisor standing there with a familiar thick file. "You know I'm going on maternity leave in a week or two," I said.

"Don't worry," she assured me. "This is just a motion. Go to Department A. It's very simple. You'll have an hour to look at the file. Don't worry about it."

When I got to the courtroom, I discovered that it was not a motion, but a trial, and that some prosecutor had informed the court that morning that the "People"—that's us—were ready to go forward. But now a complication had arisen. There were no available courtrooms in Pasadena. The closest one we could use was thirty miles away in Pomona. I immediately began to feel birth contractions.

"Your Honor," I told the judge, "there is no way I can travel that extra thirty miles back and forth every day. I'm requesting second call on this case so I can talk to my supervisor."

"Well," he replied, "the People announced ready this morning. What's the problem?"

My contractions were growing more insistent.

"I'm going on maternity leave."

He scowled. "When?"

"Right now."

He was astonished. I thought he'd fall off the bench.

By the time I'd returned to the office he'd telephoned my supervisor and screamed at her. "How *dare* you send this very pregnant woman into my courtroom," he said to her. "Don't you know we just put new carpets down?"

That did it. I went on immediate maternity leave, expecting that I'd give birth soon. I didn't. My daughter waited exactly two weeks before arriving on her appointed due date, September 3.

Four weeks later, I returned to work.

From Pasadena I then moved to juvenile court in Eastlake, East Los Angeles, where I'd get my first personal experience with the origins of the behavior we deal with in adult court. Every prosecutor should spend some time in juvenile court.

The case I remember best was that of a ten-year-old murder defendant I prosecuted. At about two o'clock one morning, he and a twelve-year-old friend had stationed themselves outside a crack house with a gun to rob people as they approached to buy drugs. One of their victims ended up dead from a bullet through his head, and now we had to figure out what to do with this child who had pulled the trigger.

I recall looking over at him, something I rarely do in court because it usually makes me angry. He was tiny for his age; his legs dangled from his chair. He was crying, too, crying for his mother. The public defender kept leaving to search for the woman, and finally found her on a bench in the back of the room. I turned to look at her and could see that she had nodded out, presumably from some drug.

This explains a lot about this case, I thought as I turned to look at the little boy again. He was still crying. Because he was so young, there were a number of issues; for example, did he understand right from wrong? With that mother, it was tenuous whether he did. It absolutely broke my heart to see him there. I wanted to put his mother in prison for child neglect.

He was too young to be sent to a state juvenile facility, and I was determined not to send him back home again. But we had to get him away from her, which meant proceeding with the case and trying to get him into some type of group home, which is eventually what happened.

I was next moved downtown, where many of the heavier felonies were tried. Someone—I can't remember who—tipped me off that I should volunteer for two-to-ten night-court duty. "This is the best-kept secret in the office," he told me. "Everybody loves it. We're doing interesting cases, too."

Night court was invented as an answer to the huge and growing volume of felony cases we were handling. There were so many prosecutions that we had begun to move cases from the criminal courts building to the civil courthouse. Because criminal proceedings always take priority over civil matters, many civil cases were being dragged out for years, which was driving the judges crazy.

Night court was the perfect solution to the problem. The courtrooms were just standing vacant in the evening, so it made sense to run a sort of second shift. That relieved the crowding problem in the civil courts building, and produced at least one unforeseen advantage—higher caliber jurors. Students, professional people, and others with busy daytime schedules always tried to avoid jury duty during the day. But they were much more apt to show up on our panels at night, which made everyone—judges, prosecutors, and public defenders—happy.

Of course, our individual caseloads were still heavy. It was one trial after another, plus preliminary hearings. Sometimes I'd have as many as twenty preliminary hearings in one night, then come back to my office from court and find another pile of twenty cases I'd never seen before on my desk, all set for preliminary hearings the next day.

I knew a lot of them would plead, or be continued, but you had to get ready for each of them because you did not know which ones you'd actually have to prosecute. And what about witnesses? Were there any? Would they show up?

Among these cases, murders were usually comparatively simple to handle. From a prosecutorial view, they are really aggravated assaults. The really difficult ones to prosecute on a moment's notice were the paper cases—fraud—where you have hundreds and hundreds of pages of documents to digest.

I remember one of them was a complex identity-theft case where the victim and defendant were both from Nigeria.

The defense contended that the defendant was actually who he said he was, and he just happened to have the same name as the victim. To counter that, I brought in an anthropology professor from UCLA who explained that in Nigeria, unlike the United States and elsewhere, individual names have very specific tribal origins, and it is therefore impossible for two Nigerians to have *exactly* the same name. The anthropologist convinced the jury, and they voted to convict.

Another memorable case involved a transient who was being charged for his alleged role in a McDonald's stickup. The public defender said his client was, in fact, innocent and sat down with me to explain why.

According to witnesses, the defendant was a well-known local panhandler, who claimed that he'd been begging outside McDonald's as usual when a stranger approached and offered to buy him a meal. Sure, thanks, he'd said, and they'd walked into the restaurant together.

The stranger's purpose was evidently to make the customers and staff think the transient was his accomplice as he jumped the counter, pulled a gun, and demanded all the cash from the registers. Then he ran out the door, leaving my defendant standing in line, still waiting for his free food. He *remained* standing there until the police arrived, and offered no resistance when they placed him under arrest.

Now, prosecutorial ethics require that you be convinced beyond a reasonable doubt of a defendant's guilt before prosecuting her or him. Based on the witness statements that the public defender showed me, as well as the testimony of the McDonald's staff, this poor panhandler had simply been duped into accompanying the robber through the door. Obviously, he knew nothing and wasn't guilty of anything, except being hungry. I dismissed the case.

NIGHT COURT ALSO brought me the Susan Dyer case, the surprise turning point in my career. Had she been assigned to another prosecutor, I would never have noticed the case. As it was, the Dyer case led to my legal reform advocacy in Sacramento, and the later formation in 1997 of our dedicated unit, STAT.

Dyer, and my subsequent campaign to improve California's stalking law, made me the de facto office expert in stalking. Although I still worked a full schedule in whatever unit I was assigned, if a difficult stalking case popped up, it was more or less automatically sent to me. Soon I was arguing in memos to the administration that we needed a stalking unit. It would require years to convince them. Until then, I prosecuted stalking cases as they were sent to me. That's how I met Robin Cloward.

In July of 1993, Robin was living at an apartment complex on 190th Street in Redondo Beach. She had recently divorced her second husband, William Cloward, because of extreme abuse.

On Monday night, July 12, 1993, William accosted Robin in a Torrance restaurant where she was dining with Allen Preger, her first husband, and Preger's niece, Mona Purillo, who was Robin's best friend. William informed Robin that her car would be vandalized that night, then he set about making good on his promise.

At about 11:00, Robin's telephone rang. Aware of how violent Cloward was, and how much Robin feared him, Preger and Mona accompanied her home that night. "Hi, this is Mike," William said when Mona answered the call. Mona, however, recognized Cloward's voice, as well as the call's origin the security phone at the entrance to the apartment complex. She hung up at once and told her uncle. Allen then ran out to Robin's car and found the windshield wipers were damaged. A .22 caliber bullet rested on top of the vehicle.

Robin's fear of William extended to concern for the safety of their two young daughters. But for all her fear, she was also remarkably practical and clearheaded. She jotted down the details of the evening's incidents, including times and places, in order to document Cloward's stalking behavior. Most important, she also listed potential witnesses. The coming weeks would be horrible for her as William continued to terrorize her, yet she documented each encounter, and identified every potential witness, down to the mailman. Once I got William in court, he wouldn't stand a chance.

On July 14, at just after seven in the morning, Cloward assaulted Robin at the apartment complex, striking her in the face and spraying her with mace. He later called Detective Mark Rodina at the Redondo Beach Police Department and admitted spraying Robin with "some shit."

At 5:00 P.M. on Friday the sixteenth, out on bail for the assault of two days before, Cloward approached Robin as she tried to exit the security gate in her car and grabbed a handful of her hair before she could drive away.

On Wednesday the twenty-first, Robin saw William again as she drove into the apartment complex. He later telephoned to threaten her and Preger.

On August 6 at 5:00 P.M., pursuant to a custody order, Robin arrived at William's house to pick up their two daughters. He met her brandishing a shovel. "I'll kill you," he said. "You have three days to live." He took a swing with the shovel, barely missing her head. As she drove away with the girls, he followed in his truck and bumped her car twice as they drove along.

About a week later, he tried to accost her in the complex's courtyard as she was walking to the laundry room. Robin ran back to her apartment.

Three days later she discovered that her car, parked in the security garage, had a smashed-in windshield.

On the twenty-ninth of August, Robin, as well as one of her daughters and Allen Preger, heard William yelling outside her apartment, "I told you to stay away from my kids. Now you're all going to get it." Robin, her daughter, and Preger all left the apartment.

Five hours later, neighbors watched as Cloward drove his car through Robin's front door. Shortly thereafter, Preger discovered that his car windshield had also been smashed.

Robin fled to her sister's house with her daughters. Late that night, as she and the girls slept in the living room, a hammer crashed through the window, landing within two feet of the children. Twenty minutes later, Preger received a voice message on his answering machine from Cloward. "I'm coming to get *you* now, Allen," he said.

At about 5:30 A.M. on the thirtieth, Preger found that someone had driven a car into the driver's door of his vehicle, badly damaging it.

Cloward was finally arrested on September 3, 1993. Since Robin had obtained a restraining order against William, we were able to charge him with felony stalking. I also charged him with assault with a deadly weapon, for throwing the hammer through the window.

During a break in one of our pretrial hearings, I watched as Cloward turned toward Robin, Robin's daughter, Mona, and Allen Preger, and made a motion with his hand as if to shoot them. I poked Mark Rodina, the investigating officer in the case, with my elbow, and Mark looked up in time to see the gesture himself.

When the judge returned to the bench, I informed him of what I'd seen, and had Robin sworn in so she could testify to it. The judge immediately doubled William's bail.

William pleaded guilty and asked for mercy from the court, but there would be none in view of the outrages he'd committed—all carefully documented by Robin in her determination to protect herself and her children from this madman who used to be her husband. At sentencing, it was reported, "No one should have to live the type of life that Robin Cloward has been living as a result of the behavior of this defendant. If the court does not take some action against this defendant, either he is going to kill her or she, in self-defense, is going to have to kill him. No one can be expected to endure the humiliation, both physical and emotional, that the victim apparently has gone through at the hands of the defendant."

William was sentenced to three years and eight months in state prison—nearly the longest sentence possible—for stalking, assault, and three criminal threat counts.

Ever since the Cloward case, I often think of Robin when advising stalking victims how best to document their experiences. A stalker will always claim in court that the victim is lying or exaggerating. But hard evidence doesn't lie. I tell these victims to always look around for witnesses who might have observed the stalker, and to write down their names, along with the dates, times, and places of the incidents. When I can corroborate a victim's story in this way, the stalker has no place to hide.

* * *

THE MICHAEL E. Gruning case came to me via the TMU
connection that I had first established via Detective Doug
Raymond in the Dyer prosecution.

Back in 1978, when Gruning, an optometrist, decided to
open his own office, he selected space on South Broadway in
downtown Los Angeles. The rent was affordable, and Gruning's research showed that this particular stretch of sidewalk
had the highest foot traffic of any street west of the Missis-
sippi. He was not deterred that it was located in one of the
seedier downtown neighborhoods. Gruning's clientele might
be down-market, but he was betting on high volume. As part
of this strategy, he even decided to accept low-paying prescrip-
tions for poor patients covered by Medi-Cal, the Medicaid program in California. Such marginally profitable customers were
often shunned by other optometrists. (Gruning also eventually
opened another office located in the high-rent area of Montana
Avenue in Santa Monica, for more high-end clientele.)

Business on Broadway was as brisk as Gruning had hoped,
although the downside of the foot traffic in that part of town
was that it wasn't always so savory. A good many of his customers came in wearing bracelets from hospital psychiatric
wards, or had recently been released from local jails.

Others made even more lasting, personal impressions.

One customer, for example, was six feet, five inches tall,
with long hair and a menacing air. He left a deposit for a pair
of glasses, and then returned with his equally intimidating
brother to ask for the money back. When Michael refused, he
vaulted the counter and chased him out of the store.

Once, another customer—a career criminal—walked in
looking for loot, armed with a .45 pistol. He locked Gruning and his two assistants in the basement, and got away with
some of the store cash. The robber was apprehended a short
time later trying to knock over a jeweler in the neighborhood.
Gruning had the satisfaction of fingering the suspect for robbing him, too. But bad news though they were, the likes of
these two could not compare with Ricky Pio Mationg.

Ricky, a wiry five feet, nine inches tall and 160 pounds, was instantly recognizable in the neighborhood for his Fu Manchu facial hair, ninja and camouflage outfits, tattoos from head to foot, and constantly crazed expression. Mationg was a heavy drug user with a long history of convictions for assault, as well as a murder charge that had been pled down.

He came into the office one day and immediately focused on one of Michael Gruning's two attractive young assistants. He then started hanging around the store. The girl was frightened to death of him, as, in fact, was nearly everyone, including her employer. Gruning finally told Ricky that his attentions were not welcome, that he was scaring away business, and that he needed to move on.

Mationg didn't take it well. He blamed Gruning for keeping him from his "loved one."

On the morning of August 4, 1994, he tried to sneak into the store behind another customer. When Michael pushed him back outside, Ricky threatened to kill him. Two weeks later, after Gruning closed and locked the store, Mationg chased him to his parked car with a knife, shouting again that he'd kill him. Somehow, Dr. Gruning managed to outrun Ricky up a steep driveway leading to his car. Although there were numerous people walking on Broadway who witnessed this chase, no one offered to help. The next morning, Ricky came to the office door and repeated the threat. "I'm going to kill you," he said to Michael.

Gruning put up a steel gate in front of his office through which patients would have to be buzzed in. Mationg was not deterred. A couple of days later, he showed up and tried to yank the steel gate open. Gruning and his two assistants huddled inside hoping the gate would hold. Mationg then grabbed a metal sign that was laying on the street and heaved it against the gate. Fortunately, the gate remained in place. He then showed up with a long-bladed knife and tried to break down the door using its handle. Gruning called 911, but Ricky disappeared before the police arrived. On the 21st, a Sunday, he saw one of Gruning's assistants working in the store and tried again to break in. Nothing was going to deter him.

Mationg's campaign was finally halted by his arrest on September 6. Jeff Dunn, a TMU detective, immediately

brought the case to me. It was a no-brainer. I looked over
the reports, interviewed Dr. Gruning and his assistants, and
filed a three-count stalking charge against Mationg—one
for Gruning, and one for each of his two assistants. Luckily
for the victims, my rewrite of California's stalking law had
gone into effect in January of 1994, so I was able to file felony
charges even though Dr. Gruning did not have a restraining
order against Mationg at that time.

I got my first close look at Ricky at the arraignment. Covered in tattoos, he seemed to be in another world. He kept
mumbling to himself in some unintelligible tongue and paid
no attention to the proceedings. I remember his lawyer looking very frustrated.

The preliminary hearing and trial proceeded without incident. Mationg was convicted on all three counts and sent off to
prison to serve the balance of his maximum, three-year sentence
(about eighteen months). Because of his clear capacity for violence and the fact that Michael Gruning was in absolute fear of
him, we took special care to make sure we'd be informed when
Ricky's release date approached. Dr. Gruning contacted both
me and Detective Dunn every couple of weeks, terrified that
Mationg had slipped through the cracks and had been released
without notification. At one point, Dr. Gruning called Detective Dunn in a panic, believing that he had seen Mationg on the
street outside his office. We immediately investigated and found
that Mationg was where we had left him—locked up.

Detective Dunn and I expected that once his prison time
was up, Mationg would be evaluated and sent to a locked-
down psychiatric facility for the term of his parole. Instead,
we were astonished to discover he was going to be released on
parole back onto the streets, which sent us scurrying to figure
out what had gone wrong. After a lot of frantic telephoning, I
finally found a contact in the prison system who could explain
the mystery.

Mationg, I learned, had been so out of control when he first
arrived to begin serving his sentence that he'd been heavily
medicated into a prolonged stupor. Basically, he was kept
unconscious the entire time he was there. No wonder on paper
he looked like a model prisoner. He hadn't been able to move,
much less act out.

We asked the authorities to take Ricky off his meds and then have him evaluated again. They did, with the results we expected. Mationg was sent off to a locked-down mental health facility for a couple more years.

I then opened another discussion with the Department of Corrections. Realizing that because of overcrowding and other issues Ricky would probably be released early in order to free up his bed, I asked that he be paroled somewhere at least thirty-five miles from Michael Gruning's optometry office. I guessed that Mationg, being a transient without apparent funds, would probably stay wherever the Department of Corrections placed him.

I was right. Ricky was paroled to San Diego and has not been heard from since, at least not in Los Angeles.

ANOTHER OF MY earliest cases involved a motorcycle gang member named Danny Hales.

His five-year relationship with Jill Thomas* imploded during the summer of 1994. Hales started to physically abuse her, knocking Thomas around, slapping and choking her. Finally, Jill threw Danny out of the house.

He responded at first by calling her dozens of times a day, sometimes begging to be taken back, sometimes threatening to kill her, as well as her family, friends, and dogs. During May and June of 1994, she filed six police reports of the threats, which were violations of a restraining order she'd taken out against him. However, for unexplained reasons, nothing was done.

Danny also menaced Jill by sending to her pager the numbers 1-8-7, the section of the California Penal Code that covers homicide. But his ultimate act of cruelty was to sneak into her backyard one day while she was at work and snatch her beloved dog.

Hales then telephoned Thomas to describe how he was torturing the animal, and how he would do the same thing to her. At other times, he'd claim he'd killed the dog, then call again

---

*Denotes pseudonym

and say it was alive. Jill pleaded with him for the truth. Danny simply laughed at her.

Late one night in July of 1994, she heard a noise and looked out her window to see Hales standing in her front yard with a flashlight and a gun. She ran to the phone to call 911, but the phone line was dead. Fearing that Danny intended to break down her door and kill her, she grabbed her gun and fired a warning shot at him. Hales ran off.

The next day, when Danny called his friend Kent Boutwell to brag about his encounter with Thomas, Boutwell accidentally recorded the call. "I just wanted to kill her," Hales declared at one point. Kent, who was friendly with Jill, later told her that Hales had also claimed to have two hundred rounds of ammunition for his gun, and how he planned to follow her to or from work, then drive up next to her and "blast" her. All he lacked, he said, was a Mack 14 semiautomatic rifle and a "hoopty ride," slang for a car.

Aware that Hales was serious about killing Thomas, Boutwell contacted the police. He later testified about the death threat, and also recalled to the court how Danny had asked him to hide Jill's dog, but Kent had refused.

The Jill Thomas case was brought to me by TMU Detective Doug Raymond, my old partner in the Susan Dyer case. After reading through the stacks of reports collected from local police departments, Doug and I set off to interview Jill at her home. I wanted to see for myself where Hales had been standing when Thomas took her shot at him.

We arrived at a small but well-kept house with a large tree in the front yard. Jill came out to greet us and took us to the side of the house where Danny had ripped the telephone wires from the wall. We then went inside to talk.

As I sat on the couch, I noticed an object moving across the floor. Distracted, I glanced at it, then almost jumped from my seat. The mobile object was a large pet iguana, casually strolling through the living room. Jill was definitely an animal lover.

As she described her ordeal of the past several months, Thomas kept returning to her utter despair over her missing dog. Danny Hales knew how much she loved that dog and what the dog meant to her. His motive for stealing the animal was pure malice.

Such pet abuse is actually quite common in stalking and domestic violence cases. The offenders have a twofold purpose: They want to inflict as much emotional injury on the victim as possible, and stealing a beloved pet certainly achieves that goal; and they are also signaling that if they could harm a poor innocent creature, imagine what harm they could do to the object of their obsession.

Thomas kept repeating to us that all she wanted to know was whether or not her dog was alive. I reassured her that I would do my best to find out once we had Hales in court. We could not force him to tell us, I said, but there were other ways of getting the information.

The jury required only a little over an hour of deliberation to convict Danny Hales of felony stalking, making criminal threats, and possession of a firearm by an ex-felon. This seemed to be the right time to bring up the missing dog. Most convicted felons facing hard time in the joint are ready to try anything to soften the impending sentence. Not Danny Hales, though. Prison or no, he stubbornly refused to tell us or the court anything of the dog's fate.

Then I had an inspiration. Just as the judge sentenced Hales to six years in state prison, I requested that he also order Hales to pay restitution for Jill's missing dog. The judge seemed to like the idea.

For Danny, it meant that half of the small wage he'd earn behind bars doing menial labor such as mopping the floors would not be credited to his canteen account (to pay for little amenities such as candy) but would go to the victim as repayment. In this case, for a stolen pet.

The judge looked down at Hales, and said, "I also order you to pay Ms. Thomas five thousand dollars in restitution for the loss of her dog."

The defense lawyer jumped to his feet and managed to blurt, "Your Honor! Five thousand dollars for that dog is ludicrous. It was only a mutt."

The judge smiled broadly as he responded, "Counsel, I also have a mutt, and to me he's priceless. The order stands—

unless, of course, Mr. Hales wishes to return the dog to Ms. Thomas."

Two weeks later, one of Danny's friends knocked on Jill's door to deliver her adored pet, which was very much alive and well.

I call that job satisfaction.

FOUR

ALTHOUGH WOMEN ARE less frequently the stalkers than the victims, they are typically every bit as diabolical and dangerous as males when they do stalk. Moreover, the problem of dealing with them is compounded by a common male reticence to admit that a woman is threatening or abusing them. Shontelle Riley was a dramatic case in point.

Shontelle Riley and John Carter* lived together for ten months, during which time, Carter later told police, Riley was often physically abusive toward him. Yet he never called 911 or filed a charge against her. According to John, Shontelle also bragged of having violently intimidated other past lovers; she boasted that one ex-boyfriend who angered her later found his tires slashed, and she allegedly hit another on the head with a hot iron. Neither incident was reported to the police.

In August of 1997, Riley appeared at Carter's house to pick up their three-year-old daughter. They quarreled, as was common. John asked her to leave. She did, but returned

---

*Denotes pseudonym

immediately and began to scream and bang on his door. When Carter's father answered, another argument erupted, and Riley sprayed him in the eyes with Mace.

The elder Carter chased Shontelle to her car. As he reached inside her vehicle to retrieve the can of Mace as evidence, she hit the gas and her car struck him, superficially injuring his knee.

This time John called the police. His family at first told investigating officers from LAPD that they wanted charges filed against Riley. However, the Carters then changed their minds. According to the police report, John Carter explained that he "does not want the suspect to go to jail or have his daughter grow up without a mother." Carter added, "Suspect is out of control and should get some help." He said that his ex-lover's behavior was the unfortunate consequence of a difficult girl-hood in a dysfunctional family. With no one willing to step forward to accuse Riley, the incident became, in police parlance, one of "mutual combat," and no charges were ultimately filed.

At the time of this incident, Shontelle Riley was in a relationship with Stephen Jones, a successful real estate broker. They had known each other for almost ten years; Jones was a mentor to Riley in the real estate business. Both of their daughters attended the same school.

Their romantic relationship had begun in 1996. Two years later, Shontelle said she was ready for marriage; Stephen, however, was not. As a later police report succinctly put it, "Riley became upset and ended their relationship"—or at least the pleasant portion of it.

She began to drive up and down Jones's street, honking the horn of her car. She'd call and make threats: "I will break your teeth out if I see you with someone else." On another occasion, Shontelle threatened, "If I see you out, I will Mace you. Don't make me mad."

When Jones deactivated a pager he'd bought for her, Riley responded with more threats. "Give me my pager code, or you will not be able to handle what I will do to you. Look, mother-fucker, this is going to get real ugly."

At 12:30 A.M. on June 26, 1998, Shontelle appeared at Stephen's front step, where she pounded on the door, demanding entrance. When he refused to let her in, Riley broke one of his porch lights and heaved planters at a picture window. Although the window didn't break, the planters were damaged.

That evening, Jones visited his father in the Baldwin Hills section of Los Angeles. On his way home at about 7:00 P.M., he was stopped in his truck for the light at the corner of La Brea Avenue and Coliseum Street when Riley pulled up alongside, jumped out of her car with a hammer, smashed his windshield, and drove off again.

In the early hours of the following morning, June 27, as Stephen and his new girlfriend slept in his upstairs bedroom, the sound of footsteps outside awakened them. Looking out the window, they saw that Shontelle was vandalizing the girlfriend's car. All four tires were slashed, and the vehicle was covered with graffiti. Riley had also spray-painted profanities on the front and side of Jones's house. When she looked up to see them peering at her through the window, Shontelle immediately ran down the street.

Jones finally contacted the police, but made no mention to them of Riley's threats against him. His two police reports were restricted to the acts of vandalism. Shontelle was arrested later that day, soon made bail, and was released. Her brief encounter with the law did not deter her in the least.

Jones owned a classic car that he kept in a garage at a condominium complex where Riley rented a unit from him. Though they had split, he allowed Shontelle to remain in the condo because of her young daughter.

When he learned that Riley had made bail on the vandalism charges, he worried that the parked car might be her next target, so he decided to move the vehicle out of harm's way. When Riley drove up to find Jones trying to get the car started, she had to be restrained by her father from attacking him.

On the twenty-ninth she telephoned Jones at least four times. As Danny Hales had done to Jill Thomas, she also punched 187—the California Penal Code section for homicide—into his pager dozens of times.

At this juncture, LAPD wisely assigned the case to Detective Bill Anderson of the TMU. During a July 1 interview with Anderson, Jones finally disclosed the threats he'd received from Riley. Anderson then searched out witnesses from Riley's past, including John Carter and other former lovers, each with his own tale of Shontelle's violent side.

When he'd completed his interviews, Anderson brought the case and Stephen Jones to my office on July 9.

I questioned Stephen Jones closely at that meeting. He repeated to me what he'd told Anderson of Riley's threats. When I asked why he hadn't reported them earlier, Stephen said he thought he could handle the situation himself, that Shontelle would eventually go away. Now he knew better.

The delay in coming forward with his accusations created potential problems for us. If we went to trial on a stalking charge, Riley's defense attorney might argue to the jury that Jones couldn't have been very fearful or concerned about the threats if he hadn't bothered to report them to the police. It might be a bogus point, but it could carry weight in court.

Jones also told me in our July 9 interview that shortly after their breakup, Riley referred to his daughter in a phone call as "that little bitch." He immediately took the child out of the school she attended with Riley's daughter. He added that he had no doubt that Shontelle would carry out her threats, if possible, and that those around him were probably at risk, too, including his father. When Riley told him what she'd done to Carter's father, she'd explained, "When I get mad at a mother-fucker, I take it out on his daddy."

Stephen Jones's delays in reporting Riley's threats notwithstanding, I filed a felony stalking charge against her on July 13, plus one count of vandalism. Judge Victoria Chaney set bail at $150,000.

Prior to the preliminary hearing, Shontelle Riley indicated that she wanted to plead guilty. When I conferred with Jones, he said that he wanted Riley to spend additional time in the county jail, but he didn't necessarily want her sent to state prison. However, both he and his girlfriend wanted restitution for the vandalism.

At the sentencing hearing, Riley successfully portrayed herself as a poor single mother who needed to take care of her child. Despite our arguments for additional jail time, the judge sentenced her to a three-year suspended prison term. That meant that she'd stay out of prison, as long as she didn't violate the terms of her felony probation, which were onerous.

She was placed in the "intensive surveillance program," the highest level of supervision that the probation department has to offer. She was required to maintain contact five days a week with her probation officer: two face-to-face visits and three telephone calls per week.

The judge issued a five-year restraining order, prohibiting Riley from having any contact, directly or through third parties, with either victim. He also ordered that Riley seek out steady psychological counseling. He wanted to see progress reports from the facility every six months.

To everyone but Riley's annoyance, extracting restitution from her for the damage she caused proved exceedingly difficult. It would require more than two years to do so.

In California, a crime victim is entitled to recover from the offender any out-of-pocket expenses directly relating to the crime. Stephen Jones wanted to be paid for the damage done to his house and truck windshield; his girlfriend wanted reimbursement for her Nissan's ruined paint job and four destroyed tires.

Beginning with our first restitution hearing in October of 1998, the judge ordered Shontelle to pay the full cost of the damage to the Nissan, about $1,850. By April 9, 2000, Riley had made a single payment of $670.

Stephen Jones wanted $212 from Riley to replace his windshield, but by far the stickier issue was the $4,000 he said he needed in order to remove all traces of Shontelle's graffiti from the exterior walls of his house. He said he'd tried covering up her mess with a coat of paint, but that he couldn't get all the colors to match unless the place was sandblasted and restuccoed.

Experts were consulted. The judge even sent a probation officer out to look at the house. The officer reported back that the colors all seemed to match to him, but this was hardly his professional specialty. Hearings followed hearings, seven in all. Riley kept coming up with excuses for not making restitution; the judge kept cutting her slack. Never have I seen anyone manipulate the court system as well as Shontelle Riley.

In the end, she grudgingly finished paying for the Nissan and reimbursed Stephen for his $212. The house wall-color controversy never did go away. In exasperation, the judge

finally told Jones that he should take Riley to small claims court
for the balance. I was furious. Jones, who obviously wanted
no contact whatsoever with Riley—he and his girlfriend both
obtained restraining orders two days after I charged Shontelle
with stalking—let the matter drop.

Riley never did give up. In the midst of the restitution fight,
her attorney moved to reduce the felony stalking to a misdemeanor and to terminate his client's probation early. I think
the judge noticed the steam coming out of my ears and denied
the motion. The good news is that the victims haven't heard
from Shontelle Riley since.

MY FIRST REVISIONS to the California stalking statute addressed
the law's most urgent shortcomings, not the full slate of
upgrades that my experience as a prosecutor told me were
necessary. I was therefore delighted in 1994 to hear from Senator Lockyer's office. They said that they now wanted to work
with me to make the stalking law even stronger. Did I have
any ideas?

You bet.

I had learned that incarceration was no obstacle to the dedicated stalker; many continued writing or calling their victims
from behind bars. Their targets, who'd thought their problems
would go away when their stalker did, were even more frightened to learn that was not true. A letter might appear all of a
sudden, or they'd get a collect call from the stalker in prison.

So I suggested inserting language to the effect that incarceration was not a bar to prosecution. If an offender persisted
from prison, we could bring a new charge of stalking against
him and anyone who helped him harass the victim.

Connected to this issue was the problem of stalkers being
released from prison without their victims' knowledge. So we
added a provision to the law that the California Department of
Corrections, or the local sheriff, must notify victims by telephone or letter of an offender's release not less than fifteen
days before the fact. Confidential victim notification forms,
to be placed in the inmate's file, would be made available to
anyone who qualified.

Governor Wilson signed the law in 1995.

Here's an example of how the first of the two changes worked in practice.

Shujaa Jasiri Silver, twenty-five, and Jean Nate (known as Peaches) Thompson, twenty-four, met and began living together with Thompson's mother, Wanda Darnell, in Northridge, a Los Angeles suburb, in 1994. Peaches, who had "Shujaa" tattooed on her left breast, was the mother of three children. On November 3, 1996, she bore Silver's son. The following May, the boy's father was convicted of rape and sent to California's Ironwood State Prison.

Shujaa and Peaches at first telephoned and wrote each other daily. By the following spring, however, Peaches was ready to end the relationship. She told Shujaa she was interested in another man, and put a block on her telephone so that Silver could no longer call her from the prison pay phone.

By June, the tone of Shujaa Silver's letters to her had darkened considerably.

"I swear you making me very upset with this not writing," he wrote on June 7. "All this situation is doing to me is making me want to Kill, Kill, Kill!! That's all that I can think about . . . Peaches, don't make me do something to you, bitch . . . I'm fuckin' breaking your fuckin' jaw when I see you. I gone just beat you to death you fuckin' piece of shit!"

His June 11 letter was similarly menacing.

"I know you are not going to write me no more. I can see your love for me is completely gone. I guess me being in prison was a sign for you to fuck somebody and leave me alone. Because your falling in love with this Son of a Bitch! Your showing me all the signs by not writing, not letting me call . . . Because you are a unfit mother. I be damned if you send my son through all these different niggas like you did [your other kids]! [My son] gone know one man. Mee. Daddy. Which he will never see you again. Because if I can't have you, then he doesn't have a mother."

On June 14, Silver at first seemed to soften. "Hi Baby," the note began, "I'm write this letter to you from deep down to apologize for me behaving the way I have. But you must understand, Baby girl, that we are both locked up in a world of hatred."

Further on he warned, "Don't make [me] hurt you."

Silver had turned violent with Peaches in the past, but the letters from prison, which she saved in a box, at first didn't concern her. But when Shujaa began mentioning his parole date, December 29, the threats seemed more serious. She moved with the children from her mother's house to live with her sister, Carmen, in Inglewood, which didn't help.

"You know what I told you would happen if you ever disrespected," Shujaa wrote on July 7. "So you did, now you scared as fuck, so you moved, thinking that would save your ass. Bitch, I'll find you."

Shujaa Silver evidently did not know that with each threat he was breaking the law. Nor did Peaches. Although as time passed, and she grew increasingly frightened, she did not take her fears to the police. In late July, she moved from Carmen's house to live with Aaron Jackson, also in Inglewood. Jackson was the father of one of her daughters.

"I found out where you stay at," Shujaa informed her in early October. "Now the question is what will happen?"

"You think I'm some kind of punk, or something?" he wrote again. "In about eighty-four days, Peaches, I'm gone show you a punk!" He also began threatening members of her family.

"Peaches," read his last letter from prison, dated December 9, "I hope I don't have to kill. If I think you don't love me, Peaches, hospital bound you will go." He enclosed a picture of her children.

She finally called Silver's parole officer in December. He told Peaches to contact the prison. She later claimed that she tried, without success, to gain anyone's attention at Ironwood.

At approximately 1:00 A.M. on the morning of December 30, 1998, Peaches, her sister, her mother, and the four children were all at Aaron Jackson's house. Jackson was with his cousin nearby. A knock came at the door. Peaches answered. It was Shujaa, who pushed his way into the living room and tried to hug her.

She ran from the house to fetch Jackson, who returned with her. A fistfight ensued, and Shujaa apparently got the worst of it. He was gone by the time the police arrived, interviewed Peaches, and took her box of letters into custody. Later that morning, when Silver called 911, complaining that he had been beaten, officers took him to the hospital, then to jail.

*   *   *

THE CASE WAS referred to our Compton branch office, where at the time I was prosecuting another stalking case. The supervisor in charge and one of his prosecutors looked over the evidence and were hesitant to file against Silver because they believed Peaches and her family would refuse to cooperate with us. There also were concerns about the victim herself. Peaches was a welfare mother with four children by four different fathers. She had no police record, but did associate with known gang members, including Silver and Jackson.

The supervisor asked me to review the case with him, too. The story revealed in the file appalled me. I immediately wanted to help the poor woman and her kids escape from this predator.

"Has anyone from the office spoken with the victim?" I asked.

No, I was told.

"Well, before we reject this case based on assumptions," I said testily, "don't you think someone should at least talk to this woman?" I made arrangements to go visit Peaches at her apartment the next day with a Compton police detective.

We found her seated in a large, beat-up old chair with her middle son, reviewing his homework with him. Her little daughter came running up to show me a picture she'd just drawn. The kids seemed happy and bright and clearly loved their mother deeply. I would do anything I could to keep this family safe.

Peaches and her mother treated us warily. No surprise. Their previous experiences with the legal system had not been positive; I realized I would have to earn their trust. Peaches told me that even though Shujaa was locked up again, she was very scared of him, fearful that he'd kill her and take away her children. She said that her first concern was their protection, and that was why she would fully cooperate with us.

I charged Shujaa Silver with stalking, principally on the evidence of his threats from prison against both Peaches and her family. Prior to the preliminary hearing, Shujaa repeatedly called Peaches from the lockup, telling her not to testify against him. Some of his friends called her with the same message.

But they misjudged this determined young mother. I remember how shocked Silver was to see Peaches in court, ready to tell the judge how he'd terrorized her and her family. Her mother took the stand, too, and I introduced copies of his many threatening letters from prison. The judge was convinced. He held Silver to answer, meaning that the case would proceed to trial within sixty days. We were partway home.

Before leaving court that day, the judge issued a protective order that prohibited Shujaa from contacting Peaches by telephone or mail. He warned the defendant there would be serious consequences if he violated the order.

Yet no sooner had Silver been taken from the courtroom to be bussed back to the men's central jail than he started calling Peaches again from the courthouse lockup! In the one hour it took me to return to my office that afternoon, Peaches had left four frantic messages that Shujaa was harassing her again. She was terrified, convinced he'd somehow get out of jail and come find her, no matter where she ran.

Fine! I thought. *If Shujaa wants to play games, he's going down.*

I called Peaches and told her that to fix the situation I needed her written declaration as to what had just occurred. I also reassured her that I'd do my best to secure state emergency victim relocation funds to move her and her family far away, where Shujaa would never find them. She agreed to write and sign the declaration.

Next I contacted the legal department at the men's central jail, seeking their advice on how to keep Shujaa Silver from calling Peaches. I was told that the only sure way was to get a court order that not only directed that the prisoner be kept from using the telephones but also specified that he be "housed accordingly"—that is, be kept in solitary confinement. They advised that the order should provide for his mail to be monitored, too.

I prepared the order, attached Peaches's declaration, and took it to the judge, who quickly signed the papers. For the next several months, as we prepared for trial, Shujaa kept his own company in jail, away from the telephones, and Peaches enjoyed her first peace and quiet in a long while.

We subsequently convicted him, and he received a three-year sentence, which with good time and work-time credits, plus time already served waiting for trial, meant he was back on the street in little more than a year. In the meantime, I'd safely relocated Peaches and her family.

By now, Silver should have figured out that his best move was to move on. Instead, he bought himself even more trouble.

I returned to the office from lunch one day in early January of 2001 to see a familiar figure sitting in the outer waiting room. He didn't recognize me, but I sure knew Shujaa Silver when I saw him.

One of our secretaries told me Silver was there to see someone in our child abduction unit. He claimed that Peaches was hiding their son from him, and said that he wanted us to help find the boy. If the matter hadn't been so deadly serious, it might have been funny. Obviously we'd done a good job in hiding Peaches, and he was using his son as an excuse to find her. Once again, however, Shujaa had outsmarted himself.

I spoke with the deputy in charge of the child abduction unit, as well as her investigator, and we decided that Shujaa should go ahead and fill out the several necessary forms, including one requiring that he provide background information on himself under the penalty of perjury. Sure enough, he neglected to document his recent prison commitments, and also stated he had a legal right to see his son, which he did not. He and Peaches had never married, and he had never legally acknowledged that the boy was his. He had no legal rights.

As soon as he signed the documents, I contacted his parole officer and explained that Mr. Silver had just perjured himself in violation of his parole. We could have filed new charges against him, but decided it was simpler to send Shujaa straight back to prison as a parole violator, and that's what we did.

FIVE

I RETURNED TO Sacramento again in 1995 to address yet another important issue. We persuaded the legislature that upon conviction of stalking, a prosecutor could request of the trial court a restraining order of up to ten years. This is not a term of probation. It stands by itself.

Civil restraining orders usually last only three years, and can anger stalkers into carrying out their threats. Under my new law, the prosecutor, not the victim, requests the order. Any violation means a substantive charge of aggravated felony.

We also inserted a provision that the court could order a convicted stalker—like Jolly Jett-Nanez Alsaybar—to register as a 290 sex offender. That meant that every year for the rest of his life—as long as he lived in California—the offender would have to register on his birthday with the local police, or whenever he moved. Failure to do so could result in additional felony charges being filed against him.

We added a confidentiality provision as well. A victim could request that her or his driving and voting records, useful for locating people, be made accessible only to law enforcement.

In 1997, we expanded a police officer's power to issue emergency protective orders in stalking and workplace violence cases. The protective order had previously been limited to cases of domestic violence, where a police officer at the scene of a domestic disturbance could call a judge and get their okay to write out a restraining order on the spot, then serve it on the offender. The order was good for five days, enough time for a victim to obtain his or her own full restraining order from a judge. State assemblyman Brooks Firestone carried the legislation for us this time. On July 22, 1997, Governor Wilson signed the bill into law.

The rise of the Internet and other electronic communications media prompted our next change, in 1998. Noting that stalkers were sending far fewer letters and a lot more e-mails to their victims, we expanded the "credible threat" language to cover the use of any electronic communication device to convey a threat. The new law covered computers and other Internet devices, plus fax machines and pagers, too.

Three years later, I prosecuted my first cyber-stalker, Marlon Estacio Pagtakhan.

Marlon was unusual in several ways. Born in 1978 in San Francisco, he was the first of four children in the family of a Filipino Navy man. ("Pagtakhan," Marlon said, was a Tagalog word meaning "wonderment.") Socially withdrawn, Marlon never lived anywhere but at home with his parents. His sole work experience was brief employment at a concession stand following his graduation from high school in 1997.

He had a passion for music, martial arts, and the Internet. He spent much of his time alone, in his room, playing his guitar, exercising, and working on his website, which was devoted in large part to the belief that his penis had been deformed in his infancy by a botched circumcision. He even posted pictures. This was why, he claimed, he was still a virgin. No woman would want to have sex with him.

Pagtakhan reported supernatural and extrasensory experiences, as well. Among them: his discovery of a psychic bond to the actress Jeri Ryan, née Jeri Lynn Zimmerman, a former Miss Illinois who was then appearing in the series *Star Trek: Voyager* as the character Seven of Nine. The isolated and troubled young man tuned into *Star Trek: Voyager* regularly.

Alone in his room, toiling away on the Internet, his concern about his supposedly mutilated penis was gradually joined by an obsession with Ryan, thirty-one, who was very alluring in her formfitting space togs. Ryan's boyfriend, Brannon Braga, thirty-three, was coproducer of the series. Marlon was aware of their relationship.

On October 20, 1999, Pagtakhan composed a note to Ryan and posted it on a Usenet site. In the subject line he typed: "Jeri Ryan...I LOVE YOU!!! Must remain abstinent." His message: "Won't you please let me be your love slave!?!?!? 'She vows never to have sex again until it's with Marlon.' "

From then on the messages to Ryan came steadily, first one every day or two, then several a day until they became a flood. On November 9 he wrote "Puck ALL Of You! Jeri Ryan loves ME!" December 12: "And whomever used my darling, for their comfort...I don't give a $hit who u r, I could beat, and pulverize you to death with my bare hands. In a bare-knuckle nude-pit fight (my debut film) I love Jeri Ryan, Jeri Ryan's da bomb! She belongs to me!" "I love you Jeri Lynn Zimmerman!" he wrote to a fans' website in early 2000. "I've been thinking of you everyday and everynight since Christmas '98." Marlon signed the post, "ViRGiN."

Meanwhile, Brannon Braga was receiving messages from Marlon, too, on the *Star Trek* site, on other fan sites, and on his own website. On February 1, 2000, for example, Pagtakhan posted the following to alt.tv.star-trek-voyager: "Brannon Braga, send me money NOW! hey you—Send me money Brannon Braga...you should know my position and send me some money! I am 'EXPECTING' some money s-o-o-n <= YeS!...i'm awaiting an—advance—from George Lucas! who's charity will come first? the Phanton Menace 'Jeri's LiL PiMP' oh yes I forgot to add...surely if you do not wish to do this, you should let me bash your cranium in with my 'FiST'! I said, 'Bash your cranium in my—FiST—!' I need not say more..."

Braga shrugged at Pagtakhan's early posts. Infamous among millions of devout *Star Trek* fans for allegedly cowriting the screenplay for *Star Trek: Generations*, in which the character of Captain Kirk is killed, Braga was accustomed to their vilification and scorn. His house had been spray-painted, and he even received death threats. The fact that Kirk's death was not his idea didn't seem to matter to the militant Trekkers, as they call themselves.

Pagtakhan employed an estimated seventy usernames—omar, LilLuvLon, and Takhan among them—at multiple sites. But he also used his own name, home address, and telephone number. Typical of most stalkers, he had little interest in hiding his true identity. He often e-mailed all night, sometimes at warp speed. During one thirty-six-hour period, he posted two thousand messages to BrannonBraga.com.

Around the middle of March of 2000, Pagtakhan enclosed some nude photos of himself with a post. In one memorable picture, Marlon posed in nothing but a hat and a strategically placed guitar. On March 22, he sent flowers to Ryan on the *Voyager* set, accompanied by a handwritten card that read, in part, "I love Jeri Bomb-Baby! Knew u don't ever need 2 cry."

At the same time, Braga's webmaster, Catherine Monson, flagged a post from Pagtakhan that mentioned the flowers. When Monson brought the post to Braga's attention, he and Ryan suddenly realized they were being harassed by the same obsessed stranger. He asked Monson to print out all Pagtakhan's posts under his various usernames that she could find. The total was more than six thousand.

The tone and content of Pagtakhan's messages were growing more worrisome, too.

Braga took this information to John Winchester, an assistant chief of security at Paramount Studios, where *Star Trek* was filmed. Winchester in turn contacted me and the Threat Management Unit at LAPD. Winchester, with whom I had worked on a number of stalking cases in the past, explained to us that Braga and Ryan wanted something done about Pagtakhan, but they were not prepared to press charges or to testify in court against him. Like many celebrities, this was not the sort of publicity they cared to have. So Winchester decided to see if a stern lecture would deter Marlon. Experience told me that it would not.

In early April, TMU Detective Alex Vargas contacted Pagtakhan by phone at his parents' house in south San Francisco.

He warned Marlon that he was flirting with arrest unless he stopped. Vargas told the suspect his behavior was inappropriate, his attempts to make contact with Jeri and Brannon were unwanted, and he was placing them in fear.

Pagtakhan didn't give the detective any arguments. He wasn't exactly contrite, Vargas reported, but Marlon was docile on the telephone, and promised to stop.

Yet he didn't.

"Pay Me Off... You can send a cashiers check for $10,000.00," he messaged Braga on May 7.

"Oh man," he wrote Ryan on May 31, "how I long to just smack that ass, so hard... spank her SO-much... and release to much 'building' tension... I want to beat her sill!... how much I would love to beat some down, is just as much as I want to 'DOMINATE' you—Oh, PLEASE let me!"

June 1 message: "I dunno, but for some reason I can just (Cave) Braga's Cranium In! Give me somethin ta brake!"

Pagtakhan demanded as much as one million dollars from Braga in his e-mails, but most consistently asked for five thousand dollars in "charity," as he called it.

June 8: "If BRANNON BRAGA isn't half JEALOUS as I AM! I WILL CAVE HIS FUCKIN SKULL IN!"

DESPITE THE ESCALATING physical threats and extortion demands, Braga and Ryan were still hesitant to press charges. So in August we tried another intervention. This time John Winchester personally telephoned Pagtakhan. The call was tape-recorded. Alex Vargas was present.

"Hello, Marlon?"

"Yes."

Winchester identified himself only as "John," an associate producer on *Star Trek*.

"We've been monitoring a number of e-mails that you've been sending to Brannon Braga and Jeri Ryan over the past few months," he said.

"And you want me to guest-appear on the show?"

"No, not exactly."

"Oh."

"The problem," Winchester explained, "is the volume of these e-mails is taking up a lot of my staff's time to read each and every one of these things. How many of these do you think you've sent since January of this year?"

"Quite a bit," Pagtakhan replied, "but since you've called, I will stop. That's all, like, you know, I actually needed."

Pagtakhan would be intermittently coherent throughout the conversation. Winchester reminded him that back in April he'd also promised Detective Vargas he would stop. "Our concern," he said, "is really why this is all going on..."

Marlon replied that Vargas had never mentioned "electronic issues."

"I don't understand," said Winchester. "Electronic issues?"

"I sent a get-well card and, yeah, he called me a stalker," Pagtakhan explained. "Like I was possibly a stalker."

"Yeah."

"But you can't stalk someone without leaving the privacy of your own home."

Obviously, Pagtakhan was not keeping up with the legal news out of Sacramento.

Winchester directed Marlon's attention to a post he sent the Braga website on April 24. "Help me," it said. "Please send five thousand dollars to get a life. I will surely stop."

"You would stop doing what?"

"Stop," Pagtakhan answered. "I would go get a life. Like I would pay off my bills. Go buy a car and get a job. Because I just need some help to get up and out of here, you know?"

"So, when you say 'I will surely stop,' does that mean stop sending e-mails or..."

"I mean, I would like get a life and get out of this room, because I don't have anything better to do, you know? If you can, like, send me some money as charity upon reading my web page, you will see a charitable charity in it. You can, you know, like stick up for the crap of the world, of today's society, and, like, just help me out of here. I will take donations, especially from *Star Trek*, because *Star Trek* is, like, you know, a very rich company."

Further along in the conversation, Pagtakhan insisted he was "a real big fan of Brannon Braga."

"Why," Winchester then asked, "would you post in your message that you want to crush his cranium, that kind of stuff, if you're a fan of his?"

Marlon answered, "I was being sarcastic, you know. You know how friends joke around? Well, I'm not exactly quite his friend here."

"Yeah, but some of it was kind of graphic. Frankly, it's a cause of concern for him."

"Yeah, you know, I don't intend to hurt anyone here. I may have been, like, you know, so farfetched and humorous, but then you couldn't understand it. But he also cannot like being coming from where you are, you know?"

"And all those sexual things you're saying about Jeri Ryan. That's really got her upset and afraid."

"Oh really? Well, she has nothing to be afraid of here."

"You get kinda graphic…"

"It's like, you know, in reality I'm the one that's being harassed here, by being, like, neglected. I could have, like, a simple fuck-off message from her…A personal stop message from her will have made me stop a long time ago, you know?"

By the end of the conversation, Pagtakhan had promised to stop whether or not he received any money from Braga. Then he resumed his postings anyway.

"Jeri," he wrote on September 7, "I am dying for my 'first' blowjob—PLEASE give me my first blowjob…and SOON!"

"SEND ME $10,000 CHARITY! If you cannot talk some 'goodwill' into Jeri Ryan," he wrote the following day.

In mid-September, I met separately with both Braga and Ryan. I needed to directly ascertain if either was truly frightened by Pagtakhan's e-mails, an essential component of any stalking prosecution.

Braga, whom I interviewed in his office at Paramount, was typical of many male victims of stalking. Although Pagtakhan's threat to bash in his skull had gotten his attention, he wasn't willing to say he was frightened for himself, only that he was frightened for Jeri Ryan.

Then I spoke with Ryan in her trailer on the *Star Trek* set between takes. She was in her full Seven of Nine costume and makeup, lending a unique eeriness to the meeting. I found her very gracious, and very afraid.

One of Pagtakhan's e-mails suggested he had come down to LA from San Francisco. That possibility, and the fact that he could be posting from anywhere, made Ryan extremely nervous. She and her son, then five, had moved into Braga's house, which she considered safer than her own. She also had recently canceled personal appearances at *Star Trek* conventions—which were quite lucrative for her—out of fear that Pagtakhan would show up to assault her.

Nevertheless, she and Braga remained unwilling to cooperate in the suspect's arrest and prosecution. So I spoke with John Winchester and Alex Vargas. It was time, we decided, for someone to pay a personal call on Marlon Pagtakhan, serve him with a restraining order, and warn Pagtakhan one final time to stop or face prosecution. The clear choice was Kevin Sleeth, a senior investigator with our office who was familiar with the Internet issues presented in the case.

We assumed by now that nothing short of arrest and incarceration would stop Pagtakhan, but Sleeth's visit would have the positive effect of further bolstering our case when, as was now inevitable, we did file charges. Marlon would be on record as having been warned three times to stop or suffer the consequences.

Sleeth consulted at length with Catherine Monson on the technical side of his investigation, and in preparation of a search warrant. Then on October 19, 2000, he visited Pagtakhan at his parents' beige-with-orange-trim tri-level on a hillside street in a middle-class neighborhood of south San Francisco. Kevin was accompanied by supervising investigator Pat McPherson from our office.

Sleeth brought with him both the search warrant and a restraining order. Kevin was also double-wired: He carried his own body wire to record the conversation, as well as a transmitter to keep the south San Francisco police officers waiting in a van on the street apprised of developments, should their assistance be necessary. The visit was not announced.

Mrs. Pagtakhan greeted Sleeth and McPherson at a side doorway above the family garage. She at first denied that her oldest child was at home.

"We need to talk to him," said McPherson.

"He was on the computer just a few minutes ago," Sleeth

added. His information came from Monson, who had been monitoring Pagtakhan's Internet activity in real time for the investigator.

"On the computer?" Mrs. Pagtakhan clearly wondered how they knew.

"Yeah," said Kevin, who had checked with Monson just before knocking. "He left us a message leaving no doubt. That's why we know he's here. Okay? Would you go get him for us?"

"He's not in big trouble?"

"He's not, really," Sleeth said. "We're just here to talk to him."

"He's inside," she said as she led the investigators not to the front door, but down into the garage, which had a door in the back that opened into Marlon's windowless, wood-paneled bedroom. The space immediately reminded Sleeth of a dungeon.

"Pit bull!" McPherson said loudly as he saw the dog, chained in the garage. He wanted to be sure the cops in the van knew of the dog in case a fracas developed.

"Is your dog tied up?" Sleeth asked Mrs. Pagtakhan, just to be sure.

"Don't worry," she assured them. "He's a friendly dog."

Marlon held his door partly ajar; he wasn't dressed. "What is it you want?" he asked.

"We need to talk to you," Sleeth answered.

"For?"

"Well, regarding Jeri Ryan. You want to talk to Jeri Ryan, right?"

"Yeah."

"Okay."

"Are we talking like an MTV fanatic here?" Pagtakhan asked.

"You know an MTV fanatic?" Kevin answered.

"Yeah. Why do you want me? If you're not going to bring me to her or her to me, I have nothing to say to you."

Marlon's words were defiant, but not his body language. Sleeth had watched his suspect's eyes and chin go down when he opened the door—a look of submission. *Alright,* the investigator thought to himself, *before this guy works himself into a frenzy, we're pretty much gonna get what we want.*

Pagtakhan shut his door, briefly, to get dressed and tidy up his room, he said. Sleeth had already seen more of Marlon than he cared to in the nude picture Pagtakhan had posted on the Internet.

As they waited, Marlon's mother offered, "We tried to tell him she is married to someone and he shouldn't do that."

"Yeah," Kevin answered. "She has a boyfriend. You know what? We don't want to see him get into trouble. So we need to talk to him about what he's doing."

Mrs. Pagtakhan then volunteered that Marlon was scheduled to enlist in the Navy in three weeks.

"He's a good guy," she said.

"Is he?" Sleeth replied.

When Marlon reopened his door, Sleeth and McPherson could see that their suspect wasn't big—about five ten and 150 pounds—but he was buff. Marlon looked like he worked out quite a lot. Sleeth noticed that throwing stars and samurai swords were mounted on the wood-paneled walls. Marlon had mentioned edged-weapon fighting in some of his posts. The investigator also saw a bamboo shanai practice sword, along with protective gear, in the room. Pagtakhan clearly took his martial arts seriously.

Sleeth also recognized a battered guitar, with only three strings, that Marlon had used in the nude self photograph. The instrument was propped up in one corner.

They spoke briefly about Pagtakhan's genital complaints, and how his hopes of suing the doctor who he claimed had mutilated him had run up against the statute of limitations. Marlon mentioned an ongoing problem with DJs and bands somehow tapping into his room and stealing music that he was composing. He also explained "my split personalities," which emerged in various postings to his website.

"So what are you right now?" Sleeth asked. "Normal?"

"Right now I'm just a type," said Pagtakhan. "I wasn't there." His conversation wouldn't get much more lucid than that.

Kevin ran down some of the more troubling communications that Jeri Ryan and Brannon Braga had received, and how adamant they were that these messages stop. He showed Pagtakhan the search warrant and restraining order, and explained that big problems loomed unless he desisted at once.

"No one's perfect," said Sleeth, "but there are certain things you can't do, and one of them is what you've been doing, okay? And that's why we're here."

"Yeah."

"I'm going to leave you with this piece of paper. This kind of basically says what you can't do. And one of the things you can't do is be around her. Also you should make no attempt to go down to Paramount Studios."

"Yeah."

"Probably more important, no more postings on web pages. No more postings to bulletin boards."

"Yeah."

"All that stuff, it's got to stop."

"Yeah."

"Okay?"

"Yeah."

"I want to make sure you really understand this."

"I really understand this."

"What do you think it means, then, this restraining order?"

"It's like a plead-out. It's a formal letter to myself where I should stop and do stop doing anything I'm doing."

"Right."

"And get together."

"Does it mean you can do it one more time?"

"No. Not at all."

"Okay."

"But you know what I'm going to do?"

"What?"

"God wants me to scan it and put it on my website and like finalize that."

"Okay," Sleeth answered. "That's your own deal. That's cool."

"That's cool, right?"

"Uh, yeah."

Shortly after Kevin Sleeth and Pat McPherson departed the Pagtakhan house, Marlon posted a video to his website. It pictured him sitting on his bed, dressed in a short-sleeved shirt.

Referring from time to time to a dictionary resting at his side, Pagtakhan denied all accusations against him. "I'm being accused of extortion," he said. "Is asking for charity a form of extortion? I think not. If Brannon Braga thinks my asking for charity from him is extortion, he is a dumbass."

He denied threatening anyone. "What is the meaning of 'threat'? A statement of what will be done to hurt or punish someone. When I say I want to kill Brannon Braga, this is literally not a threat."

Finally, "We go to stalking. Stalking is to approach a subject cowardly. Stalking is to chase, to seek, to pursue. I am not pursuing physically anyone. I have yet to leave the confines of this shit hole. I am far from a fucking stalker."

Kevin Sleeth and Catherine Monson both monitored Marlon closely on the Internet, and immediately picked up new postings from him.

"It 'turns-out' that Brannon Braga is 'MiMiCiNG' a SCARY BiOTCH—!" he posted on October 20, 2000. "(He is taking my TOO 'literally') You can view my restraining order on my homepage!"

It was time to revisit the victims.

"Brannon, Jeri," I told them in an early November meeting that Kevin and I held at Paramount with John Winchester, "the intervention is not working. You wanted us to give it a try, and we did. But he's not going to stop. It's going to escalate. He *will* turn up on your doorstep. We are going to have to file charges. If the case goes to trial, you will have to testify. I need your promise that you will. Otherwise, we're out of here. There's nothing more we can do."

We also made sure to describe for them the martial arts paraphernalia Kevin had seen in Pagtakhan's room. "This is not a guy who just shoots off his mouth," I said. "He's buffed up, and he knows how to use these weapons."

Braga and Ryan finally agreed to cooperate.

Kevin returned to the Pagtakhan household, this time with an arrest warrant along with a second search warrant, and brought Marlon back down to Los Angeles, where we charged him with stalking, extortion, and making criminal threats.

* * *

BAIL IS SET in California on a county-by-county basis by local judges.

The judge we went before to fix Pagtakhan's bail had himself been stalked by a woman who'd come into his court on a traffic violation. She'd obsessed on the judge, then terrorized both him and his family before charges were filed against her under the old law. Her bail was just $10,000. The next year, bail for felony stalking in Los Angeles county jumped to $150,000. When we stacked that with bail on the extortion and threat counts, Marlon was looking at about $250,000 in all. We would have no worries over keeping track of his whereabouts.

As it turned out, neither Brannon Braga nor Jeri Ryan would ever have to testify against Pagtakhan. The courtroom drama began and ended at Marlon's preliminary hearing, where I put Kevin Sleeth and Alex Vargas to tell the victims' stories.

When the proceedings got under way in early 2001, it quickly became apparent that Pagtakhan's attorney shared his client's mistaken belief that without a direct face-to-face confrontation there could be no stalking or extortion or threat. Armed with dozens of Marlon's most vivid and nasty Internet posts, I would have no problem establishing probable cause that he had committed the crimes for which he was charged, and should therefore go to trial for them.

The trial judge was a potential problem, however. I could see, as we placed the e-mails into evidence and explained the technical details of how Pagtakhan had been harassing Braga and Ryan, that unlike our first judge he did not quite comprehend what we were talking about. This judge was not part of the Internet generation, and there was a kind of blankness in his eyes.

So I put Catherine Monson on the stand to explain the Internet in lay terms that would make more sense to him. It worked. I can even remember the moment when the lightbulb seemed to click on above his head. The judge got it.

Once it was clear that Pagtakhan was indeed headed for

trial, his lawyer finally got it, too. He was faced with three sudden realizations: One, they didn't stand a chance on the issues; two, a jury, in all likelihood, would develop a negative opinion of Marlon; and three, forcing a two-week trial where the outcome was all but guaranteed would likely deeply annoy the judge, with possible negative consequences from their perspective.

So with Ryan's and Braga's approval, we struck a deal. Marlon would plead guilty to all counts, do a year in the Los Angeles County jail, then go on probation. If he violated that probation, Pagtakhan was looking at two more years in state prison.

Catherine Monson proved helpful in this phase of my prosecution, as well. She found a recent federal cyber-stalking case in which the government had placed very stringent probation requirements on the defendant. I checked to see if there had been any First Amendment challenges to the restrictions, found none, and concluded that the case was constitutionally sound.

According to the changes we made in 1995, I could request a ten-year restraining order against Pagtakhan, to be incorporated into his probation. Since it was clearly permissible for me to fold some of the tough federal language into the order, I did so. For a full decade, Marlon could not have control, custody, possession, or own any type of Internet-enabled device. Not just computers, either; I included other machines, such as telephones, faxes, and TVs, too. I also threw in federal language that the prohibition encompassed "any technological device that would enable the Internet now known, or that will be known in ten years."

We had Pagtakhan hemmed in. If, as he had promised three times before, he seriously meant to reform his ways, we were prepared to reward him with a comparatively light sentence: one year in jail. If, as we believed, he'd go back to stalking Braga and Ryan at his first opportunity, we had ensured he'd spend a very long time behind bars, without the people also incurring the expense of a trial.

Marlon did his year in the county jail, then returned to the San Francisco area after his release to live with a cousin. To my astonishment, his attorney had the chutzpah to petition the court for return of Pagtakhan's computer, which Kevin Sleeth had seized. The lawyer said that Marlon wished to give the machine to his cousin as a gift. I think the judge, who denied the request, was as amazed by the lawyer's nerve as I was. It was like a burglar asking for the return of his tools, or a murderer requesting his handgun be returned.

To no one's surprise, Marlon found himself a computer anyway and soon began posting messages to Braga and Ryan again, thus violating the restraining order and punching his own ticket to the joint. Yet when Kevin Sleeth showed up at his door for a third time, arrest warrant and search warrant in hand as before, Marlon actually professed surprise. "Oh, I didn't think you'd catch me this time," he said.

Besides the digital evidence that Sleeth and Catherine Monson had gathered against Pagtakhan, we also introduced forensic linguistic analysis, which tied Marlon to his Internet posts through his characteristic phrasing, use of capitals, and other writing habits. It was a slam dunk.

We sent him off to prison to complete his term, and heard nothing more from, or about, Marlon Pagtakhan until August of 2007, when he was arrested for stalking once more. He had again returned to the San Francisco Bay area, and was working for a moving company in the city of Burlingame, where, according to published reports, he lived with his mother.

His new trouble had to do, in part, with the All Pro Wrestling studio across the bay in Hayward. Marlon had joined the studio, but grew resentful at other members' alleged slights against him.

This group, both males and females, reported receiving threatening phone calls, e-mails, and text messages from Pagtakhan, and the Burlingame police stepped in to investigate. Marlon was apparently about to be charged in connection with his harassing communications when he showed up outside the All Pro studio on the evening of August 11, placed a pair of boxing gloves on the hood of his vehicle, and began screaming for the others to come outside to fight him.

He was arrested in connection with his threats as well as his alleged yearlong obsession with a female wrestler in Illinois, who performed under the name MisChif.

The Burlingame police charged Pagtakhan with fourteen counts of stalking and three counts of making threats, and jailed him under an $800,000 bond. Court-appointed psychiatrists subsequently declared Marlon incompetent to stand trial. As of June of 2008, his status remained unchanged and his trial suspended.

SIX

CASTILLO DEL LAGO—castle on the lake—was a hot spot on the Los Angeles celebrity map during the mid-1990s. The Venetian-style, multilevel hillside estate off Mulholland Highway, just below the gigantic Hollywood sign, was once home to Bugsy Siegel, the gangster who invented Las Vegas. In 1995, an even more famous and flamboyant figure, singer-actress Madonna, owned the property, which she had livened considerably with a bright coat of yellow and terra-cotta paint.

High brick and barbed-wire fences, a sturdy wrought-iron gate, electronic security systems, and armed guards afforded Madonna protection from her casual fans, as well as uninvited guests. Every few weeks someone would try to penetrate the compound's security, but they were routinely foiled.

Then came Robert Dewey Hoskins.

Basil Stephens—known as Steve—Madonna's bodyguard for the previous four years, directed the residence's security operation from his second-floor apartment, where he could monitor the multiple video cameras trained on strategic points around Castillo del Lago's perimeter. On the evening of April 7, 1995, an incursion alarm went off in his apartment. Stephens checked his screens and spied a figure climbing a pole located next to the high wall that surrounded the estate. The intruder hoisted himself up onto the wall and then dropped down onto the interior driveway leading to the house. When Stephens called out, "What are you doing here?" the intruder ran off.

The attempted trespass was a routine, low-stress event in Stephens's workday, especially since Madonna was not in residence at the time. She didn't return home from a visit to San Diego until around midnight, at which time Steve apprised his employer of what had occurred. He remained awake for the rest of the night, watching to make sure the intruder did not return.

At about 1:30 the following afternoon, as Madonna and her trainer were out on a bike ride, her personal assistant, Caresse Henry, received a call at the house from the phone box at the front gate. Henry glanced at the monitor to see a bushy-haired, heavily bearded stranger. He appeared to be fiddling with the device's wires.

"Hello," she said, tentatively. Henry was aware of the previous night's incident, and knew she was alone in the house except for a maid.

"Is Madonna home?" he asked.

"No," Caresse replied.

"This is her fucking husband!" the man shouted angrily. "I'm going to fucking kill you and everyone else!"

Rattled, Henry immediately hung up and paged Stephens, who was in his car down the hill from the house. She added a "911" to the page to ensure that he knew this was an emergency.

As she waited for Steve to arrive, the man called back twice, threatening to kill her both times.

"Don't you remember me?" the intruder asked Stephens as he arrived at the gate. "I was here last night." He directed Steve's attention to the call box where he'd attached a sheet of paper. "Give Madonna the note," he said as he departed on foot.

Stephens retrieved the message, a thick scrawl written over a printed religious tract from Tony Alamo, a virulently anti-Catholic evangelical preacher and ex-convict who at the time was serving a six-year federal sentence on a tax conviction.

The topic of Alamo's tract was incest.

"If a man has sexual intercourse with his daughter, he violates God's law," Alamo wrote under the title, "DEFILED," and continued, "for if a man take a wife and her mother, it is wickedness: They shall be burnt with fire, both he and they."

The intruder had written "Madonna Louise Ciccone" over and under "DEFILED" (Louise is Madonna's given middle name) and added "I love you" (underscored twice). "Will you be my wife for keeps. Robert Dewey Hoskins."

On the second page of the handout, Alamo wrote, "Mankind has become so wicked that if Satan and his impish army were abolished, we would be our own devil." Hoskins scratched, "I'm very sorry," (underscored once) over the printed text. "Meet me somewhair Love for Keeps" (underscored). "Robert Dewey Hoskins." Inside a separate balloon he wrote, "Be mind I'll be yours."

Stephens caught up with Hoskins and ordered him to leave at once, which touched off another screaming fit. He warned the bodyguard that he'd better deliver the note or he'd kill Stephens and marry, or kill, Madonna.

"What did you say?" Stephens asked.

"I'm going to slice her throat from ear to ear," Hoskins answered.

Stephens warned Hoskins that he'd make him regret ever coming around the property again.

"Just try it and I'll fucking kill you," Hoskins replied.

At that moment, Madonna and her trainer appeared with their bikes.

"I saw a guy standing in the roadway," she later told LAPD detective Andy Purdy. Madonna remembered the man was disheveled, unwashed, and "looked like he was homeless."

She continued, "He was near the front gate and he had a freaky look in his eyes. He looked very scary. My trainer and I rode up to the gate and we were met by Steve, who said to get in the house."

She came within two or three feet of Hoskins, but evidently he didn't recognize Madonna, who was without makeup, was dressed in a baggy jogging suit, and had her hair pushed up into a baseball cap.

* * *

THE THREAT MANAGEMENT Unit was called into the case on
April 10, and I was soon notified of the two incidents. But
until there was an arrest, there was little for me to do. The
police had a name for the stranger, but nothing more than
a description, which probably fit every third hobo in Los
Angeles. They assumed he was a transient, and surmised he
was probably camped somewhere in the brushy hillsides all
around the compound, just like dozens of other homeless individuals who made temporary shelters in the area.

Knowing that he might remain quite near the house and
could return at any time made the ensuing weeks an edgy
time, especially for Madonna. As she later told us, "This
whole thing scared me, especially that he was there twice. I
added an extra security person as an extra precaution. The
guy was never caught, so I feared that he may come back. I
was very frightened by his threats, and there was no doubt in
my mind that he could carry them out."

She was right.

At about 7:00 P.M. on Monday night, May 29, an alarm
alerted Stephens of a security breach at the front gate. He
checked the monitor in time to see Robert Hoskins, whom he
instantly recalled from their April 8 confrontation at the gate.
Hoskins was carrying a backpack and a duffel and wearing a
cowboy hat.

Stephens watched him climb the same thin pole located on
the outside of the high wall that he had climbed previously.
The pole bent in two but that did not deter Robert. He hoisted
himself up onto the wall, then dropped down on the other side.
As he tracked Hoskins's progress, Steve telephoned Protection One, Madonna's security company, to request an armed
guard be sent to the house at once. He asked that LAPD be
notified, as well.

Madonna was away in Miami, which would make Stephens's job much simpler that night. Still, his memory of the
wild-eyed intruder was sharp. He sensed there was going to
be trouble. That's why he'd asked for an armed backup. The
bodyguard also strapped on his own .45-caliber Firestar semiautomatic and grabbed a pair of handcuffs, too.

Steve had an unobstructed view of the mansion's front door from his second-floor apartment, where he remained to monitor Hoskins's movements as he waited for his backup from Protection One. Stephens watched as the intruder deliberately approached the door, put down his bags, and knocked. When there was no answer, he tried without luck to peer inside a window.

Hoskins then picked up the duffel and the backpack and walked over to the adjoining carport, where he scaled a wall to climb onto its roof. Then he walked across the carport roof toward a set of stairs that led to an upper garden and the mansion's pool area, near Madonna's bedroom. He seemed to know exactly where he was headed.

About ten to fifteen minutes into the incident, Tom Ebanks of Protection One drove through the front gate and up to the carport, where Basil Stephens met him and explained what was occurring.

Hoskins by now had reappeared on the roof of the carport. He was soaking wet, dressed only in his underwear. The duffel was hanging from one of the carport rafters. Stephens and Ebanks tried to coax him down.

"Fuck you guys!" Hoskins shouted back. "This is my house!" He then turned and ran back toward the swimming pool, with Stephens and Ebanks in pursuit. When they reached the pool, weapons drawn, they found Robert by the edge of pool, removing items from his backpack. Stephens, who feared Hoskins was digging around for a weapon, ordered him to assume a prone position on the lawn.

"Fuck you!" Hoskins snarled again as he pulled out some dry clothes and began to dress. "This is my house. I'm not going to do that!" Then he added, "Go ahead and shoot me!"

Steve holstered his .45 as Tom departed to check on the arrival of the police, leaving Stephens to cope with Hoskins on his own. The suspect was now pacing back and forth along the pool's edge, mumbling to himself and growing more and more agitated.

"I don't know why you're doing this!" he screamed. "This is my house! I'm going to fucking kill you!"

With that he lunged for Stephens's weapon.

"Tom!" Steve yelled for the absent Ebanks. "He's going for my gun!"

They grappled. Stephens had all he could handle, even though he was taller and heavier than Hoskins, in good shape, and trained in close combat. Hoskins got one hand on his throat. It felt like an iron clamp. Steve was astonished at the smaller man's strength.

With Hoskins still trying to get at his .45, Stephens managed to grab his left arm, and somehow pushed him back three or four feet. Then he drew his .45 once more and ordered Hoskins onto the ground.

"Don't move or I'll shoot!" he said. "Get back."

The threat seemed to excite Robert. "Shoot me!" he shouted. "Go ahead and shoot me!"

Then he lunged once more for the gun. Stephens, afraid for his life if Hoskins got his gun away, squared into a two-handed grip, aimed, and fired twice. One bullet hit Hoskins in the left arm, the second in the lower abdomen. He went down. Steve thought he might be dead. He'd never shot a man before.

Two of Madonna's neighbors, Nathaniel and Sara Goodman, happened to be walking their dog past the property just as Stephens pulled the trigger. Nathaniel Goodman later told LAPD that after the shots they heard "a male voice, real nervous, say, 'My God! The guy tried to grab for my gun! Oh fuck! Oh fuck!' "

Tom Ebanks remembered that Stephens looked "very scared and upset" after shooting Hoskins. Ebanks admitted that he was scared, too. "The suspect was very intimidating," he told Purdy. "He did not seem afraid of us, and that scared me."

(Although TMU had been in charge of the investigation since April 10, the homicide division at LAPD's Hollywood station had responded on May 29 because shooting was involved. From that point forward, Andy Purdy, a homicide detective, would be the lead investigator in the case.)

Stephens joined Ebanks briefly in the carport, then walked into the house to telephone Madonna with a quick report of the incident. From there, he took the elevator up to the kitchen, where he sat and watched Hoskins, who had begun to slowly stir, through the window while waiting for LAPD and the rescue ambulance, which arrived five minutes later.

Hoskins was waiting for them, too. Despite the two bullet holes in him, he somehow regained his feet, and seated himself on a ledge at poolside. Stephens approached him as he was being treated on the scene. Steve apologized to Robert for having to shoot him.

"Ah, don't worry," Hoskins answered.

Hoskins also told a uniformed officer, "I rushed that guy."

"What guy?" the cop asked.

"The security guard."

"Why?"

"Because he didn't believe that I'm Madonna's husband."

WITH ROBERT HOSKINS'S arrest, my first priority as his prosecutor was the list of charges to file. That meant ensuring Madonna's cooperation in the prosecution, which would prove by far the most difficult, annoying, and time-consuming part of the process.

She spoke with me by telephone on May 31, 1995, from her New York City apartment. I impressed on her how dangerous I believed that Robert Hoskins was, and therefore how important it would be to lock him up for as long as possible. I also told her that a successful prosecution hinged on her testimony. If she was not prepared to work with us—and this would eventually require that she testify in person against Hoskins—then there was no sense in moving forward.

Madonna told me how frightened she was, how she'd suffered nightmares and had radically altered her daily routine in response to Hoskins's intrusions. She was afraid to come back to California, she said. She also promised that she'd be there to testify when necessary. She seemed sincere at the time.

THE SUSPECT WAS transported by ambulance from Castillo del Lago to Cedars-Sinai Hospital for treatment. On the day after the shooting he was interviewed in his room by LAPD detectives Miller and Pinnaro. Miller read Miranda rights to Hoskins, who made no response. Then the officer asked, "Why do you love Madonna?"

"She's my wife," Hoskins replied.

"How long have you been married?"

"About a year."

"Where did you get married?"

"Colorado Springs, Colorado."

"Why did you try to break into the house?"

"It's my house. So is the one in Miami."

Miller asked if Hoskins would hurt Madonna.

"No," the suspect answered. "I love her and she loves me."

"Why did you fight with the guard?"

"He didn't believe it when I told him that I was married to Madonna."

"Why did you try to take the gun?"

"I was going to kill him."

"Why?"

"He didn't believe me. I love her and I have nothing in my life except her."

I ARRAIGNED HOSKINS on June 1. The original counts were:

1. Stalking Madonna
2. Making criminal threats against her
3. Making criminal threats against Basil Stephens
4. Misdemeanor assault against Stephens
5. Making criminal threats against Caresse Henry

I got my first look at Robert Dewey Hoskins at the brief arraignment. He was wearing a white (medical ward) jail jumpsuit, and was in a wheelchair, although he hardly looked like someone who'd just taken two bullets at close range. His color was good and he was very alert. He said little or nothing, as I recall.

What I remember best were his crazy eyes. I've seen lots of felons, but the only one with eyes as scary as those of Robert Hoskins was Richard Ramirez, LA's so-called Night Stalker, whose 1989 trial I attended for a day or two. After seeing him manacled in a wheelchair, it was easy to imagine how frightening Hoskins would be to someone who encountered him on the loose.

In fact, we heard a lot about that in the coming days. Because the victim was Madonna, the story was reported everywhere, and my name as Hoskins's prosecutor appeared in many of the accounts. That is how the suspect's ex-wife, Gayle, knew to contact me. She telephoned with a horrendous tale of the threats and abuse she and her five children had suffered at Hoskins's hands until their marriage ended in 1990. One child, she said, had been thrown down a staircase. Robert had threatened to kill them all on several occasions. Gayle, who was living in Florida at the time, implored me to keep him locked up at all costs.

We spoke to police in northern California, where Hoskins had once lived. Officers there, who had arrested Robert several times, feared him also. They said he often tried to grab their firearms, just as he had with Basil Stephens.

On June 13, Andy Purdy conducted a telephone interview with Hoskins's older brother, Michael, who owned a farm in Hermiston, Oregon. Michael said that Robert had lived on his property, off and on, until recently. Michael's wife, Judy, and their daughter, Hannah, had grown so frightened of him that Judy demanded that either Robert go or she would. On May 19, Michael said, they bought Robert a bus ticket to Florida: He'd said he wanted to go visit his kids. The route took him through Los Angeles, where he'd disembarked. Before leaving Hermiston, Robert told his brother and sister-in-law, "You guys will never see me again. The next time you see me will be on TV."

Robert had been obsessing on Madonna for approximately eight months, Michael reported. Robert claimed that he had visited her at Castillo del Lago several times before.

From Purdy's notes: "Robert claimed that there was a big brick wall around the place where she lived and he would often climb it and sit on the grass and in the trees while thinking of her. Robert had a white or tan raincoat that he claimed Madonna had given him. It didn't fit him too well. The sleeves were kind of small. Robert added that he and Madonna would swim in her pool, naked, and make love. Robert claimed that

he swam there a number of times. He said he partied with
Madonna and her rich friends. Robert kept insisting that he
was the 'third entity.' He never explained what he meant, but
he said it all the time. Robert also said that he saw God and
threw rocks at Him."

IT WAS ESSENTIAL that Andy Purdy interview Madonna in person. Yet when the detective tried to set up an appointment,
Lynn Shafran, one of Madonna's several attorneys, informed
him, as he wrote in his report, "...that Ciccone was not going
to submit to any form of personal interview. Shafran stated
that Ciccone was very shaken by the incident and was afraid
to return to Los Angeles because of it. I explained that an
interview was necessary to go forward with this case...But
she refused to yield."

Purdy handed the problem back to me. Through Nicholas
DeWitt, Madonna's civil attorney in Los Angeles, I was told
that Madonna was simply too busy with her various commitments—*Evita* was about to start filming—to be available as
a witness.

I replied that I would make it as easy as possible for her.
Madonna would eventually have to testify in court, I repeated,
but doing the personal interview with Purdy meant she could
avoid appearing at the preliminary hearing. Instead, the
detective could testify to what she told him; such hearsay is
admissible evidence in California at preliminary hearings. In
the end, we agreed that Andy would interview Madonna in
her apartment on the Upper West Side of Manhattan on Friday, June 9.

Purdy flew to New York with a list of questions I needed
answered to fill in the blanks. Under our agreement, once
the interview began I would join by speakerphone from my
office.

"I have become more frightened after this last incident,"
Madonna said. Having Stephens shoot someone on her property "really made this whole incident very real and scary. I have
had incidents involving obsessed fans before, but none of them
displayed the same threat as this one. When I got threats before,
or if a fan surprised me while I was out on a run or a bike ride,

I would simply alter my routine. Because of this incident I have completely halted everything I do. I don't ride my bike anymore, or exercise outside. I do not go out anymore, even here in New York. I will not go back to LA right now. I cancelled an appearance in my performance schedule in LA about four days after the May 29 incident.

"I could have been at the house when this happened, and I could have been swimming in the pool when he got there. I have had nightmares since these incidents. I have a recurring dream that [Hoskins] breaks into the house and comes into my bedroom and attacks me."

Before we finished, I once more emphasized to Madonna that her cooperation was essential to my prosecution. I explained to her again that we could not pursue the case without her personal, direct testimony under oath. She assured me she understood, and that she'd be ready for court when the time came.

There had been some long pauses and a few mysterious garbles over the speakerphone. I asked Purdy about them when he got back.

He smiled and told me how Caresse Henry had shown him to a sitting room just outside Madonna's bedroom to conduct the interview. When Purdy walked in, he saw that Madonna was sprawled in a large chair. She was wearing a black see-through dress or negligee—the detective couldn't tell which. The strange garbles, he said, were the sounds of him "losing it."

He said it looked like the type of garment purchased at Frederick's of Hollywood, or Victoria's Secret. Underneath it, she wore a black bra. On her feet were high-heeled, fuzzy-toed shoes. Her hair was wet; she had apparently just showered. And she had no makeup on.

"Hi, I'm Madonna," she'd said as he took the chair next to her.

"Yeah, you certainly are," the detective answered.

Lynn Shafran was in the room, handling the speakerphone connection with me. It was Andy's impression that Shafran was also acting as a chaperone. She hovered around Madonna in a motherly fashion, he said.

Before they got around to discussing the case, Madonna

bragged a little bit that she ran her own security company, of which she was president, and that on her own she'd arranged for all her possessions to be in the company name. No one could find anything about her through public records, she said.

"She impressed me as being a bit smarter than she was usually portrayed," Purdy remembered.

She also told him some of the history of the house on Mulholland. Her yellow-and-terra-cotta paint scheme—which her neighbors despised—was actually historically accurate to the period when Venetian-style architecture was popular, she insisted.

I was on the telephone with Lynn Shafran when Madonna stood up, revealing that besides the black bra she was wearing a thong under the black outer garment.

"It was very nice meeting you," she said to Purdy, explaining that she had a date.

Before he could rise to thank her for her time, Purdy told me, "She turned around and put her butt right in my face! Then she looked around to see my reaction. Of course, my jaw was already in my lap."

Purdy struggled to his feet and said good-bye.

"As she walked out a French door to go down the hallway," he said, "she slipped and fell. So her dramatic exit was spoiled."

ANDY PURDY AND Basil Stephens testified at Hoskins's August 29 preliminary hearing. Trial was set for October 30, 1995. Their testimony made a strong case. Our physical evidence included the bizarre note Hoskins had scribbled over Tony Alamo's religious tract, as well as a little handmade wooden heart found among Hoskins's belongings on the 29th. "To my wife Mdnna," he'd inscribed on one side, "you Robert Hoskins." On the reverse he'd printed, "Our god for keeps."

Everything was in place for trial, except for our leading lady. I had not spoken with her since early June, but had seen no reason to. I knew that Madonna was busy preparing for her starring role in *Evita*. I certainly was busy, too; just because I had the Hoskins case on my plate did not excuse me from handling a full load of other prosecutions. Stupidly, I figured a deal was a deal.

DIRECTLY FOLLOWING THE preliminary hearing, I sent Nick DeWitt a letter informing him of the trial date. In reply, Nick told me there were going to be problems, that Madonna would be recording the *Evita* soundtrack in London. He asked if she could testify via deposition, in which her testimony would be taken down by a reporter (or videotaped, or both) and then introduced in court as evidence in lieu of a personal appearance.

Nick was a civil lawyer, and that was a perfectly fine civil remedy. But it wouldn't do in a criminal proceeding. I reminded him that the U.S. Constitution guarantees a defendant the right to confront his or her accuser(s).

I did suggest one possible way around the impasse. Although it was unusual, I said, we could try what is called a "conditional examination." When a witness for good reason cannot be in court on a trial date, a judge may permit his or her testimony to be taken beforehand. In this case, Madonna would have to appear in Los Angeles in front of the judge, the court reporter, me, the defendant, and the defendant's attorney, who could conduct a cross-examination. The videotaped testimony would then be played for the jury at trial.

This compromise was soon rejected; I was told that Madonna feared making any videotape that she did not explicitly control.

Now I faced an even more complex dilemma. Hoskins was legally guaranteed a trial within sixty days of his arraignment in superior court. If Madonna couldn't make it to court on the thirtieth of October, I'd have no choice but to drop the charges, which people at my office were encouraging me to consider anyway. Their argument was sound: Madonna was well aware of the menace Hoskins posed to her, and if she was unwilling to act to neutralize that menace, that was her decision.

My answer was that Robert Hoskins posed more than a threat to a single person. He was extremely dangerous, period. If we cut him loose, I argued, he was certain to hurt somebody. I insisted on prosecuting him whether or not Madonna wanted to help.

In mid-October, I spoke to Caresse Henry. She told me that Madonna was still fearful of Hoskins. According to Henry, Madonna did not want us to drop the charges, but her schedule made a personal court appearance impossible. She was telling us, more or less, *Sorry, I have other things to do.*

I agonized a bit, then decided that I really had no alternative but to dismiss the charges against Hoskins on the thirtieth, then refile them immediately. This would start the whole process anew. But it was also our last chance. If we ran into this problem a second time, we'd have to let him go.

In an October 26 letter to Nick DeWitt, I explained the situation and my decision. I told him that if Madonna could be in Los Angeles to testify at Hoskins's new preliminary hearing date, November 14, I could videotape that testimony and use it at trial. I received no answer. Hoskins himself then made the matter moot. When he learned that Madonna would likely not appear at the second preliminary hearing, he waived it as a waste of time.

MY CAMPAIGN TO get Madonna onto the witness stand now entered its critical stage. There was no room for error. Since appeals to her conscience or sense of civic duty had failed, the alternative was to legally compel her presence. I planned to serve her with a subpoena. First, however, we had to find her.

She seemed to be avoiding Los Angeles, so we considered serving her in Miami or New York, her two other residences. Serving a subpoena out of state is a complex, multistep process that hinges on the cooperation of law enforcement agencies that are understandably more concerned about their problems than yours.

In my experience, agencies outside California are polite but pretty blunt about our chances of receiving substantive assistance. I'm sure this is true of states asking for the same sort of help from California.

However, when they learned that our target was Madonna, they were all very eager to help advance the cause of justice. Unfortunately, we had spotty and unreliable intelligence as to her whereabouts. Eager local cops notwithstanding, Madonna gave us the slip every time.

Then we got our break.

Based on a tip, we knew that when she traveled to and from her various residences she always shipped her dog in advance. When we learned in early December that the animal in question had arrived back on Mulholland Highway, Detective Purdy and his partner, Dave Lambkin, camped outside the gate at Castillo del Lago in a supposedly unmarked car, waiting to serve Ms. Ciccone with subpoenas commanding her appearance at a December 21 hearing, as well as the January 2 trial.

The stakeout didn't go well. Starting on December eleventh, then on to the fifteenth, eighteenth, and nineteenth, the detectives didn't catch a glimpse of their quarry. At approximately 9:30 on the morning of the twentieth, they returned to resume their surveillance. Fifteen minutes later, Purdy and Lambkin saw Caresse Henry being driven into the compound.

At 10:30, they decided to call Henry on her cell phone. According to Purdy's official report, when Caresse answered he advised her that he "was in possession of a subpoena for her to appear in Department 116 on December 21." Purdy noted that Henry was "upset" to hear she was being subpoenaed when she thought the matter had been dropped. Henry asked the detective to call back in fifteen minutes. When he did, the call went straight to voice mail. Undeterred, Purdy rang the house on the front gate's call box until Henry finally answered and agreed to speak to him at the gate.

In the meantime, I had received a phone message from Madonna's New York PR person, warning me to call off Purdy and Lambkin or they were going to get a restraining order against LAPD for harassing Madonna.

I laughed.

Back at the front gate, Caresse Henry approached the detectives on foot, accompanied by Madonna's trainer, and told them to go away. Madonna was suffering from an upper-respiratory problem, she said, and wouldn't be leaving the house that day.

"Well, here's a subpoena for her," Purdy said as he tried to hand it to Henry.

"I'm not taking that," she replied.

"Well, then here's one for you," he said as he gave hers

to Henry. Purdy offered to give her a ride to court. Caresse refused.

Before she stormed back into the house, he also gave her bottom copies of the two subpoenas he was carrying for Madonna. He asked her to deliver the papers, and to have Madonna tell her attorney to call me if necessary.

"She reluctantly took the copies," Purdy wrote, "and agreed to give them to Ciccone. I warned Henry of the ramifications if she failed to appear, and she agreed that she would be in court."

Detective Purdy then called me at the office and asked what they should do. According to our source, Madonna followed the same daily schedule when she was in LA. At around 2:00 each afternoon, she would go for a jog with her trainer on the dirt road that circled her house. It was now about 1:30 P.M. I asked Andy to drive away with Lambkin, get some coffee, then return to the house a little after two.

They did, and as we hoped there was Madonna in a blue jogging suit, suddenly recovered from her medical problems. She and her trainer jogged straight out of the gate and down toward the lake in front of the house, right past the two cops.

"I rolled down the window," Andy remembered, and spoke to her. "I really hate to do this to you," he said, "but it's the final step in the whole thing. We gotta go to court."

Madonna pulled a towel from her neck up over her face and said, "I don't know who you are. Get away from me." She was giggling.

According to Purdy, there were several directions Ciccone might have chosen to easily lose him. Instead, she ran along the right side of the paved road that leads down to a public park. Lambkin steered the police car alongside her as she ran. Andy leaned out the window.

"Look," he said, "I don't know your reason for this. We've bent over backward to accommodate your schedule. You need to go to court."

"If you don't get away from me," she yelled at him, "I'm going to scream!" All the noise attracted someone with a video camera, who caught part of this rolling argument, and later put it on the Internet.

Purdy asked Lambkin to drive ahead, around a curve,

where he would get out, produce his badge, and try to serve the subpoena in a civilized way. When Madonna saw them, she and her trainer crossed the roadway and headed back toward Castillo del Lago. Again, she might have easily shaken them, the detective told me, but didn't. She was still giggling.

"Can't you take a hint and take a hike?" the trainer asked when Purdy and Lambkin caught up with them.

"I just wanted to get out and arrest her," he recalled.

Purdy got out of the car and ran alongside the two. He was in a suit and street shoes, and Madonna might have easily outrun him. But she didn't. It was a game.

"Look," he said.

"No, you look," she answered as they jogged along. "I do what I want to do."

"Well," the detective replied, "in this particular case you are ordered by the court to go to court." He repeated the place, time, and date several times, then tucked the subpoena under her inner left elbow. She let the paper drop to the ground, made a rude comment, then stepped on it, leaving a muddy footprint before running off.

Purdy retrieved the duly served subpoena as Madonna jogged away, and brought the document back to me.

The next day in court, Nick DeWitt showed up without her and asked the judge to quash the subpoena. DeWitt claimed that Madonna was not a material witness.

Judge Andrew Kauffman asked if I had proof of service. Of course I had to smile. It was one of those moments that all prosecutors live for. I held up the subpoena and told the judge that not only had she been served by Detective Purdy, who was standing by me in court, but we had her muddy footprint on the first page to prove it.

Since she had chosen not to appear as commanded by the subpoena, I requested that the court issue a five-million-dollar body attachment—which is similar to an arrest warrant—on her. I was originally going to ask for a $100,000 body attachment, but changed my mind after all the trouble she had put us through. The judge granted our request.

The press, which had been all over the story since Hoskins was arrested in May, gave this new development saturation coverage. Two weeks later, when we picked a jury, almost everyone in the jury pool said they knew of the incident. Under the headline, "Madonna Ordered to Be in Court," the *Los Angeles Times* reported that "DeWitt promised Kauffman that he would get Madonna to court at the appointed time, saying she was 'not going to ignore a court order.' "

" 'She's already ignored a court order,' Kauffman dryly replied, referring to the subpoena."

The story went on, "Outside court, Saunders said she is adamant about Madonna testifying against Hoskins because stalkers are dangerous to people other than their targets. 'The issue is stalking,' Saunders said, 'not who Madonna is.' "

Not everyone agreed with me on that.

That evening I received a phone call at home from my top boss. He'd heard from one of Madonna's many attorneys, asking us to drop the body attachment. I refused to consider it, which probably explains why it took me so long to get my next promotion. I did say that if Madonna was willing to talk to me for about an hour to review what she remembered about the case, I would ask the judge to hold the body attachment until the day she was needed to testify. Otherwise, as far as I was concerned, the body attachment would issue and she would have to be in court every single day until we were ready to have her testify.

The very next morning Madonna herself called. Boy, was she angry, but she agreed to cooperate.

She may have started her career in NYC, but I was born and raised there—don't mess with a native New Yorker!

As OUR NEW trial date neared, I was moderately certain that Madonna would keep her word this time. Five million dollars would be a major financial hit, even for someone with her resources.

Two other matters concerned me more. One was the sort of defense that Deputy Public Defender E. John Myers intended to mount on Robert Dewey Hoskins's behalf, particularly if he planned to argue that his client was insane or, more likely, afflicted with what we call in California "diminished actuality."

I commonly encounter the diminished actuality defense

in my stalking prosecutions—particularly when the victim is a celebrity—so the concept merits some discussion. Prior to 1982, California law recognized a so-called diminished capacity defense, in which a defendant might be legally sane at the time of the crime but also "suffering from a mental illness that prevented him from acting with malice aforethought or with premeditation and deliberation," which meant that he could not be convicted of first-degree murder.

The diminished capacity defense applied to other crimes that required the offender's specific intent be established by the prosecution. It was also used by defense attorneys to negate such particular mental states as malice, deliberation, and premeditation. Nobody thought to challenge any of this until the infamous "Twinkie Defense" of ex-policeman Dan White, a San Francisco supervisor who'd resigned his post, thought better of it, asked Mayor George Moscone to reinstate him, and was refused.

On November 27, 1978, White assassinated Moscone and city supervisor Harvey Milk, a gay activist. White had climbed through a basement window at city hall to avoid metal detectors and confronted Moscone, demanding his job as a city supervisor back. When Moscone refused, White shot him twice at close range, then stood over Moscone's body and shot two more bullets into the mayor's brain.

White reloaded his gun and went down the hall to confront Supervisor Harvey Milk, one of America's first openly gay public officials. He shot Milk five times, killing him instantly.

At trial, defense attorneys argued that White had been suffering from depression, which caused him to commit the murders. A psychiatrist testified on White's behalf, stating that prior to the shootings, the formerly health-conscious defendant had consumed massive quantities of Twinkies, a sugar-laden, cakelike pastry popular with children. The psychiatrist told the jury that too much sugar can affect the chemical balance in the brain and worsen depression. It had diminished White's capacity to act with premeditation.

Although the defense never actually blamed the defendant's behavior on Twinkies, once the jury found him guilty of a lesser charge, voluntary manslaughter, the nickname "Twinkie Defense" was born. White was sentenced to six years in state prison. He was released on parole in 1984, and committed suicide the next year.

The broadly negative public response to the White verdict prompted an attempt by the California state legislature to do away with the diminished capacity defense altogether. Unfortunately, its replacement, the "diminished actuality" statute, creates nearly the same challenges for prosecutors as the old law did. In stalking prosecutions, for example, if a defense lawyer can convince a jury that due to diminished actuality his client could not have formed the necessary specific intent to frighten the victim, I lose my case.

To help me prepare for any eventuality in the Hoskins prosecution, I retained the noted forensic psychologist Dr. J. Reid Meloy, a foremost authority on the psychology of stalking and widely published on the subject. Reid studied all the available evidence and watched Stephens's surveillance tapes of Hoskins with me. If necessary, Reid would explain on the witness stand how Hoskins could profess his love for Madonna while at the same time want to frighten her. He also helped me prepare a motion to admit at trial his testimony, which contained invaluable information about celebrity stalkers.

Reid found no evidence that Hoskins was legally insane, which in California is determined by the so-called M'Naghten Rule: Either you don't know the nature and quality of the act, or you don't know that what you are doing is wrong. If either of those is caused by a mental disorder, you have grounds for claiming legal insanity.

So that narrowed the defense option to diminished actuality: Could Myers knock out the fact that Hoskins knew he was inducing fear? The public defender would suggest during the trial that Robert suffered from erotomania, a delusional belief that Madonna loved him. Yet he did not put on an expert willing to make that diagnosis, which severely undercut his point.

Moreover, Reid pointed out in our discussions that if you look at the note that Hoskins left for Madonna at the gate, he says nothing about believing that she loves him. "You have a future-oriented statement," he explained to me. " 'Will you be my wife for keeps.' " So in his own handwriting he gave us evidence that he did not have erotomanic delusional disorder. "A subtle detail perhaps," Reid added, "but very important."

At the time of the trial, the most popular stalking typology recognized three subtypes: erotomanics, simple obsessionals, and love obsessionals. In simple obsessional, there was a previous relationship of some kind, such as an ex-wife. The love obsessional is fanatically in love with a person. These types believe they are destined to have a relationship with her, or him, but don't necessarily believe that he or she loves them. As Meloy saw it, Hoskins probably would have been considered a love-obsessional type.

In my motion, I quoted Reid at some length:

> The psychopathology of obsessional following is, in part, a maladaptive response to social incompetence, social isolation, and loneliness. What differentiates these individuals from others, however, appears to be their aggression and pathological narcissism. The acting out of their obsession in pursuit, and in a few cases eventual violence, is likely due to a disturbance in their narcissistic economy. A real event, such as acute or chronic rejection, challenges the compensatory narcissistic fantasy that the obsessional follower is special, loved, idealized, admired, superior to, or in some way linked or destined to be with the object of pursuit. The disturbance of this narcissistic fantasy, imbued with both a sense of grandiosity and a feeling of pride, triggers feelings of shame or humiliation that are defended against with rage. This intense anger also fends off any feeling of sadness, since the capacity to grieve the loss of a whole, real, and meaningful person is not available to the obsessional follower. Instead, from a self-psychology perspective, a merging narcissistic transference is apparent, characterized by rage...Overt paranoia in the obsessional follower will likely be directed toward third parties perceived as standing in the way of the object...Intervention by third parties to help or protect the victim may acerbate paranoid beliefs by providing a vehicle that can carry the paranoid projection...

My second main concern was Madonna herself. She was a controversial entertainer. She had recently put out a book about sex that featured some pretty raw images and had offended a lot of people. That, of course, was part of her act, but I had to make sure that it didn't torpedo my prosecution. I had to be certain during jury selection, or voir dire, to weed out anyone who might have a hidden agenda or harbor some deep antagonism toward her.

The trial opened on Tuesday, January 2, 1996, before Superior Court Judge Jacqueline A. Connor in a special-security, ninth-floor courtroom of the downtown criminal courts building. Judge Connor was well-known around the courthouse for running a tight courtroom. She expected us attorneys to have our witnesses lined up and ready to go, and she did not brook unnecessary delays. Since Judge Connor was scheduled to go on vacation at the conclusion of the Hoskins trial, I was pretty sure we'd move along at her usual smart pace.

In my experience with voir dire, most prospective jurors try to avoid serving if possible. When it's a celebrity case, however, the reverse is true. Everyone wants to be chosen. This factor would make it even more difficult to ferret out the ones who might bear Madonna hidden ill will.

When we asked how many people had read about this case, all hands went up. I expected that. The story had been all over the news for months; my recent dustup with Madonna had received particularly wide press attention. There was no way someone could avoid knowing about it. In fact, if anyone in the jury pool had failed to raise his or her hand, I would have been deeply suspicious. None did.

Both John Myers and I were interested in essentially the same information about the jury, so we both listened closely as Judge Connor asked them questions such as, "Do you have any strong feelings one way or the other toward the entertainer Madonna?" I also watched each one's body language.

Eventually, that attention to detail paid off. One man in the jury pool answered all the questions correctly: He claimed to be impartial and betrayed no prejudices. But there was just something about his body language that concerned me.

So I asked him a few more questions. "Do you own any of her recordings?" I wanted to know. "Have you seen her in performance?" After a few minutes of this he finally admitted, "I do hold a slight grudge against her because I'm Catholic and I remember a video where she was misusing a crucifix."

Bingo! I knew it! That's the kind of guy who could have hung my jury for me.

Under the circumstances, the jury selection process took a while. I remember that we went through two large pools of perhaps fifty people each before we agreed on a panel of twelve, plus two alternates.

I put Nathaniel Goodman, Madonna's neighbor, on the stand, as well as Protection One security guard Tom Ebanks and Madonna's assistant, Caresse Henry, who testified to her fear of Hoskins when he appeared at the front gate on April 8. They all gave excellent testimony, as did Detective Purdy.

Bodyguard Basil Stephens was my star witness, however. We played the surveillance video with him on the stand, and went over the images frame by frame, walking the jurors through the whole sequence. I talked to some of them later, and they told me that Stephens was our most credible witness.

They might have harbored conflicted feelings about Madonna, but they loved Steve, who, of course, was also a victim. The jurors resented that Hoskins had tried to hurt him.

The huge press contingent was disappointed not to see Madonna at court that first day. I remember there were so many of them with so little to do that the photographers started photographing one another.

Day Two was like feeding hour in the shark tank.

Madonna had declined Andy Purdy's offer to drive her to court in favor of taking a black limousine, which was instantly swarmed by reporters and photographers. There was obviously no way to keep her presence in the building a secret, but we were able to avoid a mob scene in the doorway by bringing her up in the judges' elevator and putting her in an office—our version of the green room—where she made herself comfortable until I called her.

Everyone in the courtroom was waiting for her, chatting among themselves, speculating on when they'd get to see her. When I was ready, I telephoned from the bailiff's desk for her to be brought to court.

The hallway outside the courtroom was jammed with people, many of them screaming for Madonna. The sheriff's department assigned twenty deputies to form a human cordon to get her from the waiting room into court. Andy, who'd gone to considerable effort to get Madonna's brother, Chris, and some of her friends into court to hear her testify, walked over to greet her and escort her in.

She only scowled and said to the female deputy standing next to her, "Get him away from me."

The deputy asked, "Who are you?" as she tried to push Purdy away.

"I'm the investigator in this case!" he set her straight. "Let go of me!"

Three of our investigators led Ciccone through the police cordon, with Andy bringing up the rear, appropriately enough.

Then she made her grand entrance. The whole room froze for a moment of pure celebrity gawking.

Madonna was perfectly dressed for court in a plain charcoal sweater suit—not too short, not too clingy. Her hair was pulled back in a chignon. She wore tiny earrings and very little makeup. On the street, you might not have recognized her.

Robert Hoskins, at the defense table, was giving her his Charles Manson stare. Madonna, very cool, almost cold, ignored him as she sat in the witness chair. Earlier in the day, Nick DeWitt had made a final attempt to have the defendant removed from the courtroom while Madonna testified. Both John Myers and I had opposed the motion on constitutional grounds. The defendant had a right to face his accuser. I did not want the trial verdict later overturned because of error.

Judge Connor denied DeWitt's motion, explaining that to remove Hoskins might prejudice the jury, whose members she'd instructed to presume the defendant innocent until he was proven otherwise.

My job was to establish that Hoskins had put the entertainer in fear.

"You didn't want to testify, did you?" I asked Madonna.

"No."

"We had to do a body attachment, didn't we?"

"Yes."

"Why didn't you want to come to court?"

I already knew what her answer would be because she'd previously told me. "I feel incredibly disturbed," Madonna said, "that the man who repeatedly threatened my life is sitting across the room from me. I feel we are making his fantasies come true."

The jurors afterward told me that Madonna's remark made sense to them. She made sense to me, too. We *were* giving Hoskins what he wanted. Yet if we didn't, he would have walked. And once he was free again, although Madonna might have been able to protect herself against him, I was dead-certain that Robert Hoskins was going to hurt somebody if we didn't put him in prison.

She remained on the stand for about ninety minutes. We discussed our first telephone conversation, when Madonna had talked about her fears, and how Hoskins's conduct had affected her life. She testified in detail about her encounter with him, how this very strange and scary man had paused and stared at her a couple of seconds, and how weird his eyes were. She hadn't known what exactly occurred until Steve ushered her and her trainer into the house, and showed her the note from Hoskins. It wasn't so much what he'd written, she said, but the printed material from Tony Alamo below it. She'd been particularly unnerved to see her name framing DEFILED on the page. She also described how Steve had told her about Hoskins's threat to slit her throat.

Overall, Madonna was an excellent, low-key witness, willing to let the impact of her testimony rest in her words, not her appearance.

Then came E. John Myers's turn. The defense attorney was a very good-looking young man; he bore a resemblance to John Kennedy, Jr. He was wearing a brand-new suit for this, his first big trial, and had invited his parents to court to see their son in action.

As they and everyone else looked on, Myers stood up to begin his cross-examination. Madonna looked up as he rose. But she didn't just look; she stared, hungrily. I watched her eyes follow John as he walked from the counsel table over to the podium located behind where Andy Purdy and I were seated.

She was undressing him, looking him up and down. No one in the courtroom, including John's parents, could have missed it.

John was aware of it, of course, and I think he was kind of

enjoying it, until he asked Madonna, "Well, how big is your bodyguard?"

She paused, smirked, looked him up and down like a piece of meat once again, and answered, "I don't really know. How big are you?"

John turned bright red! I lost it, and had to turn my chair away so the jurors didn't see me laughing. Madonna simply smiled. I peeked at the jury and could see that they were laughing. Everyone else in the courtroom seemed just as amused, except for John's parents and Judge Connor. The laughter lasted for several seconds.

Myers eventually regained his composure, and completed his cross. But I frankly doubt that anything that transpired after Madonna's remark made much of an impression on the jury. After the trial, I teased him unmercifully.

The reporters and photographers got their second shot at Madonna as she was driven away from the judges' parking lot. But the courthouse was still under press siege later in the day when Madonna's attorney, Nick DeWitt, and I tried to sneak out the back door. They all surged toward us. Nick, who was confined to a wheelchair, nearly ended up on the pavement as a photographer inadvertently banged into him. Luckily, one of my investigators was with us and managed to grab Nick just in time. We had to push the press away to get Nick to a car.

I DIDN'T KNOW until I finished my case that the defense would call no witnesses of its own. Myers was a smart lawyer who had very little to work with. So he did what a lot of defense attorneys do: He offered multiple defenses, hoping to plant some small shred of doubt in at least one juror's mind. Through his questions of the prosecution witnesses, he tried to portray Hoskins as too deluded to understand that he was placing Madonna in fear. He also tried to make Hoskins look like a patsy instead of a predator, a poor schmo who meant no harm and was now being used by the evil Madonna to wring a little publicity out of the story.

Final arguments were Friday, January 5. John called Madonna a liar. "She comes in here and she's acting," he said. "She can't stop acting." He claimed that Madonna, Stephens, and Henry exaggerated their testimony to mask the fact that Stephens had no substantive cause for shooting Hoskins, who was guilty of nothing more than a misdemeanor trespass. After all, John said, Hoskins didn't lift a finger on the one occasion he was near Madonna, by the front gate on April 8. He scoffed at the suggestion that Hoskins did not recognize the victim. As if to make his point, Myers pulled on a pair of sunglasses in court and asked the jurors if they recognized him.

I reminded the jury of the elements of each charge and the evidence we presented to support the charges.

They came back on Monday the eighth after four or five hours of deliberation. Hoskins was smiling when he was brought in to hear their verdict. After the foreman announced guilty verdicts on all five counts, the defendant said nothing and betrayed no emotion.

Of Madonna's testimony, the foreman told reporters: "She was very real, very believable, and very credible."

Madonna later released a statement, saying she hoped "the outcome of this case lets other stalking victims know that the system can, and does, work."

My office held a big press conference on the eighteenth floor of the criminal courts building. "This sends a message to victims of stalkers that they can come forward," I told reporters, and added sarcastically that Madonna, despite her reluctance to testify, was "something of a role model" for doing so.

THE ISSUE NOW was to get Robert Dewey Hoskins as much prison time as possible for his five convictions. Unless I was proactive, he might serve as little as four years, or even less, before his release. Here's why.

In California, judges follow a formula for fixing sentences in multicount convictions. They begin with one count, generally the one that carries the highest maximum term. In this case that was stalking, for which Judge Connor could give Hoskins no more than three years because no restraining order was in place at the time of the crime. For the balance of the counts, the judge takes the mid-term for each and divides it by three.

The term for criminal threats was one-to-three years, so the midpoint sentence was two years. One-third of two years is eight months. There were three threats, so three times eight is twenty-four months, or two years. Judge Connor chose to give Hoskins a break on his misdemeanor assault conviction, so his total sentence would be five years (three for stalking plus an aggregate of two for the three criminal threats). With good time and time already spent in jail, he'd be looking at parole in about four years.

However, I had a way of possibly doubling Hoskins's sentence to ten years. That was to introduce evidence of an earlier strike, a 1975 conviction in Oregon for burglary. Although Hoskins had been a juvenile at the time of the crime, he had been tried as an adult and convicted as one, therefore qualifying the conviction as a strike. I needed to document the case, and also to show that the Oregon burglary met all the elements of burglary as defined in California law.

The defense argued that documentation or not, Judge Connor should strike the strike, so to speak. They waived a jury trial on the issue, but not a bench trial. Prior to sentencing, Judge Connor would have to conduct a mini-trial in which she'd rule whether or not the Oregon burglary qualified as a strike.

Unfortunately for me, the district attorney in Hermiston, Oregon—where the crime was committed—told me that he could not locate the necessary documentation. I was welcome to come up to their courthouse to search for myself, he added.

I had no choice. Early on January 30, 1996, Dana Thompson, an investigator from our office, and I boarded a flight for Portland, Oregon, on our way to Hermiston. I hoped to find what I needed at the courthouse, and then go interview Hoskins's older brother, Michael, who also lived in Hermiston. From Andy Purdy's earlier conversation with Michael, he seemed to understand what a menace his younger brother was. Based on how the interview went, I would consider bringing Michael to Los Angeles to testify at Robert's sentencing hearing, if he was agreeable.

Dana and I arrived in Portland, where we then boarded a snug little six-seater for Hermiston, which is in northeastern Oregon, not far from the Washington border.

A North Pacific blizzard was about to blow in; in fact,

the leading edge of the storm had already come ashore as we strapped ourselves in and taxied for takeoff.

The pilot was clearly visible from the passenger cabin, and he looked to be about sixteen years old. After takeoff, we watched in alarm as he pulled out a map, as if he didn't know where he was supposed to be flying. Dana shot me hard looks for leading him into such peril. I just hoped we didn't hit the ground too hard.

We clutched the armrests the rest of the way, finally touching down at Hermiston late in the morning. We were told that because of the impending weather the plane was leaving again for Portland in just two and a half hours, and it would be the last flight out of Hermiston. We did not want to miss it.

As it was, Hermiston was already knee-deep in snow from a previous storm. We jumped in a rental car and headed first for the courthouse, where I was lucky enough to quickly find the exact documents I needed. We then drove off to interview Michael Hoskins, who lived on a farm with his wife, Judy, and their two kids.

We arrived at the Hoskins place just after noon, which gave us an hour before we had to get back on the airplane. Michael and Judy spoke with us at their kitchen table.

They said that Bob, as they called him, had been trouble from his earliest childhood. "He was a skinny little kid," Mike remembered. "People beat up on him. In school it was terrible for him. We had a grade-school teacher who would whisper to both of us constantly, 'You're going to prison when you get older.' These things have an effect on a kid."

According to Mike, their father also routinely beat him and his brothers with a pig whip. One day after PE class, as Mike was taking a shower, a coach saw his bruises and decided to pay a visit to Dad. Unless the beatings stopped, the coach told Mr. Hoskins, "We're going to take these kids away from you."

Mike's little brother also sustained a string of horrible and debilitating physical injuries as a child. The first came when all three of the Hoskins boys—Lee, Mike, and Bob—were injured on a church hayride when their mother, Mary Lou Hoskins, accidentally hit the hay wagon with her car. Robert was hospitalized for a year, according to Mike.

Soon after he was released from the hospital, Hoskins was severely burned when a five-gallon can of gasoline blew up in his face. "You couldn't even tell he was human," Mike told us.

Then at age fourteen, Robert was helping his brother lift a big piece of scrap iron when the metal slammed down on his hand, severing a little finger.

Out of these experiences, said Mike, Hoskins developed a serious morphine dependency ("They had a heck of a time getting him off, and that's when I think his drug problem started"), as well as a violent streak. "He used to beat the hell out of [our] sister, Jill," said Mike, "beat her unmercifully, you know. He's pulled a knife on me before. He's always been violent. Always."

And angry. "He's always been angry at my parents for the way he was raised," Mike said. "Very angry. You know, everything is everybody else's fault."

In recent years, according to Mike, Bob had repeatedly threatened to kill his mother and father.

As a teenager, Robert twice stole brand-new pickup trucks from their father and crashed them both. "My dad just beat the hell out of him for that." Then at seventeen, Hoskins was arrested for the burglary in Hermiston, tried as an adult, and sent to prison. The moment he was released, Mike took him to Florida, hoping that a complete change of environment would help. It didn't. Robert was soon back in prison for carrying a gun.

He had always been exceptionally strong. Mike remembered a day when Robert picked up a full-sized telephone pole and carried it across the street by himself. He also had no fear of authority. Mike told us how his brother had pulled a knife on an Oregon police officer. "That officer I'm sure wanted to shoot him right then and he should have just shot him and [gotten] done with it right then. That's my personal feelings. But . . . that officer called backup and they finally got him under control.

"Well, at this point he knew he was in trouble for threatening a policeman's life. So he had to figure a way out of this. He goes to the jailhouse and he sticks his head in the toilet and starts flushing it, like he's going to drown himself, and they deemed him incompetent."

On another occasion, Mike watched as his younger brother took on five state troopers who were trying to subdue him. The troopers prevailed, but barely.

"He has no fear," Mike said. "He does not have any fear. You know, he's always told me, 'I want to do a Bonnie and Clyde thing.' I never really put it together until now. He wants to do the Bonnie and Clyde thing. He wants to get killed by the law.

"His exact words: 'The blue coats are gonna shut my power plant down.'"

Mike confirmed much of what I'd learned about Hoskins's marriage. He was violent and abusive with both his wife and kids. Mike once saw Robert kick his son across a room.

"He used to tell me, 'You know how I control [the boy]?'

"'How's that?'

"'Every time he's bad I take him and thump him in the balls.' And I just thought, *My God!* You know?"

Mike also had useful insights to share with us. One was his belief that Robert's heavy use of alcohol and drugs—especially crank, a form of methamphetamine that Hoskins consumed in quantity—was responsible in major part for his pathological behavior.

The second insight was more subtle. "Bob is crazy like a fox," he said several times. "He's been evaluated by some therapists, but I don't think they can see through what's really goin' on there. He needs to be really evaluated."

In Mike's view, his brother clearly had deep psychological problems, but also feigned his craziness. "He's definitely got some mental stuff going on, but I don't believe it's as bad as he wants people to believe." He explained, "He lives his life on making other people fear him. He just thrives on it, you know. It's 'I'll get my way,' you know. And he thrives on that."

Robert's obsession with Madonna, Mike and Judy agreed, began in late 1994 for no apparent reason. He'd never obsessed on a celebrity before. One day around Thanksgiving he appeared at their door with the news that Madonna had picked him up hitchhiking. They had done drugs together with her bodyguard. Later, Robert said that God told him Madonna was going to be his wife forever.

He returned from a trip to northern California with a piece

of redwood in his backpack. "This is my head from a thousand years ago," he told his brother.

"You're right," Mike replied. "That's your head. It's made of wood."

At the Hoskins family gathering for Thanksgiving, Robert told Mike that he'd driven a car off a five-hundred-foot cliff, but that God had put his hand under the car and set it safely back on the road.

After the turn of the year, he informed them that the wedding had taken place. He also seemed to start coming unglued. Robert would get high and go dancing by himself in the fields for hours.

"He got into God real heavy," said Mike. "He went out and sat all day one day, waiting for the helicopters from Washington, D.C., to come pick him up. He called the White House from this phone right here and just said his name over and over and over and over."

When Robert Hoskins boarded the bus to California for the last time in the spring of 1995, he told Mike and Judy they'd never see him again, which they hoped was a promise he'd keep. Once he was arrested at Castillo del Lago, however, Mike and Judy had gone to LA to offer what support and comfort they could.

They met with Hoskins during a courtroom break. The judge was not on the bench. I wasn't in the room, either. When Mike identified himself as the defendant's brother, a bailiff brought Robert from his holding cell into the courtroom.

"I ought to shoot you" was the first thing Hoskins said to his older brother.

"What for?" Mike asked.

"The things you been saying about me."

"Well," Mike said, "it's all been the truth, you know."

"I'm going to kill you when I get out of here," his brother answered.

Mike walked away. Robert had cut the cord.

"I think he oughta be put away somewhere, okay?" Mike said as our interview drew to a close. "I don't want to have to deal with him again unless he's healed, all right? Whether that can be done, I don't know. But this is how I personally feel about it. I don't want to have to kill him, okay? But I will if he comes around here threatening my family or me. I will. That's all there is to it."

I RETURNED TO Los Angeles more certain than ever that if Robert Dewey Hoskins went free, he would eventually seriously hurt or kill someone. The Oregon burglary conviction would buy us five extra years—if Judge Connor saw it my way. I felt that Mike Hoskins would be an effective penalty-phase prosecution witness, too. But as I pondered whether or not to ask Mike to testify, the defendant handed me exactly what I needed to seal the deal.

From August 24 onward, Hoskins had occupied a single-man cell in the county jail's module 4600—a mental observation section. On January 24, 1996, a sheriff's deputy accompanying a nurse on "pill call" through module 4600 saw Hoskins standing in his cell, waiting for his meds.

Deputy Marques also noticed the words "I Love Madonna" written on the cell wall behind Hoskins, as well as the words "The Madonna Stalker." He asked the prisoner who wrote the graffiti. "Madonna did," Hoskins answered. "She is my wife." He also added, "I'm going to slice the fuckin' bitch's throat for lying on me as soon as I get out."

Suddenly I had someone even better than Mike to put on the stand. Deputy Marques's testimony, along with pictures of the grafitti, would graphically attest to the defendant's lack of remorse, as well as how dangerous he was. I wouldn't have to put Mike Hoskins in the difficult position of testifying against his brother, plus I'd save the taxpayers the cost of bringing Mike Hoskins down from Oregon.

The defense was slow in preparing a psychiatric report that it hoped would serve as a mitigating factor as Judge Connor decided the issue of the Oregon burglary conviction and how long a sentence to hand the defendant. We finally came back to court on March 22, 1996.

I put Deputy Marques on the stand, and entered photos of Hoskins's graffiti into the record. I also handed the judge the certified documents I'd brought back from Oregon. She looked at them and said, "These are valid. They show you were tried as an adult. I find that this is a strike."

The defense submitted its very sympathetic psychiatric report, hoping that Judge Connor would cut the defendant some slack. No chance. "I don't find his mental illness to be mitigating," she said. "I find it to be an aggravating factor because it shows me he's capable of anything."

Then she slammed him with ten years' prison time.

Ordinarily, that would have concluded the case. However, the Court of Appeals caught Judge Connor in an uncharacteristic oversight. She had failed to enumerate for the record the reasons why she accepted the Oregon conviction as a strike, which meant we all—including Hoskins—would have to get together in court once more to listen to her read her reasons.

One year later, I was struck with how much better, more focused Robert Hoskins looked when they brought him in. The beard was gone. His hair had been cut. Judge Connor noticed as well.

"Oh, Mr. Hoskins," she said, "you're looking so well, so much better than the last time I saw you. They must be taking good care of you where you are."

It was the wrong thing to say. All of a sudden, the crazy look came back into Robert's eyes. While he'd been mostly quiet at trial, sometimes humming Madonna tunes under his breath and occasionally flashing that stare, now the wild and violent side of his nature exploded. Though shackled, he struggled to his feet at the defense table and started screaming at the judge.

"I don't like the way I've been treated in this court!" he yelled. "When I get out I'm coming back and I'm taking care of everyone who's in this courtroom!" Oddly enough, he didn't utter a single profanity during the brief tirade.

"Mr. Hoskins," the judge said when he had finished, "are you threatening me?"

"I'm just telling you the way it is," he replied in a nasty tone.

Any hope the defense might have nurtured that Connor would back off her stiff sentence vanished entirely.

Then I got an idea. Hoskins was threatening not just the judge, but everyone else in the courtroom. I looked over to the court reporter to make sure she was taking it all down.

After Judge Connor ordered Hoskins removed from the

court, I requested a copy of the transcript and made sure it accompanied Hoskins, with the rest of his record, when they shipped him back to prison. As I hoped, the outburst cost him all the good time he'd earned, helping to ensure that he'd serve every day possible of his sentence.

As it turned out, Hoskins kept acting up from time to time while in prison, and so served his full ten-year term. As he was nearing his release date, I requested that he be given a psychological evaluation. According to procedure, a psychiatrist, a psychologist, and a psychiatric social worker interviewed him, and concluded that he posed too great a danger to be released.

As a consequence, the state of California placed Hoskins under a conservatorship and sent him to Atascadero State Hospital, a locked-down psychiatric facility, where he remains today.

SEVEN

THE STEADY ROTATION in and out of various prosecution units found me, in January of 1995, in the Organized Crime/Anti-Terrorist Unit, where I had just completed a trial involving the newly emergent Russian Mafia in the United States. The defendant was a hired assassin who had unsuccessfully tried to place a bomb in a car carrying a powerful member of the organization's Brooklyn operation. He'd crossed the wrong wires and blown off his right hand.

The police responded to the explosion, and traced a trail of blood from the scene to the defendant, who was sitting nearby on a curb, smoke still curling up from his hair. The defense maintained that he had not been planting a bomb, just trying to steal a car, and had the exceptional bad luck to have picked a car with a bomb in it. The jurors were not persuaded.

At sentencing, the defendant actually begged the judge not to send him to prison because he was crippled. That ploy didn't work, either.

Shortly after this trial, I received a phone call from Sergeant Karen Green, known as KG, a twenty-seven-year veteran of the Los Angeles County Sheriff's Department and a good friend of mine, who often came to me with strange and difficult cases. This one would prove no different.

At one minute to midnight on January 10, 1995, Karen told me, Fern Collins, an investigator with the Los Angeles County Department of Consumer Affairs, had received the first in a series of disturbing messages on her office telephone. The caller was Thomas Clark Agee, thirty-one, an emotionally troubled San Franciscan with a long history of mental problems.

Agee's issue was with The Scriptorium, a Beverly Hills autograph shop, which he claimed had overcharged him for a signed photograph of the late actress Jean Harlow. Collins had looked into the matter for him, and endeavored without success to mediate the dispute with the shop's owner, Charles Sachs. Recently, the investigator had informed Agee by letter that she could do no more.

Her answering machine automatically timed-out his first call, but not before he said he was still waiting for Collins to retrieve his five thousand dollars from Chuck (as Agee referred to him) Sachs.

At 12:07 A.M., Agee left a second rambling telephone message. "You know, I'm a very smart person," he said. "I just want you to know that, Fern."

He telephoned once again at 12:13 A.M. "How'd you like to spend a whole lot of money on a criminal defense attorney?" he asked. "Gosh! Talk about money! Boy, you could spend your whole life savings on that, Fern.

"You know, everything requires competence. You have to always be competent. That's the important thing…That's why there are all these crazy crimes and people goin' and shootin' people is basically because there are incompetent employees…"

Tom was just warming up.

"I've worked in the public sector, okay? So you know you're talkin' to someone that's got a brain, okay? I mean, I know all the shenanigans, all that kind of stuff. You're not fooling me one bit. So, like I said, I will be checking my account, and I shouldn't have to call you anymore…All the proof is basically there. It's a matter of doing your job—not being lazy, sitting around collecting taxpayers' money and not doing your job."

Agee left a fourth message at 1:47 A.M.: "You know," he said, "I can't make you do anything, Fern Collins, but I can make you wish you did something."

COLLINS WAS NOT unduly concerned about Tom Agee's multiple "messages of a peculiar nature," as she later described them. She met lots of difficult people as a consumer investigator, and was used to dealing with them. Even so, Tom Agee was an odd duck.

For one thing, he had kept introducing screwy conditions to the negotiations with Sachs. The December 7, 1994, entry on her complaint sheet, for example, summarized a telephone call with Agee. "If [Sachs] doesn't want to deposit the money [in Agee's bank account,] he can buy a lady's watch instead." Collins noted parenthetically: "Totally irrational!"

She filed a Security Incident Report on January 11. This routine, one-page document was destined for Sergeant Green, who at the time was serving with Lieutenant Lee Taylor, also of the sheriff's office, as LA County's two-person Office of Security Management.

Whenever any of the county's 93,000 employees experienced or witnessed cases of veiled, potential, or actual threats, the employee was expected to file an incident report with Green and Taylor. The two officers also handled all crimes committed in, or on, any of the county's 6,300 properties. Their job was to bring each case to the attention of the appropriate local law enforcement agency. They also prepared a quarterly statistical report on threats and crimes for LA County's thirty-nine department heads and supervisors.

KG and Taylor referred quite a few stalking and threat cases to the TMU, with whom they coordinated closely. KG and I also worked together frequently. Whenever she had a case that looked like it might fall between the cracks, she usually called me, as she eventually did in the developing Agee matter.

She read Fern Collins's incident report, met with the investigator, and made copies of her message tapes. Since Tom Agee hadn't made an actionable threat against Collins, there was nothing to be done at the time except to monitor the case. Some weeks later, Agee did call Collins at her office from his apartment in San Francisco, twice, to let her know that he would not be contacting her again.

That appeared to end the episode, or so Fern Collins supposed.

Not Tom Agee.

At 6:09 P.M. on February 8, he reached Charles Sachs's answering machine and spoke disjointedly for a few minutes about various high-quality ladies' wristwatches he was considering for purchase. He also mentioned there was a sale on parakeet paraphernalia at his local Woolworth's. Sachs later told police that Agee sounded drunk.

Then he switched abruptly to a vicious riff on Jews. "They're the one minority that all the other minorities don't like," Agee said. "They're just so into money. I tell ya, I don't know what it is about the Jews. It's a sickness. They always, you know, 'Oh, don't murder people. It's wrong to murder people.' But boy, they just bring it all on themselves, really."

The tape machine cut him off.

At 6:58 P.M., Tom telephoned a second time with more pointed threats against Sachs. "I don't wanna go down to LA," he said, "but it seems like you want me to go down to LA and shoot up a bunch of people. That seems to be what you want me to do. Like I said, get out that Uzi. Shoot up a bunch of people, then shoot yourself. I mean, that seems to be, you know, what you want because I figure if I can't convince you to deposit the money in the account, I'll probably not get my money anyway ... You're a sick, sick man. I mean, you're like a Nazi war criminal ... You have this ability to create violence, Chuck. I don't know. A lot of Jewish people have that ability to create violence in other people. They're obnoxious and they know how to set people off."

Agee called Sachs again at 2:45 A.M., this time to excoriate a federal judge in San Francisco who had earlier ordered him sent to a government psychiatric facility. "That Marilyn Hall Patel, she's a goddamn whore!" Agee screamed. "She's a goddamn whore! You know she is!"

The shopkeeper and the federal judge were not acquainted.

Agee focused again on Sachs. "You goddamn motherfucker!" he screamed. "Do you understand me, Chuck? Do you understand me!"

3:02 A.M. "Your whole family oughta be murdered."

Twelve minutes later, "I just don't know what's the matter with you, Chuck. I mean, if you're just uncivilized or what. I mean, you're just basically a creep. You know, you don't deserve to live. I mean, your family and anything like that...Pay the goddamn money and get it over with! Fuckin' asshole!"

3:22 A.M. "Marilyn Hall Patel you know is a fuckin' whore!"

3:32 A.M. "I'm gonna nail that fuckin' bitch! The fuckin' bitch! Nail that fuckin' bitch! Nail my former employer. That asshole! Load that mental illness crap on me!"

3:53 A.M. "You know, God, I hope O.J. walks. I really do. He doesn't deserve this."

4:08 A.M. "I'm sick of people fuckin' shit about me, Chuck, you know. Just fuckin' shoot 'em up, you know? That's the only way to do it. I'm gonna kill 'em...These judges are bureaucrats and they're just a bunch of arrogant scum. They're low-life pigs. They don't even deserve to be around. They really don't!...Now, I want my money."

As it happened, both Charles Sachs and Tom Agee then went to the Beverly Hills police; the former with his tape recordings of Agee's threats, the latter looking for help in retrieving his five thousand dollars. Both were disappointed. BHPD did not arrest Agee for terrorizing Sachs. Agee was told his problem was not a police matter. As he later recollected, Detective Paul Edholm advised that "buyer beware" should have guided him. When Agee persisted that he'd been defrauded, Edholm suggested he try the Consumer Affairs Department. According to Agee, when he *still* kept calling, Edholm hung up on him.

For several weeks neither Sachs nor Fern Collins received any calls or phone messages from Tom Agee.

HE BEGAN AGAIN at 1:50 A.M. on March 18 with Charles Sachs. Tom had more thoughts on expensive women's watches and on what sorts of deals he might get on a Breguet versus a Patek Phillippe. He repeated the specific model numbers for each of the several timepieces he had in mind. Sachs later told me that

Agee dressed like a derelict, but he sure knew his upmarket timepieces.

Agee also read aloud to Sachs a fund-raising letter, written by California senator Dianne Feinstein, on behalf of Emily's List, a Democratic fund-raising organization to which Agee said he was a contributor. Evidently his politics were liberal. Feinstein popped up in his monologues frequently.

He said he "very desperately" needed $5,750 at once, which Charles should put into his account at the California Federal Bank. He promised to take Sachs on a vacation to Hawaii if the money was forthcoming. "It's gonna be one of those cheap ones," Tom said. "You're gonna have to pay for your own food over there in Hawaii. I'm not gonna do that."

The tape then ran out.

In his next message, Agee bizarrely compared Sachs to Leon Klinghoffer, the sixty-nine-year-old retiree from New York who was infamously murdered by Palestinian terrorists aboard the cruise ship *Achille Lauro* in October of 1985. The wheelchair-bound Klinghoffer had been shot in the head and chest and thrown overboard.

"He was just being obnoxious," said Agee, "totally obnoxious. He should've been quiet and behaved himself, and he wouldn't have gotten killed. You know, I just don't like this testing the bounds of human behavior. I'm not gonna bother suing you, Chuck, so why don't you go ahead and sue me?"

The message ended, "I don't have the patience to go to court. I really don't. I, uh, handle things out of court, not in court. And I have my way. You know, I really do."

The next night the first call came at 10:02. "I don't know why you wanna be this stubborn little bastard. Oh, and by the way, tell that detective, uh, whatever his name, Edholm and Fern Collins, tell 'em I think they're both a bunch of fuckin' assholes..."

Three more calls followed in rapid succession. In one, Agee offered to find Sachs a deal on a Breguet—"I think I can probably get it to you at fifty percent off"—and again lashed out at Edholm and Collins in another. "They're a bunch of stupid morons," he said, "a bunch of white trash. They're nothin' but trash, scum, loser, low-life idiots."

"I don't see anything wrong with killing people," Tom said in the midst of his tirade.

A week later, he went after both Fern Collins and Charles Sachs on the same night.

At 11:17 P.M. on the twenty-sixth, he read into Collins's machine a news account of a New Jersey man who'd just been charged with killing four men and wounding another while robbing a post office where he once worked. The suspect had explained that he needed the money, about five thousand dollars, to pay his back rent.

"Anyway," said Agee, "I just wanted to let you know that the phone company as of tomorrow...is going to be cutting off my phone."

At 11:26 the topics were watches, again, Emily's List, and parakeets. "Um, basically, you can hear the parakeets here," he said. "Come on, come on! Yeah. They're really happy. I'm taking very good care of them."

Agee added, "I'm kinda gettin' tired of dealin' with, you know, incompetent government employees...I'm getting a little bit fed up about it."

Eight minutes later: "You know, you can call the police and waste taxpayers' money and stuff and be a stupid Irish Mick government employee that you are. But let me make it perfectly clear: I'm gonna kill you. I'm definitely gonna kill you. I'm literally gonna kill you. I don't know if I'm gonna use a gun, or I'm gonna slit your throat, but at this point you really don't deserve to live...You choose to side with Mr. Sachs, so stay on Mr. Sachs's side. That's fine. I'm gonna kill you. Okay. I'm gonna kill ya. I'm gonna find ya, and I'm gonna kill ya. And you know, I'll kill people around you and whatever. I really will."

Agee elaborated in the next message to Fern, recorded at 11:41. "Let me just warn you that if you *do* decide to call the police, and try to have me put in jail and go through the whole bunch of malarkey, then I will definitely kill you. Because I will get out of jail eventually and I *will* do it. So you know, it's up to you. You know I will get you...You're nothing but a slimy Irish Mick. You're scum. You're just nothing but a prostitute."

At 11:59, he called Charles Sachs. "You should have heard

some of the stuff I said to Fern," he boasted. "Oh boy! I called her an Irish Mick. Yeah, and she is. She's a fuckin' stupid little Irish Mick whore. That's what she is."

The last message came at 12:09 A.M. "I tell you, there's nothin' better than killin' people," Agee said, then mentioned how much he admired O. J. Simpson. "I like O.J.," he said. "He's a good guy, you know? His wife really knows how to push his buttons. Hey, you know, when you push people's buttons, you just gotta expect all that." End of message.

CHARLES SACHS WAS intelligent, educated, well-spoken, and absolutely unstrung by this second barrage of messages from Tom Agee. When we later met in my office, he told me that Agee had originally struck him as quirky, but there was no hint in his behavior that a simple transaction between them could get so far out of hand.

He said that Agee had come to him almost a year earlier in search of an autographed photo of Jean Harlow, apparently a rare item that Sachs didn't have in stock.

Agee did not look prosperous to Sachs, who questioned whether this would-be client could afford the signed picture. Agee, however, was determined to have it. According to what he told the Scriptorium's proprietor, his mother, who lived on the East Coast, would cover the cost of the photo.

Charles told me he agreed to search his fellow dealers for the item. He said that he warned Tom repeatedly that since he would have to personally pay for the picture, his usual ten-day refund policy on Scriptorium catalog items would not be in effect. Once Tom accepted the Harlow, she was his.

He did later agree to Fern Collins's proposed compromise, which was to sell the photo for Agee on consignment. But when the picture arrived in the mail damaged, Sachs declined to have anything further to do with Agee.

The harassment had begun not long thereafter, but only recently had it escalated into death threats. What scared Sachs the most, he said, was Agee's virulent anti-Semitism, and the remark about the Uzi. Charles knew that Tom could easily find him, and he was deeply worried for his family, as well as himself.

Fern Collins retrieved her messages on the morning of March 28, listened to them, and immediately went to the assistant director of her department, Evelyn Stein, who in turn contacted KG.

In her subsequent Security Incident Report, dated the twenty-ninth, Collins wrote: "These messages were of a significantly different nature from the January messages. He specifically told me that he was going to kill me! He told me that he hasn't decided whether he was going to slit my throat, or shoot me in the head, but that he definitely was going to kill me. Much of the tapes were also rambling but he interspersed clear threats of physical violence...

"It appears to me that this individual is highly unstable and I do fear that he is capable of carrying out these threats. I am requesting that immediate steps be taken by the appropriate agency to arrest Thomas Agee and protect me from any further action that he might take."

Fern then enrolled in a martial arts class and bought pepper spray, which she carried in her purse.

KAREN GREEN DID not have much to go on, just her suspect's name and address. So she called the U.S. Marshal's Service in San Francisco and spoke to a woman named Marty Glenn. After identifying herself, KG asked Glenn if the marshals knew anything about a Thomas C. Agee, who was making serious threats to kill people in Los Angeles.

"Whoa!" answered Glenn. "I know Thomas Agee. We've had problems with him in the past."

"You're kidding!" Green exclaimed.

"Oh, no," said Glenn. "He's tried to intimidate a federal judge who shipped him off to Rochester, Minnesota, for psychiatric treatment."

KG then spoke with James Sullivan, the chief deputy marshal, who confirmed what Marty Glenn had told her. Tom Agee had indeed been sent to a federal medical center in 1992, but had committed no known federal crimes since. If anyone could file a charge against Agee that would stick, it would be Sergeant Green, Sullivan said. He added that the marshals were ready to be of any assistance possible.

Fortunately for Charles Sachs, KG's investigation led her to him. She interviewed him, gathered up the Agee voice mails as evidence, and wrote a report detailing the threats made against both Sachs and Collins. Her next stop was my office, where we listened together to the taped messages. I asked her to set up an interview at my office with both victims as soon as possible.

I interviewed them separately. It was easy for me to see how the two victims feared for their lives. Agee didn't just threaten them; he did so with bloodcurdling menace in his voice. I agreed to file charges.

Right after speaking with KG, James Sullivan personally visited Agee, along with a detail of marshals and some SWAT team officers from the San Francisco police department. The idea was to assess the suspect's emotional state. Sullivan reported back to KG that Agee appeared to be heavily sedated, and for the moment posed no threat to anyone, or himself.

He lived in government-subsidized housing on a very marginal stretch of Ellis Street. The apartment was full of parakeets.

Over the coming weeks, as we prepared the charges, Sullivan called on the suspect several times and telephoned him on a number of occasions, trying to establish rapport. If Agee had planned to act on any of his threats during this period, the constant attention of a senior U.S. marshal must surely have given him pause. It did not, however, moderate his rage.

"Tell that bitch Fern Collins I want my money and I want it now," Agee wrote Sullivan in pencil on April 2. "I don't have any more time to play her silly little games . . ."

"Mr. Sullivan," he added further on, "when you talk to Fern Collins, tell her this . . . Tom Agee's got a little Buyer Beware of his own. Tell her Tom Agee thinks it's real cool when a person murders another person. Tom Agee thinks there's nothing wrong with murdering people."

In an April 14 letter to Sullivan, again in pencil, Agee began, "I have come to the conclusion that you are not going to get my six thousand dollars back from down in Los Angeles." Thus, to Agee's mind, the marshal had joined the growing list of conspirators.

"Mr. Sullivan," he continued, "you don't strike me as an

arrogant person, however I do believe you have a big ego and a lot of pride. You don't deal with the concept of helping someone out who's been in jail, especially your jail, you're just going along with the federal status quo... Everybody including you, Mr. Sullivan, [is] programmed like robots to be anti–Tom Agee.

"Federal Judge Marilyn Hall Patel is someone with low self-esteem, feelings of inadequacy, unsure of herself, lethargic, depressed, behaves in an arrogant manner in order to cover up for her own mistakes, resents anyone whom she feels is superior to her, can't handle responsibility, can't handle confrontation, is very sneaky and will attempt to sidestep important issues.

"In regard to money, Mr. Sullivan, you and Judge Patel are a lot alike. Judge Patel can't deal [with] awarding and getting me money. It would hurt her pride. It would literally burn her up inside. Judge Patel is jealous of Tom Agee. She would much rather tear Tom Agee down because of her jealousy. I believe Judge Patel won't get me my money, her ego just can't handle it, she doesn't have it in her. Judge Patel is gambling on not giving me money by pointing out my mental history..."

Sullivan's willingness to babysit Agee for us was a helpful courtesy that KG in particular appreciated, and a sterling example of interagency cooperation.

I filed five charges, all felonies, against Agee:

1. Stalking Fern Collins
2. Making criminal threats against her
3. Dissuading a witness by force or threat (Collins)
4. Threatening an employee of an elected official (Collins)
5. Stalking Charles Sachs

On May 3, a Los Angeles judge signed Tom Agee's arrest warrant. Two days later, KG and Lee Taylor flew north to execute the warrant.

Deputy Marshals Tom Bauman and Mike McCloud met them at the Oakland Airport and drove them into San Francisco to meet with James Sullivan at the marshals' office on Golden Gate Avenue. The group then moved to SFPD, where an arrest strategy was worked out among the marshals and members of the police SWAT team, under a Sergeant Callejas at SFPD. To help ensure that Agee would be at home when they arrived, James Sullivan had made a lunch appointment with him, and arranged to pick him up at noon.

The operation proceeded without a hitch. KG and Lee Taylor—both in business suits—entered the building just before noon while the rest of the team deployed outside.

"Hi," KG said to the security guard, "I have a lunch date today with Tom Agee."

"Oh, he just left," the guard replied, probably assuming that the two investigators were social workers. "But I'm sure he'll be right back." The guard allowed Green and Taylor up to Agee's apartment, 7-B, which was locked. No one answered their knock, but from inside KG heard a racket that she recognized as parakeets, lots of parakeets. Before heading back downstairs, they let a group of SWAT officers up a back stairway, just in case.

Back downstairs in the lobby, the guard pointed out Agee, a tallish white male of medium to heavy build walking toward the door. Preferring to arrest him in the open, where there was less chance of a civilian getting hurt, KG quickly moved out the door to confront Agee in front of the building.

"Tom Agee?" she asked

"Yes." He looked startled.

"My name is Karen Green. I'm with the Los Angeles Sheriff's Department, and I have a warrant for your arrest."

The marshals and SWAT team members stationed around the entrance closed in on Agee and swiftly handcuffed him. He offered no resistance. As he was being driven away, KG and Lee Taylor went back inside, identified themselves to the guard, and asked to be let into Agee's apartment.

When they opened the door, they discovered a flock of parakeets flying freely around the room. Their chirping created a din, and the apartment stank of their droppings.

Anxious to get Agee back to Los Angeles as soon as possible, KG left the parakeets in the apartment. The next day, with Agee now securely behind bars, Lee Taylor left a little sketch on her desk. It depicted a parakeet lying on its back, with its legs sticking up in the air, and a cartoon bubble stating, "KG did it." KG, an animal lover, immediately called San

Francisco to arrange for the local SPCA to rescue Tom Agee's orphaned birds.

WE PUT AGEE in the Los Angeles county men's central jail under $150,000 bail—later raised to $300,000—and went to work piecing together his background information.

We found that his mental problems apparently stretched back into his boyhood. Tom and one older brother were raised in a well-to-do New Jersey family—he said his father was a stockbroker. He was educated both in public schools and in at least three different private institutions for emotionally disturbed children. Agee received his high school diploma at age nineteen in June of 1983.

His work history began at a Dunkin' Donuts, where he worked for two months, and then a pizza restaurant, also for two months. His mother subsequently secured for him a job at a resort in Vermont, which he said he quit because he was being "harassed."

In 1984, Tom briefly relocated to San Diego, where he could not find work, then moved up to San Francisco, where he lived with an uncle—who later became custodian of his parakeets—until he found a position as a nursing home orderly. Agee kept that job for five months. He left because of unspecified conflicts with the patients. A year of unemployment ensued, and then five months as a clerk/typist working for the Department of the Army.

He enrolled at San Francisco City College, but soon dropped out. More jobs as a clerk/typist followed—at the U.S. Small Business Administration (one year), the National Park Service (four months), and the General Services Administration (six months)—until, on June 4, 1989, the U.S. Consumer Product Safety Commission office on Battery Street in San Francisco hired Tom Agee, then twenty-five, as a clerk/typist.

His first year of work at the commission appears to have passed without incident. However, according to a later affidavit, in the summer of 1990 Tom Agee seemed to start coming apart.

In July, he and fellow employee Laura Uribe got into such a loud and heated discussion that commission coworkers had to step in to end the argument. In August, he started a fist-pounding fight with Lee D. Baxter, the commission's regional director, who ordered Agee out of his office. A short while later, Agee picked an argument with Joy Rizzitello, and then wouldn't leave her alone in the office.

By January of 1991 Agee was routinely missing work, and disrupted the office when he did show up. In an effort to minimize his impact on coworkers, Lee Baxter moved Tom to the reception desk. There, he started yet another set-to when Joel Swisher, a public affairs officer, complained that he could not read a telephone message that Agee had taken down. According to Swisher, Tom replied abusively to him.

On advice of his psychiatrist, Agee checked himself into the California Pacific Medical Center in San Francisco for treatment and counseling on February 21, 1991. He was discharged on March 7. While at the center, he told one of the doctors who examined him that he was hearing voices. In recent months, he reported, he "began to feel singled out and persecuted by his supervisors." The doctor noted that Agee believed "they are trying to edge him out of his job."

The consensus diagnosis at the center was that Tom suffered from a combination of paranoia and schizophrenia. He was given medications to help him control his disorders, but he warned the doctors that he would not take his pills.

He went back to work at the commission, sporadically, through April 25, when Agee showed up for one hour and never returned. In May, Agee caused a disturbance at the residence of Alfred F. Limberg, Jr., a former supervisor. The police were called, and Tom was taken into custody. No charges were filed.

In late July of 1991, Lee Baxter fired him for "insubordination." His termination papers were sent to him by U.S. mail.

A few days later, an individual identifying himself only as "a friend of Thomas Agee" delivered to Baxter at the Battery Street office a large yellow envelope, addressed to the regional director in Tom's hand. Among the estimated 150–200 documents that the envelope contained were various of Agee's personal bills, with handwritten instructions for Baxter to pay them.

As we looked deeper into Agee's past, we found it full of

parallels to the behavior for which I planned to send him to prison. It was dismaying to me to see how far back Agee's pattern of criminal conduct went, and how ineffective the system had been in dealing with him. We needed better remedies.

"Mr. Baxter," Agee wrote, "when an individual doesn't have any money his mind becomes very irrational. People get real funky when they don't have any money. Money is my best medicine, it's my best friend. I really don't have the patience left to file a grievance or go through any proper procedure. I need my bills paid now."

Just as he'd later tell Fern Collins about the New Jersey man who killed four men and wounded another while robbing his old employer, the post office, Agee included in documents he sent Baxter a number of newspaper stories about various disgruntled employees around the nation who acted out their workplace frustrations with firearms. These included a Maryland bank employee who shot and killed three coworkers, and the city hall murders of George Moscone and Harvey Milk by Dan White. Another article looked at the Charles Manson killings of 1969. Several reported on a discharged California airline employee who murdered a pilot during a flight, killing forty-four people in all.

"I never forgot when that airline crash happened back in December 1987," Agee wrote. "I had the same attitude about it back then as I do now. I remember I had a certain fascination about it because it told about that factor of his boss fucking with him and I definitely sympathized with the criminal."

Also among the papers Agee sent to Baxter was a document generated at the medical center the previous February. Written by a doctor, it read, in part: "Because of paranoid psychosis, Mr. Agee is unable to accept treatment and behaving in such a way that he is in jeopardy of losing his job, apartment, and friends and becoming destitute and homeless."

Frightened for his safety as well as that of his employees, Baxter notified the Federal Protective Service (FPS), the security force for federal buildings. Over the coming weeks, he reported three threatening telephone calls from Agee, and received yet another large envelope full of Agee's bills, more news clips, and several movie videos. As Officer David Skultery of the FPS noted in a later affidavit, "All these movies contain graphic scenes in which persons are violently killed with knives."

On October 31, 1991, Baxter swore out a complaint against Agee. "I believe Tom Agee wants to kill me," he wrote. "He had letters and voluminous photocopied items sent to my office. One of the letters said he couldn't buy a firearm *legally* because he had been hospitalized for a mental condition. News stories and articles related to murders. One was a 'boss' killed by a 'fired' employee. I believe Tom is mentally ill and is capable of violence. I fear that he [could] 'snap' and come into our office and kill or harm anyone in the area."

On December 4, Jeffrey Bornstein, an assistant U.S. attorney, indicted Agee under Title 18 of the U.S. Code's Crimes and Criminal Procedure, Threats to Government Employees provision. Specifically, Bornstein alleged that Agee "did knowingly and intentionally engage in a course of conduct designed to impede, intimidate, and interfere with Lee D. Baxter...and other employees...while such employees were engaged in or on account of the performance of their official duties..."

Joan S. Brennan, a magistrate judge, ordered a pretrial psychiatric evaluation, which was carried out at Mills-Peninsula Hospital. Dr. Donald Newman interviewed Agee for an hour at the jail, and also reviewed previous psychiatric reports. Dr. Newman concluded that the stresses of life on his own were probably too much for Tom, and that a "structured environment" might suit him better.

Agee was found incompetent to stand trial. On May 19, 1992, by order of Judge Patel, he was sent to the Federal Medical Center at Rochester, Minnesota, for further evaluation and "restoration of competency to stand trial."

That goal proved elusive. On his August 4 discharge from the center, Agee was described as "poorly compliant with treatment." He refused to take his antipsychotic meds, so they were administered "involuntarily." The consensus conclusion was that the patient was still not competent to stand trial. Given the minimal progress Tom had made at Rochester, there was scant hope he would achieve the necessary improvement "in the foreseeable future."

Then they cut him loose.

* * *

IN EARLY JUNE of 1995, about a month after his arrest in San Francisco by KG and Lee Taylor, Agee wrote to both Judge Patel and me. It wasn't difficult to infer his state of mind. "You and that Nazi-loving Jew boy Jeffrey Bornstein," he wrote Patel, "still haven't gotten my billions of dollars owed to me from those Nazis and the U.S. Consumer Product Safety Commission. Tell that suing Jew Jeffrey Bornstein that it's a fact that it's a lot less complicated to shoot up a bunch of people than it is to go through a complicated civil suit. Law suits are too much trouble, it's so hard to collect money you're owed from people or the government, yet it's so easy to kill people. It's so very simple."

"Dear Rhoda"—Agee for some reason called me Rhoda—began the most unusual letter I've ever received from a defendant. "Los Angeles is a city full of liars, even LA police chief Willie Williams can't tell the truth. They ought to call this town Lie Angeles. I don't even plan on setting foot inside Beverly Hills. That town is full of criminals. That Beverly Hells detective Paul Edholm is probably a crook. I'm scared of Beverly Hills. If I set foot in that Ku Klux Klan Nazi town I would probably get arrested for no reason at all by some crooked Beverly Hells cop."

He informed me that the San Francisco Housing Authority was pressuring him to give up his apartment on Ellis Street, which he hoped to give to a friend "if someone buys me a one-bedroom, one-bath condo in West Hollywood with garage." That someone, Agee had decided, was me.

"Ms. Rhoda Saunders," he continued, "I've always enjoyed Los Angeles and I promise I'll pay my property taxes and monthly condominium dues. All I'm asking you to do is buy me a condo outright so I don't have a mortgage." He had scribbled in the margins: "If you want to buy me, Tom Agee, a mansion in Bel-Air, I promise I won't stop you." He included a couple of pages of apartment listings from the *Los Angeles Times* and had circled several of the listings that he found suitable.

A week later, on advice of his counsel, Brian Getz, Agee waived his right to a preliminary hearing. Judge Jacqueline Connor, already scheduled to hear the Hoskins case, was named to preside at Tom Agee's trial, too. One of her first actions was to order a psychiatric evaluation to determine if he was competent to go forward.

In September of 1995, Bruce H. Gross, director of the Institute of Psychiatry, Law, and Behavioral Science at the University of Southern California, and Dr. Howard Askins, a fellow at the institute, interviewed Agee for ninety minutes, and also reviewed the ever-lengthening list of previous psychiatric evaluations, as well as the evidence against him, including transcriptions of his threatening calls to Fern Collins and Charles Sachs.

Gross and Askins found Agee incompetent to stand trial. On October 12, Judge Connor committed Tom to Patton State Hospital in San Bernardino County. On December 22, doctors at Patton certified that Agee was now competent to stand trial, and that he'd promised them he'd take his meds throughout the course of the proceedings.

Before leaving San Bernardino, Tom wrote a letter to Senator Dianne Feinstein, in which he complained that Judge Connors and I were "still stalking me with my case."

He went on, "These two women want Tom Agee to be a physically violent person. Senator, I don't believe in physical violence, but those two women strongly encourage people like myself to be violent. These two women want violence."

ON MAY 7, 1996, just before we went to trial, I received a Mother's Day card from Agee. "Happy Mother's Day, Ms. Saunders," it read. "I hope it's a good one. May you never end up in a nursing home or board in care home. Sincerely, Thomas C. Agee, AKA—*Unibomber*."

Agee opted for a bench trial, and his lawyer advanced the diminished actuality defense. In essence, the defense contended that Agee was so mentally disturbed that he did not understand that he was placing Charles Sachs and Fern Collins in fear. Although the defendant did have a long series of psychiatric commitments, the diminished actuality argument was fairly easy for me to overcome.

I pointed out that the sheer malice in the multiple messages reflected intent to frighten. I argued that he was sane enough to be aware in detail of current events, such as the Simpson trial. And I emphasized his numerous anti-Semitic diatribes against Sachs, particularly when Agee compared Charles Sachs to Leon Klinghoffer.

When Charles testified, he told the court that Agee's rabid anti-Semitism persuaded him more than anything else that the threats were real. I also argued that his disgusting bigotry extended to Fern Collins in his use of pejorative terms about her Irish ancestry.

The defendant behaved himself throughout the two-day trial; he looked like a scared and confused schoolboy through most of it. But I knew better. Easily the high point of the proceedings for him was the appearance of his mother, Cynthia, as a defense witness. She took the stand after a lunch break. Tom burst into a huge smile when he first saw her; it was obvious that he loved her and was thrilled that she had come. Given Tom's history, his boyish delight struck me as sad and rather touching.

"Mom! Mom!" he called to her. "Did you eat? Are you hungry?" Before she could reply, he reached into the big pocket of his jail-issue jumpsuit, produced a baloney sandwich he'd saved from lunch, and lobbed it across the courtroom, past the judge, into her lap. "Okay, thank you!" Mrs. Agee answered as she caught the sandwich.

Nor was the excitement over.

Cynthia Agee's job on the witness stand was to convince Judge Connors that her son was sick, not a criminal. She recounted Tom's severe psychiatric problems from boyhood, and his numerous commitments for treatment. As she was walking us through the various episodes, she suddenly stopped, looked down at her feet, and said in a perplexed voice, "Where are my shoes?"

Huh? I thought as I glanced at Agee's attorney, who could only shrug.

It turned out that Mrs. Agee had been wearing high heels that pinched her feet. When she came into court, she had removed them and placed them at the back of the room, next to a trash can. Now she had suddenly remembered them.

"Have you seen a pair of shoes around here?" Judge Connors asked a bailiff.

"I did," he answered, "and I threw them away." Any extraneous item found in a courtroom is considered a security breach and is routinely discarded.

To complicate the matter, the garbage had been collected. So the judge stopped the trial while the bailiff went looking for the missing shoes, which he located somewhere in the building after a brief search.

JUDGE CONNORS FOUND Tom Agee guilty on all counts and gave him a total of fifty-six months in state prison. Because of the time he had already served in the county jail, plus good-behavior and work time in prison, Agee was released within two years and was reevaluated. Somehow, Tom persuaded his interviewers that he was ready to rejoin the wider world.

We all expected him right back in our laps, and were moderately surprised when we heard nothing from or about him. I had hoped that his family finally found him a structured environment, where Tom would pose no threat to others or to himself. With the felony convictions on his record, another arrest would lead to an extended incarceration.

He gradually slipped from my mind altogether until October 1, 2004, when Sergeant Jack Douglas of the Beverly Hills PD called to warn me that Tom Agee was up to his old tricks. Dr. Tuan Anh Duong, a San Francisco physician who had been treating Agee for various physical ailments, had just notified SFPD that his patient had made credible criminal threats against a list of twenty-eight individuals, and I was among them. Agee was not yet in custody, but was believed to be in the Bay Area. I immediately notified our Bureau of Investigation, which oversees our security. They obtained a DMV photo of Agee and printed a poster warning personnel in our office about him. I added an all-cap message instructing us to be notified immediately if Thomas Agee called or showed up, and taped it to the front door of our office.

Agee was at large for three or four days before the San Francisco police picked him up. He was ultimately charged with thirty-seven counts of making criminal threats. I learned more about the incident in a so-called Tarasoff letter that Dr. Duong sent me on October 5.

Tarasoff letters, a common part of my business, are named for Tatiana Tarasoff, a University of California coed who was stalked and stabbed to death in the early 1970s by Prosenjit Poddar, an Indian architectural student. Poddar had disclosed his intention to kill Tarasoff in a therapy session with a university psychologist, who notified the university police of what Poddar had said.

However, Tarasoff's family believed that they should have been warned of the peril, as well. The Tarasoffs sued and lost in court and on appeal, but then won in the California state Supreme Court in 1976.

Noting that doctors have been held negligent for failing to diagnose a contagious disease, or not notifying at-risk family members of it, the court held that a therapist has a legal obligation to warn someone if a patient plans to harm them. "The discharge of this duty," the court said, "may require the therapist to take one or more of various steps. Thus, it may call for him to warn the intended victim, to notify the police, or to take whatever steps are reasonably necessary under the circumstances."

Usually, a letter suffices.

"In the course of my care and treatment of Mr. Agee," Dr. Duong informed me in my Tarasoff letter, "he has provided a list of twenty-eight individuals he considers to be his enemies. He has subsequently made written statements to me to the effect that he believes that 'killing a bunch of people seems to be the only solution to the hurts that have been caused me by those twenty-eight people whose names you have.' He further wrote that 'it is okay to murder a bunch of people' with an assault rifle."

I had lots of familiar company on the list. Besides Fern Collins and Charles Sachs, there was KG (but no Lee Taylor), James Sullivan, Judge Connors, and Paul Edholm. From the 1991 case I recognized Judge Patel, Jeff Bornstein, Lee Baxter, and a long list of others who had worked with Agee at the Consumer Product Safety Commission. He even included Joan Brennan, the federal magistrate who had first ordered a competency evaluation. Tom Agee has a long and excellent memory.

"Mr. Agee's statements," Dr. Duong continued, "oral and

in writing, involve various angry, denigrating, and hostile remarks against these various individuals, but include the aforementioned references to imagined or contemplated acts of violence."

Agee also threatened Senator Dianne Feinstein, according to Dr. Duong. Following his arrest, they found photos he'd taken of himself standing in front of her residence. I knew that James J. Molinari, James Sullivan's boss at the marshals, had moved on to become head of security for Feinstein. So I called Sullivan in Washington, D.C., where he, too, had a new job as second-in-command at Interpol. I told him of Agee's threat against the senator.

Sullivan contacted Molinari, who had been told nothing by the San Francisco police or the local district attorney, and was furious.

As for Agee, the San Francisco authorities were faced with a tricky issue. Since he hadn't personally sent the list to any of us named on it, it would be difficult to argue that Tom had a specific intent to put any of us in fear—although I sure as hell was fearful when I learned about it! Eventually, the prosecutors in San Francisco worked out a deal whereby Agee pled out to a single count of making criminal threats in exchange for a year of psychotherapy at a local facility.

That is the last we've heard of him, and I hope it stays that way.

EIGHT

NINETEEN NINETY-SEVEN WAS easily my favorite year.

It was the year that our Stalking and Threat Assessment Team was finally established, which meant both ratification for me and empowerment. After years of battling to make it happen, the advent of STAT was a form of official sanction. It also meant that, at last, I'd be given the tools to do the job.

It also was the year that I reconnected with my first child, Doug. It had been thirty years since I'd made the hardest choice of my life, to give him up to my first husband's uncle and aunt, and then be asked not even to visit him. The decision had laid heavy on my heart ever since.

Doug hadn't left my mind for a moment. Now that he was a grown man, presumably on his own in the world, I wondered if he knew why his mother had been missing from his life. If not, he needed an explanation, and to hear from me the truth that I'd always loved him.

I was inspired to some extent by the success we had begun to see among cyber-stalkers in their pursuit of victims. Although it was still pretty early in the Internet age, these people were ferreting out all sorts of information using computers and modems. I figured if they could do it, maybe I could, too.

My search was relatively simple, since my first husband has a very unusual surname. It didn't take long to discover that he was working as a photographer in North Carolina. I called him, and we talked a bit about our son. At the end of the conversation, he gave me his aunt and uncle's telephone number. They were living in Florida.

I couldn't anticipate what sort of greeting I'd receive from these people more than three decades after they'd told me that my visits to Doug were too emotionally trying for them, and would I please not come around anymore. To my relief, they were very cordial—quite wonderful, in fact. They were happy to hear from me, and curious to know my purpose. When I told them, they immediately agreed to contact Doug, who lived near New York City, and give him my telephone number.

When I picked up the receiver and heard his voice, it was the single best moment of my life. He was very guarded, as I expected, and full of questions, which I was delighted to answer. I learned a little bit about him, too. No, I didn't have any grandkids yet. He wasn't even married. Yes, he had a good job. He was a master mechanic.

The next questions were when and where to meet. Since I traveled to New York frequently, the earliest and easiest place for our mother and child reunion was there. Doug chose a Chinese restaurant he liked on the east side of Manhattan. My other children, Sean and Shannon, came along, too. They had always known about their older half-brother, and were understandably curious to check him out. Both were deeply impressed when he came to the meeting astride a motorcycle he'd personally built from scratch.

Although I hadn't seen Doug since his infancy—and had no pictures, either—I instantly recognized him from his very bright blue eyes as he crossed the street. They're my eyes. Sean has them, too. Doug also recognized us from a distance, which created a happy air of anticipation for all four of us there on the streets of New York. It was a rare moment of nervousness and joy.

We spent two hours together at that first meeting, my adult child and I trying to get a sense of each other, exploring each other's hearts and minds. I was thrilled. Doug was leery, though plainly interested to learn the truth of matters that had been a mystery to him for his entire life. He was clearly taken with his two articulate and outgoing siblings.

Our next meeting was at his apartment. He gradually grew comfortable enough to tell me of the considerable pain he'd felt wondering why I gave him up. I explained my desperate circumstances at the time. I was young, a teenager with no money or job or even any marketable skills. His father was well-intentioned but unreliable.

By contrast, his aunt and uncle were very good and responsible people, with three daughters and a deep wish to raise a son. I knew them quite well; they'd babysat Doug on several occasions. When they offered to take him, I had no reasonable choice but to accept, as much as it pained me to do so. My first responsibility was my son's well-being.

As I told him this story, understanding began to supplant the doubt in his eyes. Thirty years had created quite a distance, but as I began to build a little trust, we were able to move on to other topics, such as my career or his taste in books. I learned he was widely read and very bright, which naturally made me very proud. He was impressed with my improbable path to success, and sustained in his own ambitions by my example of what hard work and determination can yield.

By the summer of 1997 I had been the de facto "go to" prosecutor for stalking cases for six years. Throughout most of that time, I had argued in memo after memo the necessity of a stand-alone stalking unit in the office. Each year I was told that there was no money in the budget. When I persisted, it was suggested that I go out myself and find some grant money to fund the unit.

Normally, prosecutors at my level are assigned new cases by regular turns, the Hobson's choice approach. But as I continued to rotate in and out of our various divisions, I was expected to handle threat and stalking cases as they arose. For example, when the Madonna matter broke in 1995, I was working what we call CT-13, the general trial unit that handles mostly drug cases, but also theft and the occasional murder trial. These are heard in the thirteenth-floor courtrooms of the criminal courts building in downtown Los Angeles.

This created a professional absurdity. I was expected to handle a very sensitive, high-profile prosecution while also doing fifteen to twenty preliminary hearings a day or jury trials on every imaginable type of case. The demands on my time were extraordinary, complicated by the scarcity of available computers in the office. For example, to get time at the computer and printer in order to work on the Madonna case, I had to stay in the office most nights until midnight and later, basically working two shifts, plus weekends.

Naturally, I'd sometimes overlook details such as dinner. I remember the night a couple of law clerks took pity on me and brought up some takeout. Another time a colleague gave me a set of sweats she kept in the office. "Take off that suit and those high heels," she said, "and put these on. You'll be a lot more comfortable if you're going to spend the night here."

In July of 1997, another mortar landed in my lap. I was assigned at the time to the Workers' Comp Fraud unit. On Saturday, July 12, I received a call at home from a detective. He said there had been some strange happenings over at Steven Spielberg's house. LAPD didn't quite know what to make of it.

The only thing unusual about such a call was the alleged victim's identity. The stalking laws I'd written were still relatively new and not thoroughly understood by every police investigator in Los Angeles, or elsewhere in California; likewise for private security services and in-house corporate security operations, including those at the motion picture studios. Frequently, the police called simply to seek my guidance on a case. Sometimes they'd call in the hope that once I heard the details I'd reject it as a candidate for possible prosecution.

Not this time.

I grabbed a pen and took some notes. According to the officer's sketchy information, on June 29 Jonathan Norman, thirty-one, had driven a white Jeep Cherokee up to the gate of Spielberg's Pacific Palisades residence, where he pushed the intercom button. When confronted by Steven Lopez, a security guard, Norman said he worked for Spielberg's business partner, David Geffen, and that he'd been sent to deliver a personal message from Geffen to Spielberg. Aware that the whole family had departed six days earlier for Ireland, where Spielberg would direct his new movie, *Saving Private Ryan*, Lopez took down the Cherokee's tag numbers—3SZK711—and instructed Norman to leave. The police were not called.

Nothing more was seen of Jonathan Norman at the Spielberg residence until about 1:30 A.M. on July 11, when another security officer, William Hunter, noticed Norman parked in a Land Rover, just opposite the entry gate. The vehicle was identical in almost every detail to the Land Rover that Spielberg's wife, actress Kate Capshaw, then drove.

Hunter asked Norman why he was parked there. Norman said he had engine trouble. When Hunter instructed him to try the ignition, however, the Land Rover started right up. The security guard ordered Norman to move on, and he did so without further incident.

Then at about seven that same morning, Spielberg's neighbors began phoning reports to LAPD that a strange man carrying a large stick was running loose across their backyards, leaping over their fences as he went. One neighbor said the stranger was flapping his arms like a bird.

Jonathan Norman was back.

The police and Spielberg's private security guards went in search of the interloper. When security officer Terry Costello finally found him hiding under some bushes, he discovered his quarry was big and incredibly buff; Norman was a demon weight lifter.

When police questioned Norman at the scene, he told them his name was David Spielberg, Steven's newly adopted son. He said he'd been "running away from the jackal"—which turned out to be the Spielbergs' watchdog.

When the officers told him to stand up and raise his hands, Norman dropped a black day planner to the ground. In it they discovered photos of both Spielberg's and David Geffen's heads pasted onto pictures of naked male bodies. They also found handwritten notes. Norman had entered Spielberg's name; the names of all his family members, including his kids and mother; plus addresses, phone numbers, birth dates, and other personal information. There was also a good deal of personal information about Geffen's and Spielberg's other business associates.

The LAPD officers took Jonathan and his day planner to the West LA station, where he floated yet another tale. He told a Threat Management Unit detective that his name was Jonathan Spielberg, and again claimed that he'd recently been adopted by the famous director. Norman said he'd been to a party at Jack Nicholson's house, where he and Nicholson had gotten into a fight, so he'd left. He claimed he was running around the neighborhood because jackals were after him.

The police detained their suspect long enough to have a DRE—drug recognition expert—evaluate him. He was clean. Not knowing what to do next, the officers asked Norman to voluntarily accompany them to a local mental clinic for evaluation. He agreed. He also verbally consented to a search of his Brentwood apartment. Even though by now the LAPD also knew of the June 29 episode with Steven Lopez, as well as the front-gate confrontation earlier that morning with William Hunter, the officers returned his day planner to Norman and then left him at the clinic. A couple of minutes later, he walked away.

This was an uncharacteristic lapse on the part of the police. Unfortunately, it would not be their last in the Norman investigation, which was plagued with screwups and other problems.

When officers searched Jonathan's Brentwood apartment, pursuant to his verbal consent, they didn't find any weapons, but they did note that Norman had collected hundreds and hundreds of pages of information about Spielberg, much of it from the Internet. There were pictures as well, and news clips about the director and his films, particularly *Jurassic Park*. Inexplicably, officers especially trained to deal with threatening behavior and stalkers didn't bother to take a single sheet of paper from Norman's apartment into evidence. They just left everything there.

Late on the afternoon of the eleventh, Jonathan returned once more to the Spielberg compound. Using a windshield sunscreen to hide his face from the surveillance cameras—an alert guard recognized him anyway—Norman backed the Land Rover up to the gate, as if he intended to crash through it, then drove off. A brief search turned up the abandoned SUV parked a short distance away. Police staked it out.

Twenty minutes later, they watched their suspect approach the vehicle on foot, wearing a baggy set of sweatpants and a sweatshirt. Officers grabbed him once more. He was found to be carrying a large roll of gray duct tape tucked inside the waistband of his sweatpants. A pair of handcuffs was inserted into the center of the roll. He also had a razor knife—a box cutter—with him.

Inside the Land Rover were two additional sets of handcuffs, plus several containers of razor blades. He had no explanation for the handcuffs, duct tape, razor blades, and box cutter in the vehicle, nor did he discuss the handwritten "Assorted Toys" list police also retrieved from the Land Rover. The list included mentions of items such as "strap-on dildos," "3 dog collars," "4 pair nipple clippers," "beebee gun," plus "cloraform/shocker." Condoms were found, as well. The glove box also turned up rental papers for the car, which matched the company that the Cherokee's license plate had also been registered to.

On the strength of his repeated behavior, statements, and the "rape kit," Norman was taken to the psychiatric unit at Harbor-UCLA Medical Center. On the way, he told his LAPD escorts, "I work for David Geffen. He and Steven Spielberg are physically passionate. Steven told me to come over and act the persona of a rapist. My lovers and I take turns wearing handcuffs. They want me to be personified in Judaism and have adopted me as their godson. I find them highly attractive."

When a doctor asked what he was doing at the Spielberg residence, Norman replied, "I guess making a fool of myself."

Based on what I learned in that first call from the LAPD, I had three major concerns. Of paramount importance was Spielberg himself. The first thing I needed to know was whether the director had yet been informed of the incidents. I contacted one of his several lawyers to find out.

"Does Spielberg know about this?"

"Not yet," he replied. "He will be told."

"Well," I said, "there isn't a whole lot we can do until we find out what his reaction is."

I then explained that any prosecution would hinge on this. To prove stalking, you not only must establish the stalker's *intent* to place the victim in fear, but you also must show that the victim *actually was* in reasonable fear for his or her safety. Even then you aren't necessarily home free, especially if your victim, like Madonna, resists taking part in the prosecution.

There was a practical security concern, as well. Oftentimes, the people around a celebrity will withhold news of a stalker threat because they don't want to upset the target. This can be extremely dangerous.

Celebrities don't always have bodyguards with them. They go to the supermarket. They take their kids to school. They're especially vulnerable if they're unaware that someone means to harm them. John Lennon's murder by Mark David Chapman is a case in point. It was no coincidence that among Jonathan Norman's possessions we later found several press accounts of Lennon's ambush death.

My next, related concern was with Norman's whereabouts. He had been placed under a psychiatric hold at Harbor-UCLA, which was ordinarily good for seventy-two hours. If it wasn't extended, there was no way to keep him locked up.

The way to calm these concerns was to get Norman charged and jailed under a stiff enough bond to ensure he'd be off the streets at least until trial. But to charge him I needed facts—evidence—primarily in the form of written reports from police detectives. The security officers at Spielberg's house needed to be interviewed. We needed to find out where and how Norman had acquired his vehicles. We definitely needed to look at the evidence that the LAPD officers had neglected to seize when they searched his apartment.

Yet from the outset I could not get the new TMU detective assigned to the case to stop procrastinating and produce some investigative reports for me. I had previously enjoyed a strong professional relationship with the TMU squad, but the new guy simply did not seem to take the case seriously.

I think I know why. This detective seemed to reason that there was no way that we'd sustain a stalking charge because the victim was not at home—or even in the country—while Norman stalked him. Therefore, why bother to pursue it? He was dead wrong, I thought, and eventually the California Court of Appeal would agree with me.

My apprehensions over Jonathan Norman only intensified

as we began to look into his altogether unusual, and often violent, past.

Born October 24, 1966, Jonathan was the fourth of four sons in the family of George I. Norman, Jr., and his wife, Frances, of Salt Lake City. In August of 1997, completely coincidental to the concurrent events in Los Angeles, *Esquire* magazine published a lengthy article by journalist Ivan Solotaroff about the elder Norman, entitled "America's Greatest Living Criminal Genius Sends His Regards."

According to Solotaroff, as well as two subsequent pieces in the Salt Lake City *Tribune* by reporters Vince Horiuchi and Brian Maffly, the Norman family lived extraordinarily well through the late 1960s and early '70s. Their house, at the base of Mount Olympus in the southeast section of Salt Lake City, was vast—Dad's suit closet alone was six hundred square feet—and featured a huge swimming pool with his monogram (GIN) on the bottom. Lots of celebrity guests, from Bob Hope to Buddy Ebsen, were known to drop by. There was extra garage space for George's three Stutz Bearcats—the one Mrs. Norman drove was upholstered in blue mink—as well as a Jaguar XKE, two Rolls-Royces, and a Lincoln. The chauffeur occasionally drove Jonathan and his older brothers the short distance to school.

The domestic opulence and George's free spending ways (supposedly, Tony Lama himself cut the elder Norman's cowboy boots) impressed his friends and business partners as intended—until it turned out that he was a crook. In March of 1973, the family's world of privilege imploded when Dad flew to Denver with his attorney, future U.S. senator Orrin Hatch, to face sentencing on a federal conviction for embezzling five hundred thousand dollars. But instead of surrendering to begin a two-year prison term, Norman stole a judge's Cadillac Seville and lit out for Idaho, and then points unknown. George Norman would remain at large for twenty-three years, until he was finally apprehended in Nashville, Tennessee, in November of 1996.

The U.S. Marshals Service appears to have been just a step or two behind Norman for much of that time, nearly arresting him on a couple of occasions. According to Solotaroff, Norman worked behind a screen of aliases to invest widely in ventures from McDonald's franchises to Thoroughbreds, real estate, and minerals. He fleeced any number of business partners, too. Estimated profits from Norman's various deals ran as high as $150 million.

Back home in Salt Lake City, Frances (who had divorced George in 1984 and moved to California) and the four boys relied partly on the kindness of friends. But according to Solotaroff, George also "traveled in and out of Salt Lake City at will, disguised as a monk or ski bum. When he couldn't get there, he sent his family money orders drawn at the local supermarkets."

George later remarried. His attractive new wife—a talented golfer who set course records at several country clubs the pair joined—was half his age. Together, they became active in Republican politics, too. Witnesses, who knew them as Tom and Liz DeAngelis, remembered photos of their friend Tom with Presidents Reagan and George H. W. Bush displayed in a Texas residence the DeAngelises owned for a time.

George and Liz also found time in their busy lives to welcome Jesus into their hearts. When Norman was arrested by the marshals in the parking lot of a Comfort Suites, he was driving a Continental bearing the bumper sticker, PRAYER CHANGES THINGS. George I. Norman, Jr., died in 2006.

Family friends told the *Tribune* reporters that the abrupt loss of their father and his long odyssey on the lam had a devastating impact on Jonathan and his three older brothers, one of whom later did time for his part in the murder of a Maryland drug dealer. Jonathan was soon expelled from grade school for assaulting his fellow pupils. By age thirteen he was smoking marijuana. By the time he finished high school, he was using methamphetamine.

One boyhood acquaintance, Jim Irvine, told us of Norman's violent tendencies. He recalled that Jonathan had enjoyed torturing animals, and before he finally acknowledged his homosexuality, said Irvine, Jonathan had dated a girl whom he beat severely on at least one occasion.

Jonathan, who matured into a handsome young man, attended UCLA and earned a bachelor's degree in economics in 1990. George gave his youngest boy a new BMW as a graduation present. Weeks later, according to Irvine, he was a

My mother, Sylvia, on her
wedding day in March 1945.
Courtesy of Rhonda Saunders, Esq.

Me and my grandfather Louis
in the Bronx, 1947.
Courtesy of Rhonda Saunders, Esq.

My grandfather Samuel,
and my father, Irving, in
his army uniform, circa
1944.
*Courtesy of Rhonda Saunders,
Esq.*

My time on the stage—in *Anything Goes* (circa 1968) and *Showboat* (circa 1969). *Courtesy of Rhonda Saunders, Esq.*

Me at eighteen, when I was just starting my theatrical career. *Courtesy of Rhonda Saunders, Esq.*

My graduation from
Immaculate Heart College
in 1979.
Courtesy of Rhonda Saunders, Esq.

My graduation from
USC Law School,
with my husband,
Ralph, and son Sean,
1982.
*Courtesy of Rhonda
Saunders, Esq.*

"Be on Alert" flyers of Susan Dyer, which were distributed throughout my office.

Special Bulletin

WATCH BRIEFING
OFFENDER OF INTEREST

NOT WANTED - NOT WANTED

NAME: DYER, SUSAN

DOB: 10-25-1962

PHYSICAL: FW / 39; BRO; BRO; 507; 150

LKA: ▮▮▮ Harvard Street, Santa Monica
(Former residence of brother)

Add'l Res: Transient, living out of vehicle

CDL: ▮▮▮
FBI: ▮▮▮

Criminal History: 417.8PC; 245(A)(2)PC; 459PC; 136.1(C)(1)PC

Photo: 02-24-1998

Vehicle: 1982 Mercedes Benz, mustard yellow in color; 4-door; CA VLN: ▮▮▮

Susan DYER was convicted in 1991 of Assault with a Firearm and Exhibiting a Firearm. Prior to this conviction, DYER had been continually stalking a female victim. At one point, DYER had been living under the crawl space of victim's house without the victim's knowledge. DYER's conviction includes threatening to shoot a SWAT Team officer, as well as the victim's friends, following an incident wherein DYER barricaded herself inside victim's residence.

DYER was released following a verdict that found DYER to be mentally competent. DYER is living in the above-listed vehicle and has been contacting the victim's family members as of January 2002.

**DISTRICT ATTORNEY'S OFFICE
BUREAU OF INVESTIGATION
SECURITY ALERT**

Date: 12-30-04	INFORMATION ONLY

SUSAN DYER

Driver's License: ▮▮▮   **Date of Birth:** 10-25-62   **Sex:** Female   **hair:** Brown   **Eyes:** Brown   **Height:** 5-7/150

Addresses used: ▮▮▮

In 1992, DDA Ronda Saunders convicted Dyer on 417.8 P.C. Exhibit firearm & 245(A)(2)P.C. Assault w/firearm (Case No. BA045707), which Dyer stalked her victim. She was sentenced to 9 yrs prison. When Dyer was released on parole there were several violations and she was placed at Patton State Hospital where she refused treatment and completed her parole status on 1-28-00. After a suitability hearing she was release in October 2000. Dyer has recently left several hostile voice mail messages on DDA Saunders' office telephone. Dyer continues to deny any wrongdoing and believes she was wrongfully convicted. Dyer is believed to be dangerous and a potential threat. If seen, notify the command center at 213-974-▮▮▮.

Mug shot of Susan Dyer, in 1995.

Mug shot of Dante Soiu,
convicted of stalking actress
Gwyneth Paltrow.

Letter left by Robert Hoskins at the front gate of
Castillo del Lago, Madonna's estate.

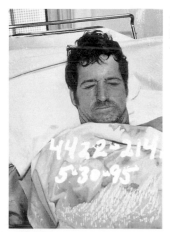

Hoskins, shortly after being shot by Basil Stephens.
Andrew Purdy

Pool area at Madonna's estate, where Hoskins confronted Stephens.

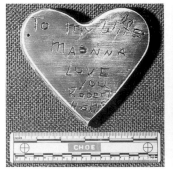

Carved wooden heart inscribed to Madonna from Robert Hoskins, found among his belongings the day he was arrested.

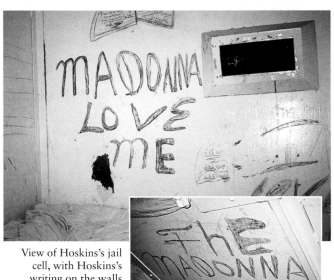

View of Hoskins's jail cell, with Hoskins's writing on the walls and under the bunk.

Mug shot of Jonathan Norman wearing his "Rambo" outfit.

Assorted toys: 2 sizes of strapon; small, medium, large, Huge Di..
3 Eye Masks
3 Cuffs
4 pair nipple clippers
3 Dog Collars
— Check for nipple shockers...
3 Jacks w/same key
— Beebee Gun at Sportsmart
4 Packs of Blades at local grocery store.
— Vibraform, Shocker.

Party Mag for Equipmen
and supplies

Staples
Eddie
Pleasure Chest
Dry Cleaners

Tomorrow:
Pet store
Marshells

Norman's "toy list," recovered from his car at the time of his arrest for stalking Steven Spielberg.

Lieutenant Karen Green (KG), of the Los Angeles County Sheriff's Department, shortly before her retirement.
James Buddy Fowler

Stick drawing of dead parakeet by Lieutenant Lee Taylor, left on KG's desk the day after Thomas Agee's arrest.
Lee E. Taylor

CALIFORNIA DEPARTMENT OF MOTOR VEHICLES IMAGE

THOMAS CLARK AGEE

	EXPIRES: ▉	CLASS: ▉	SEX: ▉
HAIR: ▉	EYES: ▉	HEIGHT: ▉	WEIGHT: ▉

DATE OF BIRTH: ▉

ADDRESS: ▉

PHOTO DATE:	PHOTO OFFICE:	APPLICATION DATE:	APPLICATION OFFICE:
	▉	▉	
ISSUE DATE: N/A	ISSUE OFFICE: N/A	RESTRICTIONS: 0	

SIGNATURE:

Thomas C. agee

FINGERPRINT:

This photograph is a true copy of the photograph that is contained on the Department of Motor Vehicles photo database and delivered over the Department of Justice communications network.

Date: _____ /s/ _____

PLEASE NOTIFY DA INVESTIGATORS IMMEDIATELY IF

THOMAS AGEE SHOWS UP AT THE OFFICE OR CALLS.

HE MAY BE ARMED AND DANGEROUS.

RHONDA

Photo alert of Thomas Agee posted in my front office.

Snapshot of Marie Poynton in happier days. *Sarah Barra*

Left: The knife used by Richard Poynton to kill his wife.
Right: Damage to the car Poynton used to ram his wife's vehicle.

Front and back of envelope sent to actress Jeri Ryan
by Marlon Pagtakhan.

Me with Maria Noelle Sulgatti and her hero, Lieutenant Randy
Osborne of the Glendale Police Department,
who captured Jolly Jett-Nanez Alsaybar.
Marie Johnson

Whipple Street, where Janice Sugita shot her victim.
Shannon B. Wainwright

Michael Brewer, Esq., my colleague and cocounsel
on the Dante Soiu case.
Courtesy of The Brewer Law Firm of Southern California

Investigator Kevin Sleeth, who arrested Marlon
Pagtakhan on two different occasions.
Hector Alvarado

Me and Rick Pfaff (LASD, retired) reviewing cases in my office.
Brentford Ferreira

Me and my longtime assistant, Marie Johnson.
Shannon B. Wainwright

passenger in the BMW when his old high school friend missed a turn at eighty miles an hour and totaled the sports car.

In 1994, Norman appeared at Cedars-Sinai Hospital in Los Angeles, claiming that his father, then still a fugitive, was monitoring him. He asked to have the phantom monitors removed. The young man was put in restraints and held overnight for observation.

Approximately one year later, Jonathan was arrested in Santa Monica for attacking a group of Jewish senior citizens. While driving his Jeep, he saw the elderly people crossing the street in front of him and sped up in an attempt to run them over. He failed, so he put the Jeep in reverse and tried again. When that didn't work, he jumped out of his vehicle, ran up to one of the women in the group, threw her to the ground, and started kicking her back and head.

One of the men in the group tried to stop him. Norman turned his anger on him, punching and kicking the man until police arrived and arrested him. On June 24, 1995, Norman pled guilty to two counts of assault with intent to commit great bodily injury. Seven other counts were dropped. He was sentenced to three years in state prison, and was released after serving less than two years, just a few months prior to his visit to the Spielberg gate.

The fact that Norman's previous victims were Jewish bothered Spielberg's security firm, Berman and Ely, Inc., more than anything else. Because of the subjects and slant of some of the projects their client had been involved with, including *Schindler's List*, *Shoah*, and *The Color Purple*, word had circulated that the Ku Klux Klan and other right-wing hate organizations had put the director on a hit list. That complicated his security arrangements. When Spielberg made public appearances, for example, his team had to worry about potential bombers and snipers, unusual problems for an entertainment figure.

SPIELBERG HEARD NOTHING about Jonathan Norman's attempted incursions, or intentions toward him, for several days, even though I placed numerous phone calls to his lawyers and security people emphasizing to them the importance of obtaining his reaction. Everybody was kind of twiddling their thumbs, not wanting to upset him, I was told. These people mistakenly believed that Norman would be kept indefinitely at Harbor-UCLA, betraying a basic ignorance of how fast California processes mental cases in and out of its public psychiatric facilities. I knew different.

When I told them that Norman was to be released on the seventeenth, a call was finally placed to Ireland by Spielberg's personal attorney and close friend, Bruce Ramer (for whom the mechanical shark in Spielberg's first great cinema success, *Jaws*, was named).

Ramer ran down Norman's behavior and reported the handcuffs, duct tape, and box cutter, as well the day planner with its lists of names, phone numbers, and addresses. Ramer also disclosed that the suspect was about to be released.

Bruce Ramer shared this revelation with Spielberg by telephone. "It was not an easy message to deliver," the lawyer later testified. "He was in the midst of directing a film and obviously focused, and it's not the kind of information one comfortably passes on to a friend, let alone a client."

The bizarre news naturally terrified Spielberg, who told me he was so shocked that he reflexively hung up on Ramer. He couldn't talk. His throat closed up on him. "I reacted to the information at first with disbelief," he said in court, "then I became quite frightened. I was very upset. Had Jonathan Norman actually confronted me, I genuinely in my heart of hearts believe that I would have been raped or maimed or killed."

Once he regained his composure and got Ramer back on the telephone, Spielberg ordered increased security at his compound and for all his family members. The number of security personnel was tripled, as was the security budget. He also made it clear, then and later, that he would cooperate in Norman's prosecution.

We'd just cleared another major hurdle. Not only was my victim willing to testify, but we could clearly meet the legal test of Norman causing fear both objectively and subjectively. Spielberg was, in fact, terrified. Now we had to figure a way to get Norman off the streets until I could indict him.

On July 17, the day of his release from the psychiatric hospital, Jonathan and his friend, Chuck Markovich, went to the movies to see *The Lost World*, the sequel to *Jurassic Park*. All through the film, Norman kept nudging Markovich, saying, "I'm the baby tyrannosaurus! I'm the baby tyrannosaurus!"

In fact, he was toast. While Jonathan and Chuck were at the movie, I was on the phone with Jonathan's parole officer, Lionel Coulter, describing Norman's recent stalking conduct. At the very least, I hoped for a "parole hold," to buy us some time.

The news from Coulter was better than anything I imagined. One term of Norman's parole was that he could not use drugs, and was subject to random testing to see that he didn't. On June 12, Lionel told me, Jonathan had tested dirty for methamphetamine, as well as again on July 7. The parole officer had already decided to put Norman back into custody.

While Jonathan was enjoying the movie, Coulter was preparing the warrant that would send him back to prison.

As Norman was being held in the county lockup, he received a twenty minute visit from Rick Vigil, a security consultant working for Spielberg in conjunction with Berman and Ely. Vigil needed to know if Norman was part of a group or had acted alone.

Norman assured him that he did not belong to any organization, nor was he a political, religious, or social extremist. "I just wanted to be friends and live on the estate," he told Vigil.

In a very matter-of-fact tone, he said he'd been high on drugs for a week straight before trying to enter the Spielberg compound. Norman also told Vigil that he'd intended to tie up Spielberg and rape him. Vigil asked what he'd do if Spielberg's wife walked in on him. "I'd tie her up and make her watch," he said.

What if Spielberg turned out to be heterosexual? "I think I can turn him," Norman replied.

OUR FIRST IMPORTANT break in the case came via one of Spielberg's law firms, which in its independent inquiry into Norman's background and associations had hired a private investigator who turned up Chuck Markovich, Norman's friend and would-be lover, who was willing—and eager—to talk. Markovich was interviewed at the West LA police station, while I listened to the taped interview in a separate room.

Chuck was an ordinary-looking guy, very much in love with the handsome Jonathan, who did not return his affection. Markovich said that Norman refused to have sex with him, but did live with him from time to time, and allowed Chuck to support him with the meager proceeds from a string of low-paying jobs.

Their long, abusive relationship antedated Jonathan's imprisonment, and included at least one police complaint in which Markovich alleged that Norman had attacked him, knocking out a couple of teeth. Norman had been charged with felony assault.

Markovich then wrote letters to the prosecutor, elaborating on how violent Norman was and how afraid he, Chuck, was of Jonathan. On the eve of prosecution, however, he changed his mind, refused to testify, and the case was dropped.

Markovich now recalled that Norman had started obsessing over Spielberg while in prison, but could offer no explanation why. The moment he was released, Jonathan began collecting information about Spielberg from the Internet. Markovich was with him the day Norman bought a star map on Sunset Boulevard in order to locate Spielberg's residence.

Weeks before the first incident in late June, Norman began to cruise past the address regularly, insisting that Chuck accompany him on these excursions. On July 9, two days before his arrest, he told Markovich he'd decided to convert to Judaism and be Bar Mitzvahed. He also said he'd found a place to climb over the wall surrounding Spielberg's compound, and that he intended to rape the director.

Markovich warned Norman not to try it. He argued that Spielberg was obviously surrounded by security. Jonathan not only was sure to fail but would be arrested if he tried out his plan.

Norman stayed home that night; Markovich believed he had talked him out of raping Spielberg. However, the following afternoon Chuck came home from work to find Jonathan masturbating over pictures of Spielberg. Jealous and angry, Markovich started a fight. Norman stormed off. The next time he heard from Jonathan was by telephone from Harbor-UCLA.

Chuck had given us critically useful information, but there was still more. He said Norman's landlord was about to evict him, and that he intended to go to Norman's apartment to clean it out.

As I listened I inwardly screamed, "That's evidence! My God! Do something before it's destroyed!"

At the time of the "jackal" incident, Norman had consented to a search of his apartment, but the consent was stale—that is, after two months it was too old to use and could present potential problems down the road. Moreover, it had been verbal, not written, as is much preferred. To be on firm legal grounds, I wanted a search warrant. As soon as the interview was over, I said to the TMU detective, "We need a search warrant, now. Get a search warrant. We know there's stuff there. We need this if we're going to file charges. I especially want to look at the hard drive on his computer."

Next day, I asked, "Search warrant?"

"No, no search warrant."

The detective told me he didn't know how to do a search warrant for a computer. So I sent over a template to follow. Still nothing. Nothing was happening.

My office noticed the problem.

"Why hasn't anything been filed?" I was asked on several occasions.

"Because I don't have any reports," I answered. "LAPD is dropping the ball."

I requested that we use our investigators, who are very, very good. No, I was told. Just make LAPD do their job.

The head of the office called to say that Spielberg's attorneys were pressing him daily for details of our progress. Again I explained that I had no reports on which to base my complaint. I asked again if I could use our investigators to get the job done.

"This is a serious problem," I said. "Please, can I have our investigators do this case?" He gave me the okay. So I called Pat McPherson, one of our very best investigators, who was immediately on my wavelength: If you have a case, jump on it.

We wrote a search warrant for Norman's apartment in a

couple of hours, then McPherson headed out, only to discover that Chuck Markovich had arrived hours before him and completely emptied the place. Although by now it was early evening, McPherson found a judge who agreed to a change of the address on the warrant to Markovich's residence. When Pat finally got to Chuck's house with his search warrant, he discovered that Markovich had the incriminating material all spread out. He was preparing to destroy everything.

McPherson recovered a blue diary in which Norman had recorded his sexual fantasies about Spielberg. He'd also written a very chilling scenario in which he would wait in the shadows for "a man" to come home. He'd sneak up behind him, bind and gag the man, put a "screaming mask" on him, and then brutally rape him.

Pat found a receipt from a local spy shop for night goggles and similar gear, as well as the "star map" Norman had used to find Spielberg's house. Scattered on Markovich's bed were hundreds of pieces of paper with personal and professional information about Spielberg that Norman had downloaded from the Internet. McPherson also found the day planner that had been given back to Norman by LAPD. Unfortunately, the incriminating photos of Spielberg's and David Geffen's heads had been removed from the pictures of the naked male bodies.

McPherson did excellent work, but I still needed numerous witnesses interviewed. Even though our investigators were technically on the case, for political reasons we could not exclude LAPD. So I called a meeting in our conference room, hoping to get everyone pointed in the same direction. Pat McPherson attended, as did three TMU investigators. I asked the new detective, who so far had shown very little enthusiasm for the case, to bring his Norman notebook, a running account of the case that each LAPD detective is expected to maintain. He produced a single page with Norman's name written on it and nothing more.

I hit the ceiling. Numerous witnesses need to be interviewed, I told the group. These included Spielberg's neighbors, the security guards, employees at the auto rental place where Norman had picked up the Land Rover identical to Kate Capshaw's, as well as the police officers who had participated in each of the incidents.

I took the list of witnesses and assigned each person in the room several people to interview immediately. I told them that I also needed pictures of the various locations and copies of the Spielberg security people's surveillance tapes.

OUR STAND-ALONE STALKING unit was finally approved and up and running in early August 1997. Thenceforth, all stalking cases within the county of Los Angeles would be prosecuted by the Stalking and Threat Assessment Team, or STAT, as we called it. All prosecutions would be vertical as well, meaning that a single prosecutor would be in charge from beginning to end. If we were overwhelmed with cases, we would give guidance to the prosecutor handling the case.

The dedicated part of our mission was a key element; from now on, I would be handling stalking, threat, and workplace violence cases exclusively, free from the distractions of other prosecutorial responsibilities. It would make me that much more effective.

STAT originally consisted of me, one other prosecutor, an investigator, and a victims' advocate, whose job was to help the victims in our cases gain access to such resources as psychological counseling, secure financial restitution from the offender, or help with physical relocation from the state of California. Since there was no office space available for us in the beginning, I worked out of the library until room could be found in the Hall of Records. We were not the state's first stalking unit—after all the years of delay, San Diego had beaten us to the punch—but I doubt that any similar unit then or later was any more effective than ours.

We had broad responsibilities, including jurisdiction to file charges anywhere in the county. Within a few months, most of the police agencies in LA County knew to bring their stalking, threat, and workplace violence cases to us, or to seek us out for help and advice. We were ready to assist them at any level, from organizing a case to investigating it to bringing it to trial. Consequently, the number of stalking cases filed for prosecution rose significantly.

Part of my job was to travel around the state and country, educating law enforcement agencies and prosecutors about stalking. The *Los Angeles Times* and *People* magazine wrote about us, which brought many more victims to our attention, especially in instances where local authorities had failed to help these individuals. Within two years, we had doubled the number of prosecutors and investigators working with the STAT team.

STEVEN SPIELBERG WAS among the very first stalking victims to benefit from STAT's enhanced capabilities, although it would require me to go to the mat with my immediate supervisor in order to retain control of the case.

As is always true, I needed to speak directly with the victim, the sooner the better. Spielberg was more than willing. In fact, his lawyers offered to fly me to Ireland to conduct the interview. I was tempted, but reluctantly declined the offer to avoid any possible appearance of a conflict of interest. So it was arranged that we'd meet soon after Spielberg returned from Ireland in September.

As the date approached, however, my immediate supervisor called me into his office to say, "The administration doesn't feel you should interview Mr. Spielberg. I will." In other words, I wasn't worthy of talking to the famous man.

This supervisor didn't have a clue what the case was about. I grew *very* upset. What sent me over the edge, however, was his next remark. "When you take this before the grand jury," he said, "I'll handle Spielberg, and you'll do the rest of the witnesses."

"All right," I replied, shoving the case file across his desk at him, "I'm out of it."

The next day, we spoke once again. He told me the administration definitely wanted me to stay on as prosecutor—I'd been working on the case seven days a week, and nobody else in the office, besides Pat McPherson, knew the case like I did. I would be allowed to question Spielberg in front of the grand jury, but with his assistance. However, at the upcoming meeting, I was not to talk to Spielberg—or say anything to him, for that matter.

So on September 26, 1997, this self-important supervisor and I, along with a TMU detective and Pat McPherson, met with Spielberg in his DreamWorks office at Paramount Studios. The session did not unfold as my supervisor had hoped.

I had recently broken my arm while roller-skating with my daughter. When Spielberg walked into the room, he had a cast on his left arm, too. We exchanged smiles as he walked directly over to me.

"I know who you are," he said. "You're the woman who wrote the stalking law." He'd done his homework.

Spielberg had a list of questions that only I or Pat could answer. That left the titular head of our delegation with little to do but listen. Spielberg wanted to know what was going on, how the investigation was going, what role I expected him to play. The one question we could not answer was why. "Why did this man want to rape me?" he asked, then permitted himself a small joke. "I never thought of myself as a sex symbol."

We spoke for an hour or more. I was impressed, and touched, by his evident love and concern for his wife, mother, and children. He was terrified for them. No airs. Just a down to-earth and honest guy. He promised me that he would always be available when I needed him to testify. This was a very welcome change from the wars with Madonna over her cooperation. I inwardly swore to myself that I'd do everything in my power to protect Steven Spielberg and his family.

I specifically remember him saying that it was not just that Norman had showed up with handcuffs, but that he'd brought three sets of handcuffs. That showed Spielberg that Norman planned to hurt his kids or wife, not just him. He also noted the irony that he, a card-carrying liberal, would willingly be part of a coordinated effort to take away someone's freedom and put him behind bars. That's how horrified he was, and afraid for his family. He was especially fixed on Norman's remark to Markovich that he'd found just the right spot to climb the wall that surrounded the compound. "My seven-year-old son plays right by that wall," he said. "What if he had gotten over it? What would he have done to my son?"

We wanted to get the case before the grand jury as quickly as possible lest the parole hold on Norman be lifted. The earliest date we could get was Wednesday, October 8.

We sent an unmarked car for Spielberg, which brought him and his attorney Bruce Ramer in through the underground judges' entrance, and then up to the thirteenth floor in the judges' elevator, thereby avoiding any contact with the public. So far the press hadn't uncovered the story, and I was determined to keep things that way for as long as possible. That was a major reason for taking my case to a grand jury—which meets in secret—rather than to a preliminary hearing before a judge, which is a public proceeding. If at all possible, I wanted to avoid a repeat of the media frenzy that accompanied the Hoskins prosecution of 1996.

It required a full day to put on all my witnesses. Spielberg, who testified for about forty-five minutes, and Chuck Markovich, who appeared before the grand jurors for two hours or more, were the most important.

I asked Spielberg to begin with the phone call from Bruce Ramer.

"He said the man came stating that he was in some way related to me," he remembered as twenty-two grand jurors intently followed every word. "Later he said he had a desire to hurt me, to rape me. He brought with him items that were found in his car and on his person, multiple sets of handcuffs, duct tape, and a razor knife. And he was very bold and brazen, stating that he was there to do me harm."

I knew from my own discussion with Spielberg that the incident had shaken him. Now it was important for the grand jurors to see just how scared the director was.

"When you were informed of these incidents," I asked, "what was your immediate reaction?"

"Well," he answered, "disbelief was my immediate reaction. I didn't believe it because nothing like this had ever happened to me before... When Bruce gave me more details of his state of mind and what he perceived to be an honest and very realistic threat to myself and my family, I became completely panicked and upset and very afraid to tell my wife."

In fact, he said, he said nothing to his wife for a couple of days, and never told any of their seven children.

"What was your reaction when you heard about the duct tape and knife and handcuffs?"

"What anyone's reaction would be—that he was there for a mission. Had he not been caught he would have—you know, thank God he was caught—he would have completed his mission. I really felt my life was in danger."

"You were frightened?"

"I was frightened. I have seven children, and I was mainly frightened for their safety."

Spielberg explained how he beefed up security at his Pacific Palisades residence, and at his mother's kosher restaurant in Los Angeles, as well as his and his family's personal security while in Ireland, and then in London, shooting *Saving Private Ryan*. Spielberg testified that his fear as he was filming battle scenes in Ireland was that Norman, if at large, might easily make his way armed, and unnoticed, onto the set. Norman could start shooting real bullets, and the sound would be masked by the battle noises. He also revealed that he'd obtained a restraining order, even though Jonathan Norman was locked up.

"I'm very distraught over the possibility that this man could come out of jail and go right back on the war path again," he said. "I'm completely concerned for my children. My children go to public schools. They are on the street a lot. They are out there exposed. It's something that obsesses me. I think about this all the time. It's always on my mind. It's gotten somewhat in the way of my work…I have dreams that have kept me up at night."

Toward the end of his testimony, I showed Spielberg the detailed list of his family members that Norman had made. He read it aloud to the jury.

"Looking at that," I asked, "what is your reaction?"

"Well, you know, it's chilling," Spielberg replied. "It's absolutely chilling."

I had to be a bit more careful with Chuck Markovich, whose affection for the accused might possibly cloud his memory on the stand. Prior to his testimony, I showed Chuck the audiotape of his earlier interview, conducted at the West LA police station. Then I told him he had better be truthful. I warned that if his testimony differed from what he had told the LAPD detective, I'd play that tape in front of the jurors to impeach him. He meekly told me that he would tell the truth.

He was obviously very nervous, but he just as obviously

enjoyed all the attention. That was his main motivation—being the center of attention—which had never before happened to him.

Chuck discussed the photos of Spielberg's and Geffen's heads pasted over naked male bodies. He recalled how Norman had said he wanted to rape Spielberg. He talked about buying the star map and cruising the Spielberg residence. He remembered his friend saying that he wanted to rent a Land Rover exactly like the one Kate Capshaw drove so he could get past the gate. He also testified about the physical evidence, including Jonathan's diary, which Pat McPherson had seized at his house.

Markovich touched on Norman's relationship with his father, George Norman, as well.

"Jonathan's father left him when he was six years old," Chuck said, "and he's never been able to deal with that. His father's been a fugitive, and he's always wanted a father. I mean, he still talks to him, but he was never there. His father is very anti-gay."

It was Chuck's opinion that David Geffen, who is openly gay, was more of a father figure to his friend than was Jonathan's own father.

Because grand jurors in California serve for a full year, a majority of those who are picked are older or retired people who generally don't have daily demands on their time. Since they could sort through the physical evidence as they wished after the testimony concluded, I made a point of warning them that Jonathan Norman's diary had a good deal of obscene, disturbing material in it. I didn't want their sensibilities offended.

"When you go through this blue diary," I said, "I need to warn you that it's rather explicit. So keep that in mind. The part that starts off in the center with 'Steven Spielberg has a sexy look.' It gets a little graphic. What this will show, however, is the extent of his obsession and the fact that he didn't want just a father figure. He didn't want a lover in the normal sense of the word. He wanted violence. He makes reference in here to 'rape boy.' You can see this for yourself."

So I went outside to wait for them to hand down the indictment, expecting it to take no time at all. After about twenty minutes, I started worrying. *What could possibly be holding them up?* I wondered. Five or six minutes later, they finally voted as I'd hoped and expected.

A short time afterward, the grand jury advisor came up to me. "The indictment would have come down much sooner," he said, "but the minute you left they all dove to take a look at that diary."

WE CHARGED NORMAN with one count of felony stalking at his November 6 arraignment. A conviction on that charge alone would have earned him just a three-year sentence, which would be substantially reduced by time already served. With his two previous felony convictions in the Santa Monica case, however, Norman faced a potential sentence of twenty-five years to life under California's three strikes law. That was my goal.

The first necessary legal step was to allege these two prior strikes at his arraignment—which we did; then prove them at the sentencing hearing—which we would. Bail was set at one million dollars.

To help ensure that he received a fair trial, both his public defender and I requested that the grand jury testimony be sealed. Just in case of a leak, I redacted all mentions of the victim from the transcript and inserted "John Doe."

Superior Court Judge John Reid sealed both the transcript and the indictment, and so did Superior Court Judge Robert Perry when he took over the case. By early December, however, the press had picked up bits and pieces of the story. They knew it involved Steven Spielberg and a parolee named Jonathan Norman, but had trouble getting anyone in my office or LAPD or among Spielberg's representatives or even from the state Bureau of Corrections to comment.

I knew it couldn't last.

On Thursday, December 4, reporters Norma Meyer and Paul Pringle broke the story in the *San Diego Union-Tribune*. Under the headline "Extraordinary Secrecy Engulfs Alleged Spielberg Stalking," Meyer and Pringle reported, "In what seems to be the system's attempt to protect a celebrity, all documents in the case have been sealed from public view and the alleged victim's name stricken from the indictment that was handed down secretly by a grand jury. The county's district attorney, the police, and the defendant's court-appointed lawyer won't even confirm that Spielberg is the alleged victim."

Meyer and Pringle had called me for comment. "I'm not at liberty to discuss it. Bye, now," I told them, which they accurately reported in their piece.

No surprise that the story immediately showed up everywhere. "Stalker Terror for Spielberg" was the headline in the *Scottish Daily Record*. "Stalker Grabbed at Spielberg's Mansion" screamed the *Daily Mirror* of London.

The Copley News Service filed suit, demanding the case records be unsealed. At first Judge Perry resisted, but a couple of weeks prior to the trial he threw in the towel, saying that the transcript was going to get out anyway. By then, much of what had been testified to had already appeared in the papers, though not necessarily in complete or accurate detail.

On December 18, the grand jury transcript was published on the Internet.

Shortly thereafter, Judge Perry bowed out of the case. At a pretrial hearing, he'd asked the public defender and I to approach the bench, where Perry ruefully told us how a fellow judge, from Santa Monica, had recently approached him at a Christmas party. The judge wanted to know why Perry was handling a case downtown that originated in Brentwood, which was in their jurisdiction. To keep the peace, Judge Perry transferred the case to Santa Monica.

Fortunately, another excellent superior court judge, Steven Suzukawa, was assigned to preside. Unfortunately, I now had to deal with the Santa Monica courthouse, which was notorious for major security problems. Three prisoners had escaped from the place in recent years.

Most Los Angeles courthouses feature a lockup adjacent to every courtroom, so that prisoners can be distributed safely, one at a time, to a secure, individual lockup at the back of each courtroom. Not Santa Monica, which was scheduled to be replaced by a modern new courthouse near Los Angeles International Airport. In Santa Monica, all prisoners were brought from jail to a holding tank, then marched together in their restraints like an indoor chain gang to each courtroom, where, one by one, they were unlocked from the group and taken inside. You could hear them clanking along together from quite a distance.

WE HAD A lot of witnesses and evidence to put on in the Norman case, which would take two weeks to complete—a relatively long criminal trial. A couple of days in advance of jury selection, I set up a makeshift office in the library of our Santa Monica office—I seemed fated to spend a good portion of my professional life operating out of libraries—and went to work on trial preparation.

Part of my work was to prepare questions for the judge to ask potential jurors during voir dire. They included, "Have you or anyone close to you ever been the victim of stalking, harassment, or sexual assault?" Another was: "Have you or anyone close to you ever been accused of stalking, harassment, or sexual assault?" I also asked if any of them had strong feelings, one way or the other, about the victim in this case, or any of the movies he'd made. As was true with Madonna, I didn't want anyone with an anti-Spielberg agenda sitting on my jury.

On the day of the trial, I arrived at the courthouse at six, two hours early, hoping to avoid the throng of reporters and photographers certain to show up. The early arrival did me no good.

As I walked up to the courthouse door, two photographers and a reporter came out of nowhere to snap my picture and start peppering me with questions, which I ignored. I got inside and past the metal detectors, which were up and operational much earlier than usual, and flashed my badge at a pair of security men. They let me through, and prevented the three newsmen from following any farther.

I headed upstairs to my library office on the second floor to get ready for jury selection. Pat McPherson arrived a short while later. I'd designated Pat as investigating officer in the case, which meant that he'd sit with me at the counsel table throughout the trial.

I was tense but focused, ready to get started, when I received a telephone call informing me that none other than the first stalker I'd prosecuted, Susan Dyer, was at large and nowhere to be found! Just the news I needed to hear moments before I was to begin a lengthy, high-profile trial in which I'd receive daily scrutiny from my office, my peers in the legal trade, and the worldwide media. I had good reason to be concerned.

Although Judge J. D. Smith had ordered Dyer sent to a prison with psychiatric facilities in 1992, she was not seen by a mental health professional until shortly before her scheduled release from Valley State Prison for Women in 1996. Just before she was due for parole, I was sent a Tarasoff letter from a staff psychologist at Valley State.

The doctor warned me that Susan's comments to her and others about Jane, Detective Raymond, and myself persuaded her that we were in great danger if Susan, who had been diagnosed at the prison as a paranoid schizophrenic, was released. Because of the diagnosis and warning, we had been able to keep her incarcerated for two more years.

My caller, Susan's parole officer, told me that Dyer had managed to slip off her electronic monitor and had disappeared. If she was looking for me, she wouldn't have to search far. Thanks to the press coverage, the time, place, and principal figures in the Spielberg trial were known to everyone in Los Angeles.

I wasn't about to ask for a trial postponement while we waited for Susan to be picked up, so I put aside my fears and did my best to focus on my business while in court. However, I was filled with trepidation after court each of the several days before Dyer was finally found by her parole officer—in Santa Monica. She was returned to prison for an additional year.

My other distraction was a pair of civil attorneys dispatched from one of Spielberg's law firms to attend the trial. I'm not sure what their orders were, but they insisted on advising me at every turn, even though they knew squat about criminal law.

These attorneys sat in the front row, and at each break pelted me with well-meaning but useless advice on how to conduct the trial. To deal with them, I perfected what I called my "civil lawyer nod," which, with a fixed smile, I used to convey my seeming agreement with their insights while in fact I had tuned them out completely while I focused on my work.

The defendant came clanking down the hallway with his brother inmates each day to court, outfitted with a restraint that was concealed from the jurors beneath his white shirt and dark trousers. He was always brought in and seated before the jury arrived.

Norman seemed to make a point of not looking at the witnesses as they testified, Spielberg in particular. However, my secretary told me that during the victim's testimony, whenever the defense lawyer and I were called to the bench to confer with Judge Suzukawa, Jonathan turned his head and stared at Spielberg.

His defense would be diminished actuality—no surprise—caused by a drug-induced psychosis. An expert would testify to this at trial. The defense's second contention boiled down to a question: How can there be stalking when the victim is eight thousand miles away? My job was to knock down both arguments, while at the same time proving all the elements of the crime necessary to convince the jury to find Norman guilty.

The first issue was fairly easy to dispose of, thanks in great part to Chuck Markovich, who provided us with a chronology of the important dates in Jonathan's preparations for his planned assault on Steven Spielberg. I conceded that Norman was a methamphetamine user, but I argued that his brain was not all that clouded by the drug.

I showed, for example, that Norman had started writing about Spielberg in his blue diary, in detail, as far back as early June. But my best evidence came from the car rental agencies he patronized as the dates of his planned assaults approached.

I put an Enterprise branch manager on the stand, who testified that on June 25, 1997, four days before he first appeared at Spielberg's gate, Norman tried to rent a Land Rover that was the same year, model, and color as Kate Capshaw's. He was told that the vehicle could be found, but that it would take a week or two. According to the manager, Jonathan seemed very lucid as he explained his needs. He settled on the white Jeep in the interim.

She added that he claimed he was in the entertainment industry, and wanted an entertainment industry discount on the car, which he received.

In a June 28 entry in his blue journal, Jonathan wrote about surveilling his neighbors in Brentwood, whose properties were protected by tall security fences. He fantasized about waiting in the shadows to accost a man walking alone late at night. "I would come up behind him and put a gun to his head," Norman wrote, "and dress and sound and act very nasty." He continued that he'd force the victim to put on a piece of gear called a "screaming muzzle" and then handcuff him, as well.

Chuck Markovich would help me demonstrate how the phrase "dress and sound and act very nasty" was important to my case. On the stand, he testified that Norman always dressed in a starched white cotton dress shirt and black trousers. This was practically his uniform. Chuck could hardly recall seeing Jonathan wearing anything else.

Yet when he was arrested he was wearing a sweatshirt and sweatpants, very unusual attire for his friend, Markovich told the court. Later, when Chuck visited Jonathan at the psychiatric hospital, Norman struck a pose and asked, "Don't I look like Rambo?" In other words, I argued to the jury, Jonathan thought he looked tough and scary, just as he'd written in his diary.

July 8 was a key date. It was the day that Enterprise alerted Norman that the exact Land Rover he wanted was now available. I was also able to produce, again thanks to Chuck, a receipt dated July 8 for three sets of handcuffs that Norman purchased at a sex-gear shop called the Pleasure Chest. These two actions reflected how his mind was working, how his plan was progressing. This was not drug-induced psychosis; it was careful preparation.

I had one other way of showing that Norman's obsession and stalking had nothing to do with the influence of methamphet- amine. Prior to the trial, a deputy sheriff working in the Way- side jail where Jonathan was being held telephoned me with very useful news.

The deputy told me that Norman had carved Spielberg's

name into a foam cup. He explained that he took the cup to his supervisors, who ordered him to search Jonathan's cell.

As deputies approached, Norman kicked several sheets of paper under his bunk. One turned out to be a map he had sketched showing the location of Spielberg's residence, as well as David Geffen's and those of several of their business associates. Next to the Spielberg address he'd written "SS" and drawn a heart around it. He'd also recreated, from memory, much of the personal information about Spielberg's family and business partners that had been discovered among the papers seized at Chuck Markovich's apartment.

I reminded the jury that Norman had not been near methamphetamine for months prior to producing these documents because he'd been locked up. No psychosis underlay the behavior that had landed him in court as the defendant, I said. Jonathan Norman was demonstrably sane and in full control of his faculties throughout these criminal episodes. He was strange, yes, and obviously dangerous. But he was not crazy, not for a minute.

We made case law on the second issue of Spielberg's absence when Norman's stalking occurred. It was nearly the same as passing another statute.

I argued that it was immaterial whether or not Steven Spielberg was in Ireland while Jonathan Norman stalked him in Pacific Palisades. First, we had established criminal intent—mens rea, as we lawyers call it. In Jonathan Norman's *mind*, the only place that mattered in this argument, Spielberg was inside the house. Jonathan Norman's criminal intent was to stalk, and possibly rape, Steven Spielberg. He did not know his intended victim was out of the country.

Second, Norman had clearly put Spielberg in fear. The director testified in detail to the terror he felt, even several time zones removed. "Nowadays," he said, "it's very simple for someone to buy an airplane ticket and be in Ireland in less than eight hours."

AT THE START of the trial, the press was skeptical of Spielberg. As the first story in the San Diego paper speculated, reporters thought the director was getting celebrity treatment. Early in the trial, I remember questions such as, "Isn't it true that the only reason you filed charges against Jonathan Norman is because Steven Spielberg was the victim?"

Spielberg's testimony changed all that.

He surprised me that morning with a big hug, which seemed to startle his civil attorneys, who obviously had a very different relationship with him. Pat McPherson joined us as we discussed his testimony in a little room just off the courtroom. As Pat and I started to leave, Spielberg playfully viewed the investigator through his fingers as if framing McPherson for a movie shot. To this day, whenever I see Pat, I tease him about his near miss at becoming a movie star.

On the stand, when Spielberg explained that he came to court because it seemed the only way to protect his children, wife, and mother, I looked back at the audience. Believe it or not, a couple of reporters had actually teared up. They'd finally understood what this trial was about.

The jurors never took their eyes off of Spielberg. As he testified, he was no longer a famous Hollywood celebrity, but a husband and father who loved his family and would walk through hell to ensure their safety. His last statement to the jury was, "I believe this was a man with a mission, and that mission was me."

MY INTERPRETATION OF the law I had written prevailed in court, and the jury duly convicted Norman of stalking. But we still had a way to go. Confident as I was of my position, I knew it would be scrutinized again in the state court of appeal. An even more pressing concern was the upcoming sentencing hearing. The defense waived Norman's right to a jury at the hearing, so it was left to Judge Suzukawa to decide whether the defendant was to be a long-term guest of the state.

First, we held a presentencing hearing that lasted for several days. The single legal issue was whether the two felony counts from Norman's 1995 Santa Monica case were strikes, as we alleged at arraignment, or not, as the defense argued.

Under the plea bargain, the prosecutor in the prior case had allowed Norman to plead guilty to two counts of assault with intent to inflict great bodily injury, which is not a strike in California. Assault with a deadly weapon, on the other hand, is a strike. My only hope was to look behind the plea, so to speak, to see what was actually said in court.

Eureka! According to the official transcript, when the prosecutor took the plea bargain in July of 1995, he specifically asked Norman, who was under oath, to admit that he had assaulted the victims with his vehicle, which in that instance legally *was* a deadly weapon. Norman did. Moreover, the transcript showed that the prosecutor had pointedly warned Norman that if he committed another felony, it could be the third strike that would send him away for twenty-five years to life.

Therefore, I argued, the two assault convictions qualified as strikes. Judge Suzukawa agreed, but he still had the discretion to ignore one or both of the strikes at sentencing. This meant that Jonathan Norman might receive three years (which, because of time already served and other factors, really meant immediate release); six years if the judge counted only one of the earlier strikes; or twenty-five years to life, with no possibility of parole for at least twenty-five years, if he invoked the full three-strikes penalty. There were no other sentencing options.

Part of my strategy for persuading Judge Suzukawa to slam Norman was to put Spielberg on the stand once more at the sentencing hearing to give victim impact testimony. Although the director had booked the Los Angeles Philharmonic for the day—he was working with the symphony on music for *Saving Private Ryan*—he canceled the recording session in order to honor his promise to appear whenever I needed him. Here was another welcome contrast to my experience with Madonna.

Once again, he was a very effective witness, forcefully imploring the judge to put Jonathan Norman away in prison for as long as was legally possible. Judge Suzukawa didn't take much convincing. In June of 1998, he meted out the severest penalty possible. Almost exactly one year after his first attempt to get at the famous director, Norman was now looking at a quarter-century, minimum, in state prison.

*   *   *

I WON IN the court of appeal, too. "To state the obvious," the justices wrote, "there is nothing in the language of the statute to
require a concurrence of act and reaction. By its plain terms, all
that is required for a conviction...is proof that the defendant, (1)
with the apparent ability to carry out his threat, (2) has willfully,
maliciously, and repeatedly harassed his victim, (3) with the
intent to place the victim in reasonable fear for his safety, and
(4) has, in fact, caused his victim to reasonably fear for his safety
or the safety of his family.

"Indeed, by its current provision that stalking can occur
by the use of an 'electronic communication device,' including a computer, the statute necessarily encompasses situations
where there is a delay between the defendant's harassment and
his victim's awareness of the defendant's conduct. By way of
simplistic example, a threat communicated by e-mail may not
be received for hours or days or even weeks (depending upon
the frequency with which the recipient checks his e-mail) in
which event the victim's fear, on reading the e-mail, would
occur hours or days or weeks after the threat is made."

I can't overemphasize the importance and value of this
language, particularly the bit about e-mail. Had the justices
ruled otherwise, then we probably could not have prosecuted
Marlon Pagtakhan for stalking Jeri Ryan and Brannon Braga,
because neither victim read his e-mails until well after he had
sent them. After the decision came down, a number of district
attorneys around the state contacted me to report their pleasure that for the first time they were specifically empowered
to prosecute offenders for stalking by e-mail.

Finally, it was gratifying to read how emphatically the
appeals court agreed with me on Norman's two previous strikes.
"We summarily reject Norman's contention that it was 'grossly
unfair' for the trial court to deny his motion to dismiss one or
both of the prior strikes. The trial court's decision was based on
Norman's prior conduct—which was exceedingly violent—and
his present conduct, which threatened more violence. As the
trial court noted, Norman was specifically warned by the prosecutor at the time of his 1995 plea that another felony conviction
would result in a sentence of twenty-five years to life. Knowing

that, Norman was out of custody a mere seven months before he began stalking Spielberg. As the court observed, Norman presents a danger to society. As the record discloses, the trial court considered the 'entire picture' and understandably concluded that Norman fit 'within the parameters of the three-strikes law.' The motion was properly denied."

NINE

EVEN IN THE bizarre company of celebrity stalkers, Dante Michael Soiu was singularly strange.

In early 1999, Soiu (pronounced "saw you"), who had just turned fifty, spent his days as "Dr. Love," applying balm to troubled hearts via the Internet from a public library computer in Columbus, Ohio. The size of Dr. Love's online following is unknown, but the site was popular enough to have commercial sponsors.

He also offered enlightenment to the famous and the powerful. By Soiu's estimate, he sent the first President Bush three thousand personal notes on a variety of topics. President Clinton received a hundred or two. These dealt mainly with Clinton's "sexual problems," as Dante described it—especially Monica Lewinsky.

According to Soiu, he also addressed what he believed was Clinton's sociopathy in his letters. He copied one of them to the Republican National Committee. "They must have laughed at it," he said, "but everybody in the library said it fits him to a T."

Dante thought of himself as a spiritual as well as a practical advisor, with special access to God. Accordingly, he reached out by letter to Dr. Laura Schlessinger; Ted Turner, as well as Turner's then-wife, Jane Fonda; plus actors Robert Urich, William Shatner, and Val Kilmer.

"Every one of these people had a specific problem that I would want to work on to solve," he eventually explained in court. "That's primarily the sort of gift that I would have. I would...take on their personality and pray for them, and then whatever problem they'd have they'd come out of."

Dante's letter writing seems not to have stirred much serious concern among law enforcement agencies. He did have a lengthy arrest record—fifteen minor offenses such as theft and trespass—but no history of violence.

Soiu typed away for as much as eight hours each day at the library in his cyber-guru mode, then he headed out for his evening's work, delivering pizzas. He recalled how he'd surprised a young female customer with a kiss on the hand, and two hours later, according to Dante, her boyfriend threatened to kill him. Eventually the police got involved, and Soiu lost his pizza delivery job.

His first mental problems seem to have surfaced in the late 1960s, when he was a scholarship student in the Asia Studies program at Xavier University in Cincinnati. He was hospitalized at least twice for unspecified treatment.

Soiu, whose estimated IQ is in the bright-normal range of 110–119, graduated with a 3.54 grade point average in 1971. He took a minor in theology at Xavier, too.

From 1976 to 1978, he studied toward an MBA in accounting at the University of Cincinnati, and worked as a tax preparer. In the early 1980s, he was a student at the Rhema Bible Training Center in Broken Arrow, Oklahoma.

Intelligent and self-directed as he apparently was, Soiu was unable to get much traction in either his professional or his personal life. He had no career, and later admitted that he'd never been able to sustain a long-term relationship with a woman. He was faced with chronic money problems, suffered from low self-esteem, and worried that he was homosexual. Psychiatrists and psychologists would later diagnose him as bipolar, delusional, schizophrenic, and narcissistic.

In March of 1999, he began to experience what he called

"unusual supernatural manifestations" in and around Columbus, which would soon bring him to my attention in Los Angeles.

As Soiu told the story, one day he happened into a movie house where *Shakespeare in Love*, starring Joseph Fiennes and Gwyneth Paltrow, was playing. Movies and television were important sources of inspiration for him. "Lord," Dante said, "if you want me to see this movie, open the door." The door opened, and "I walked in and I sat down and I saw this movie."

Paltrow, who played Viola de Lesseps, the Bard's lover and the muse for *Romeo and Juliet* in the movie, triggered Soiu's string of "manifestations," most of which he described as miraculous. He heard music from the movie, for example, whenever he turned on his radio. Other times, if Dante thought of Paltrow while visiting his bank, money arrived the next day in the mail.

He prayed, he said, and took such events as a sign "that I was either connected to, or going to be connected to, Gwyneth Paltrow in some manner. What I heard from that prayer was, 'If you love this woman totally, unconditionally, and make a commitment to her, eventually she would become your mate because she is... psychic. She does meditations... She is perfectly in tune with herself.'

"In fact, to me she was the most perfect, pure, spiritual-type woman that existed on my level. I thought that was rather unique."

Lucky Gwyneth.

Soiu turned his energies to researching Paltrow's life. He picked up from the fanzines and grocery-store tabloids that she was dating the actor Ben Affleck, who also appeared in *Shakespeare in Love*. He found a movie star guide book in his local library that listed the address in Santa Monica where her parents, producer/director Bruce Paltrow and actress Blythe Danner, lived.

On March 21, 1999, millions of movie fans around the world, including Dante Michael Soiu, watched on television as a radiant Gwyneth Paltrow accepted the Best Actress Oscar for her role in *Shakespeare in Love*. (The movie took seven Academy Awards in all, including Best Picture, against competition that included Steven Spielberg's *Saving Private Ryan*.) A few days later, a letter postmarked Columbus, Ohio, arrived for Paltrow at her parents' house, where Gwyneth was staying, as she customarily did when in Los Angeles.

Receiving mail of any sort at the Santa Monica house was unusual for her. Although she'd lived there as a child, in the seven years since she'd first started appearing in major movies, Paltrow could recall getting maybe two other letters at the residence. She later told me that she felt guilty for attracting this stranger's unwanted attention to the family house. But it was the content and tone of the letter that chilled her.

Blythe Danner was at home when the letter arrived, so mother and daughter read it together in the den.

"First," Soiu demanded, "do not marry Ben Affleck. He's a slob."

He also grandly claimed that he could make miracles happen. But what scared Paltrow was his assumed intimacy. "I am more than a fan," he wrote. "I have formed a soul union with you."

Soon, letters and packages began arriving from Columbus almost daily, sometimes several a day. At first, Soiu confined himself for the most part to quoting scripture and recommending self-help books. In one that he sent her, *Ten Stupid Things Men Do to Mess Up Their Lives*, he scribbled "Ben Affleck" next to each chapter heading.

Typical spiritual messages included "The Gospel of marriage is the Gospel of two people becoming one, like you and Jesus Christ!" He also shared with her a letter he'd written to then first lady Hillary Clinton, proposing the establishment of a cabinet-level Department of Love, Family, and Relationships. Soiu wrote Clinton that he and his lovely wife, Gwyneth, eagerly volunteered to head up the new agency.

Fearful at where the correspondence might lead, Paltrow decided to retain Dennis Bridwell, head of Galahad Protective Services, Inc., to deal with Soiu for her. Bridwell, a former marine, had known Paltrow since the early days of her film career, and had provided protection for her on a number of occasions. In the past, he'd also read her fan mail for her, looking among the many letters for signs of trouble.

"They were for the most part pretty innocuous," Bridwell

remembers. "'I love you,' and so on. That's how they all start out. With most of them, however, you can tell early on whether they're going to take a wild turn." What he read in the first messages from Dante Soiu concerned him.

The clues include inappropriate requests, such as asking for a face-to-face meeting, solicitations for money, or any reference to something personal. In Soiu's case, his claim of a direct connection to God and the ability to perform miracles set off Bridwell's alarm. He told the Paltrows to gather the letters and packages, unopened, as they arrived, and to leave them for Galahad to sort through.

Dennis also contacted me, which he commonly did when a client was being stalked. Over the years we had worked many stalking and threat cases together. Just like LAPD, he was interested in knowing what the law said about a case, and in working out strategies with me for effectively dealing with a threat with a minimum of publicity.

He explained to me what was occurring with Paltrow and Soiu, and promised to keep me posted as the case unfolded. As of then, Dante Soiu had stayed within the law. But we both knew better than to expect he'd continue to do so.

As days passed with no response from the object of his obsession, Soiu's messages grew more explicit and less coherent. "If you are not obedient," he wrote in a letter that arrived April 8, "you will perish, and we don't want that because the Devil likes to destroy those who are not obedient to him...but I like making babies with you."

Four days later, there came a package containing the cover to a book, *Ordinary Women/Extraordinary Sex*, together with several letters. "I am glad we're nymphomaniacs for each other," read one of them. "I have to eat and wash up after our messes."

"If your parents want to steal from us," read another, "which is stealing from God...God will strike them. A curse is laid upon them in Malachi 4:10 for stealing from God." Dante also wrote a frightening letter to Gwyneth, asserting that she was filled with a cancerlike sin. He said he was going to take "God's scalpel" and cut the "sin" out of her.

Later, a vibrating penis arrived with "Because I Love You" inscribed on it. Dante also mentioned that Gwyneth's spirit had been visiting his apartment on a nightly basis and that he could hear her speaking to him from the magazine racks at the supermarket. He also referred to Ben Affleck again. "I will beat the Hell out of the guy."

It was as if Soiu and Marlon Pagtakhan had attended the same writing class.

Dennis Bridwell examined and cataloged the contents of each article that arrived in the mail, sparing his client the unpleasantness of dealing directly with such raunchy, distasteful, and troubling material. But Bridwell was experienced enough to know that for her own safety he'd be foolish to hide from Paltrow what she was receiving from Ohio. She needed to be aware and alert. What was more, if we were to make a case against Soiu, Gwyneth needed to have personal knowledge of his actions in order for me to prove she was reasonably frightened by them.

There was slim chance that Soiu would stop. Bridwell saw him as an erotomanic stalker, convinced not only that Paltrow reciprocated his love but that she was covertly communicating with him by codes and in supernatural ways. "I've never known of anybody ever being cured of this type of delusion," he says. Neither have I.

However, such a "profile," as Bridwell refers to stalkers such as Soiu, will sometimes jump from one perceived love relationship to another. "He might see another actor on television," Dennis explains, "and think *Wow! She's fascinating and she's talking to me through the television!* In that case, he might then fall off our radar."

Not Dante Soiu.

ON MAY 28, 1999, Blythe Danner was out in the front yard of the house, playing with the family dog, when a stranger acting overly familiar approached from the sidewalk. He introduced himself; she didn't recognize his name. Then he repeated it and Danner realized that the man who'd been terrorizing her family by mail for the past two months now stood in front of her.

"Oh, you're Dante," she said, as she watched him reach in and out of a bag he was carrying. This scared her even more. She thought he was going to pull out a gun.

There had been a recent mention in a periodical that her husband had cancer. Soiu told her that he'd learned directly from God that someone in the house had the disease. He was digging in his sack for bottles of vitamins from one of his website's sponsors that he said were effective against it.

Danner wasn't interested in his cures or his conversation. She told Soiu that he was frightening the family and asked him to please stop.

He promised her he would.

"I'll stop."

Soiu noticed a pile of letters and packages by the house, and realized they had all come from him. Danner handed him some of the articles to take back.

"I felt almost slighted," he later said in court. "I felt like all this effort was just going down the tubes and they weren't even looking at it, and any inspiration, genius, work, talent, creativity was just being not even looked at. I felt kind of bad about that.

"So I thought, *Well, maybe my next step is I'll try harder. If I fail, I always try harder because I have a positive faith about success. You just try harder, and you'll make it.*"

Danner recalled that Soiu said he understood he was scaring them, promised to stop, and left. The next day, Bruce Paltrow discovered a note that Dante had written and attached to the gate. It read: "I want to thank you for forgiving me, for I have been a pain to you." Paltrow gave the note to Bridwell's business partner, Dan Palmer.

THE LETTERS AND packages did not stop. On June 3 there arrived a photo of a nude couple locked in a sexual pose. "Gwyn" was written on the female; "Dante" on the male. Soiu included multiple copies of the picture with a note: "The extra copies are for your mom. We will be having an open marriage, just between us three. A trinity relationship. Privately."

At about this time, Dennis Bridwell organized a meeting at the Paltrow house. I needed to see where Soiu had accosted Danner, and I wanted to gauge how close we might be to filing a case against him. To do that, as always, I needed to find out directly from Gwyneth what she knew and how it had affected her.

I drove to their address with Ed Messenger, one of our investigators. Since Soiu had now crossed state lines and made threats through the U.S. mail, this was nominally a federal case. So Special Agent Jim Davidson of the FBI joined the discussion, as did Dennis Bridwell.

Gwyneth and her father greeted us, and showed us all inside to the dining room for our meeting. It was a pleasant, unpretentious house. They were remodeling at the time, and Bruce apologized for all the loose lumber and displaced furniture. Gwyneth offered me coffee, which I never refuse. I noticed that she went to fix it herself. The Paltrows didn't have household help.

I remember walking into the kitchen with her to get something, and noticing Steven Spielberg's photo on the refrigerator. Gwyneth told me Spielberg was her godfather. I was vaguely aware that she and Madonna were also good friends, but that coincidence wouldn't really hit me until trial time.

During a short interlude of small talk, I for some reason mentioned my background in the musical stage. This led to a discussion of live theater—both Gwyneth and her mother did a lot of it, particularly at the annual summer Williamstown Festival at Williams College in western Massachusetts—and then the realization that we three had all known and worked with the late Nikos Psacharopoulos.

Nikos was a cofounder of the Williamstown Festival, and one of its guiding lights for many years. He had directed both Blythe and Gwyneth in a number of plays there. I knew him from the New York City Opera, where he had directed me in a production of the Poulenc opera *Dialogues of the Carmelites*. I loved talking about my days in the theater, and Nikos gave us a somewhat more life-affirming bond than did Dante Soiu.

None of us gathered in the Paltrow dining room that day were surprised to hear from Gwyneth that although she was frightened of Soiu, she was not as yet prepared to prosecute him. She knew that the moment a case was filed, some reporter would ferret it out at the courthouse.

Like all celebrities, particularly those in the entertainment business, Paltrow did not want her problem to become a media event, which it likely would. I told her that Dante Soiu was not going to go away, and that the harassment almost assuredly would escalate. I also told her that I was ready, willing, and able to file against him right away. She wasn't, but I knew it was only a matter of time.

After the meeting, I contacted the U.S. Attorney's office in Columbus to inform them of the pornography Soiu was sending through the mail. The federal test for pornography is the local standard of morality at the receiving, or consuming, end. What offends community standards in Topeka, Kansas, will not be the same as Baltimore, Maryland. The Los Angeles standard is considered pretty low; the type of photographs Soiu was sending could be found on any Los Angeles street corner newspaper rack. Therefore, the pictures Paltrow was receiving did not meet the feds' criteria for filing. I couldn't argue with that logic.

We also arranged via Davidson for his bureau colleagues in Columbus to pay a call on Soiu. The objective was similar to Kevin Sleeth's when he visited Marlon Pagtakhan at his home in San Francisco: We wanted to gather whatever information we could, and also make it explicitly clear to Dante, again, that he was scaring Gwyneth and her family. In this way, we'd preclude any possibility of the defendant later claiming in court that he had no idea he was scaring anyone.

Bruce Paltrow asked Dennis if the FBI's entry into the case might persuade Soiu to stop altogether.

"No, Bruce," Dennis said. "I'm sorry to tell you that it's not going to be over."

"What do you mean?" Gwyneth's father replied.

"Soiu believes he's ordained by God to be your daughter's husband. Anyone that delusional believes the FBI has no power over God."

Paltrow was incredulous. "If the FBI knocked on my door," he said, "I'd stop what I was doing."

"Yeah," Dennis answered, "you and I both would. But he won't. He might for a short time, but then he'll continue."

"We'll see," Paltrow said after a brief pause. Then he added with a smile that they could always dispose of Soiu in the way such problems were handled in his old Brooklyn neighborhood.

"I don't particularly want to go to jail, thanks," said Bridwell.

They left it at that.

After consulting with Agent Davidson, Dennis also contacted FBI Agent Tom Ingram in Columbus, who'd be the one visiting Soiu on June 29. Bridwell wanted to brief the FBI man on his subject. From what he knew of erotomanics and from the profile's correspondence, Bridwell told Ingram to expect posters of Paltrow on the walls, a shrine to her somewhere in the apartment, and probably some item Dante considered special on his nightstand. There would also be a crucifix above his bed.

"Holy shit!" Ingram reported by telephone to Bridwell after the visit. "You were right, down to the letter, with all this stuff and how it was situated."

Ingram had great news to report, too. When he and his partner had arrived at Soiu's apartment, they'd found a note on the door announcing Dante's wedding to Gwyneth Paltrow. Dante answered their knock, and asked them in with the air of a man who was flattered to have been brought to the attention of the FBI.

Ingram, who audiotaped the interview, handled it brilliantly. Instead of saying, "We're here because you're scaring Gwyneth Paltrow," he asked, "Do you know why we're here?"

"Uh, either to stop sending letters," Soiu blurted in reply, "or they feel hyper, they feel fearful, they feel, uh, bad with relationship to the Paltrows. "

"No," Ingram said. "The family feels pretty threatened, okay?"

"Oh-oh, big."

"We're here to tell you to stop. They feel threatened and not to do it."

"Okay."

He made my case for me in that single first sentence. It showed that Soiu was totally aware of what he was doing. He was conscious that he was frightening the Paltrows, yet he was not going to stop. We could have arrested him on the spot but Gwyneth wasn't yet ready to go forward with the prosecution. She and her parents were still hoping that Soiu would simply go away.

Ingram contacted Soiu once again a month later and also spoke with him by telephone. By then Dante had set up an e-mail account—under the username mylovemywife—to which he posted his messages. There would be in excess of twelve hundred in all, all counted and cataloged by Dennis Bridwell. He admitted to Ingram that he'd opened the e-mail account and also that he was still sending packages, even though he'd been told not to and knew it was wrong.

OVER THE COMING months, Soiu sent Paltrow everything imaginable, from pizzas to undergarments from Victoria's Secret, investment ideas, poetry, an engagement ring, a fiber-optic angel, books and articles on various types of businesses, sex toys including a "Venus Penis" and "vibro balls," lots of pornography, articles on travel, chocolates, flowers, and a number of wedding-themed CDs, including *Great Wedding Songs, The Classic Wedding Album*, and *Your Perfect Wedding*.

In one letter, he explained how she could give up her silly career in acting and get rich with him instead, running a Kinko's franchise. He also proposed a couple of partnership ideas to Bruce Paltrow, later explaining, "I thought if I acted like maybe a good son-in-law or close to a good son-in-law...that would make them feel like this guy could be suitable for their family or suitable to be involved with them." Before he was finally stopped, the material Soiu mailed to the Paltrows would fill a whole room at Bridwell's office in the San Fernando Valley, floor to ceiling.

IN EARLY MAY of 2000, Soiu wrote Paltrow that he'd received a sign from a billboard as he was driving in Columbus. It was time, the billboard told him. He was coming back to California for her. Although he'd often mentioned such a return trip in his letters, Dennis Bridwell believed that this time Soiu was really on his way.

Dennis alerted the Paltrows—their daughter was not in Los Angeles—as well as me, Ed Messenger, Jim Davidson, and the Santa Monica Police Department to expect Soiu at any time. His plan was to wait for Soiu outside the Paltrows' house and make a citizen's arrest when he appeared.

Soiu showed up as Bridwell expected on Saturday afternoon, May 13. He rang the intercom. Bruce Paltrow saw him through the window and ordered him via the intercom to leave. Blythe Danner anxiously telephoned Bridwell with the news that Soiu was in town. Danner also gave Bridwell a telephone number that Soiu had thoughtfully left at the door should any member of the family wish to call him.

Dennis headed for Santa Monica, and he dialed the number along the way. He wanted to make sure that Soiu hadn't been scared off.

"Hello," a male voice answered.

"Dante?" Bridwell asked.

"Yes."

"Where are you?"

"Los Angeles."

Click.

That was good news. Soiu was still in town (Santa Monica is technically an unincorporated city within the county of Los Angeles) and undoubtedly planning another excursion to the Paltrow house. Bridwell would be there, and the ugly, fourteen-month saga could at last be ended.

When he arrived, Dennis suggested that Bruce and Blythe go out to dinner. Both were happy to oblige. A couple of hours later, around 10:00 that night, Soiu arrived on foot, carrying a bag, and walked up to the door.

Bridwell walked up behind him, identified himself, informed Dante he was under citizen's arrest for stalking, and put a pair of handcuffs on him. It was over in a moment. Soiu didn't physically resist, but he did argue that he was visiting the Paltrows by invitation. The bag Dante was carrying contained books. Bridwell summoned the Santa Monica police, and five minutes later Dante Soiu was on his way to jail.

When he was frisked for weapons, a small pocket knife was found, along with a cell phone and a little blonde Barbie doll from McDonald's that bore a resemblance to Gwyneth.

When the Santa Monica police went to his hotel room the next day, they found a copy of Alex Comfort's *The Joy of Sex* and a box of condoms.

DENNIS AND I did everything we could to keep this case secret from the press, and we succeeded. Instead of calling 911 after arresting Soiu—which would create a trail for an enterprising reporter to follow—Bridwell had quietly handed him over to the Santa Monica police. Using the same law that permitted me to identify Steven Spielberg as John Doe, I listed Gwyneth Paltrow as Jane Doe. This law protects victims of sexual predators from having their names listed in a charging complaint, which is a public record. We'd sail past the preliminary hearing and Gwyneth's trial testimony before any reporter figured out who the victim was in this case.

The trial venue helped, too. I filed the case at the airport courthouse, which sits incongruously in an industrial area near Los Angeles International Airport. Big cases are rarely tried in this out-of-the-way building; reporters don't monitor it very closely. Unlike the courthouse in Santa Monica, which it replaced, the airport courthouse was extremely secure, and there would be no chance for Soiu to escape. It was perfect for us.

Trial preparation went smoothly, too. Usually I'm forced to scurry around, looking for witnesses, making sure the evidence was ready. Bridwell had everything organized in a fifty-page catalog that made management of the physical evidence a breeze. Gwyneth and her parents were also helpful and very cooperative.

The preliminary hearing was held on July 18. Under the same Proposition 115 provision that had allowed me to put Detective Andy Purdy on for Madonna at the Hoskins preliminary hearing, I had Special Agent Jim Davidson testify for all three Paltrows. Among the forty exhibits we entered into evidence—almost all of which were notes and objects Soiu had sent Paltrow, including letters he'd written to her from jail since his arrest—I also introduced into evidence a transcript and tape of Special Agent Tom Ingram's June 29, 1999, interview with Dante in his apartment, in which Soiu readily admitted knowing that he was scaring Gwyneth and her family.

The case against him was so strong that there was never a doubt he'd be held to answer in Superior Court after his preliminary hearing, and he was. "Held to answer" means that the magistrate hearing the preliminary hearing has found that there is sufficient evidence to go forward in Superior Court with a felony trial. As the date for trial approached, a couple of material witnesses were out of the country. Soiu refused to waive time for his trial, so I was forced to dismiss and immediately refile the case. Soiu waived his right to have another preliminary hearing because he realized that Gwyneth was not going to testify at that hearing, and the fastest way to get himself into her presence was to proceed to trial as soon as possible.

The trial was reset for December of 2000. However, I was about to begin another lengthy and serious trial in which a Los Angeles fire captain had solicited the murder of his wife. There was a good possibility that that trial would overlap Soiu's; therefore I decided to bring in a backup prosecutor, Michael Brewer, from STAT, so that I would not have to drop the Soiu charges twice, and thus set Soiu free.

Michael, a former public defender who'd joined our office that January, sat in on my interviews with Gwyneth and her parents, visited Dennis Bridwell's evidence room with me, and otherwise prepared himself to pick the jury and conduct the all-important direct examination of the victim. Even if I returned in time to start the trial, I wanted Michael to do the direct examination of Gwyneth Paltrow because he was up for a promotion in the office and I figured it would advance his cause. I didn't reckon with the petty jealousy of a certain supervisor.

Regardless, shortly before trial, Michael and I needed to conduct an important review of the physical evidence with the victim, who would be required to identify and discuss some of the materials in court. I recall the day we were all in a room at the airport courthouse with Gwyneth, going over the items that we intended to enter as evidence.

Michael, who would be questioning her on the stand, was the logical person to lead the review. There were a lot of very graphic documents and sexual objects in our selection of evidence, but everything went smoothly, until Brewer got to the Venus Penis.

For reasons he can't explain, instead of showing Paltrow the Venus Penis, he asked her if she'd seen it.

"I was trying to be matter-of-fact, you know. 'Uh, did you see the Venus Penis?' " he recalls asking.

Then, he continues, "Gwyneth Paltrow, movie star, one of the most beautiful women in the world, turns to me and says, 'No. What is that?' All of a sudden I'm the deer in the headlights. I realize what I've done. I look at Rhonda, and ask, 'Rhonda?' She looks back and says, 'Oh no. You brought it up. You need to explain it.'

"I'm red-faced, blushing. I can't look at Paltrow. In a soft, stuttering manner, I say, 'It's kind of, uh, fourteen-inch purple strap-on vibrator, uh, with ridges.' When I finished there was a long silence. I sheepishly look up. Gwyneth was just looking at me. Then, seriously as she can, she says, 'No I didn't see that, but I really enjoyed your explanation.' "

THE FACTS OF the Soiu case were never at issue, but their interpretation was. Eleanor Schneir, the very capable public defender who represented Dante Soiu, pleaded him not guilty of stalking, which was the underlying charge in the case.

Ellie Schneir would contend in court that her client was so delusional that he did not appreciate that his actions might frighten Paltrow, nor was that ever his intent—the diminished actuality defense again.

When my fears of a schedule conflict were confirmed, Michael Brewer stepped in until I finished my other trial. He and Ellie Schneir picked a jury on Thursday, December 7, 2000. The next day they delivered their opening statements, and our first witness, the victim, took the stand. Our timing was dictated in part by Gwyneth's schedule. She had to have her testimony finished in time to get to Scotland for Madonna's wedding to Guy Ritchie. Paltrow was one of the bridesmaids.

We had so far kept the proceedings out of the press, no small achievement in light of the many ways in which newspeople are alerted to such things. If Gwyneth could just give her testimony and leave, we'd succeed completely. It almost didn't happen. There was a prosecutor at the airport court who came up to Michael and loudly said, "Oh, I heard that Paltrow's supposed to be here today. Where's Gwyneth?" Had reporters been lurking, the remark would have doubtlessly sparked a scene like those at the Madonna trial. Luckily, the press was otherwise engaged. When the media hordes did descend the next day, they were too late.

My office also threw up a second obstacle to the effective, professional prosecution of the case. Brewer remembers that the same meddling supervisor who'd tried to insinuate himself into the Norman prosecution called him on the eve of trial to ask, "What the hell are you doing?"

Michael said he was helping me out because I was engaged in another trial and didn't want the case dismissed, something of which the supervisor was well aware.

"Nobody ran it by me."

"I didn't know I needed to," Brewer explained.

Michael later received a personal upbraiding from this supervisor. "He was really pissed," Brewer remembers of the meeting.

Michael started his direct examination of Paltrow with the first letter she had received from Soiu. "I felt there was something very dark about the letter," she testified, "something very dark about the tone of it."

She described how Dennis Bridwell had kept her apprised of the material that Soiu was sending and of its evolving nature. "I was told that some of the things he said in the letters were threatening to my parents," she remembered, "that since God had told him personally that we were supposed to be together and my parents were keeping him from me, or keeping us apart, that God would smite my parents or that they would die because they were keeping us apart. If I was resisting our union that I was a sinner and that bad things would happen to me."

"What," Brewer then asked, "were you told about sexual objects that had been received from this person?"

"That he started to send hard-core pornography in the mail, very explicit pornographic pictures," Paltrow answered, "and he had written his name over the man and my name over the woman . . . and that some of the letters described in detail what kind of sexual acts he was going to perform with me, or on me, and that he started to send dildos and vibrators and things of that nature."

At this point, Soiu had Schneir interrupt Paltrow's testimony so that he could change his plea to guilty. He explained that he wanted to spare the Paltrows the stress of further testimony. More likely, in my view, he realized how effective a witness Gwyneth was, and that the jury was completely sympathetic to her.

"My client is thinking that maybe he should spend some time in the hospital," Schneir told Judge O'Neill in a sidebar conference with Michael Brewer, out of the jury's hearing. "I don't know how to do this. I don't know if the court wants to go to a break and talk to him, but he and I have been discussing it since she walked in the door. I told him not to tell me to stop the proceeding unless he was sure." Soiu had indicated that he wanted to plead guilty to the charge of stalking and then go on to the issue of his sanity. He had tried this tactic earlier in the trial but then backed out of it at the last minute.

"Which is something I don't want to keep doing," said the judge, "and I'm sure you don't want to keep doing, bouncing back and forth."

Judge O'Neill excused the jury, and spoke from the bench to Soiu, who announced that he wished to change his plea to guilty. The judge slowly and carefully questioned him on the decision, asking several times if he'd discussed it with his lawyer, and explaining the rights he'd give up if he did change his plea.

"Do you understand all those rights, sir?" the judge asked.

"Yes," Soiu answered.

"Do you give up each of those rights?"

"In a sense, I..."

"Dante," said Schneir, "it's a yes or no question. It's not 'in a sense'... The question is, do you give up the right to have this jury decide whether or not you're guilty of these charges? Otherwise we resume the proceeding."

"If we can continue with the trial and see if I'm sane or not," Soiu said.

"All right," answered O'Neill. "We'll be in recess."

* * *

AFTER THE BREAK, Brewer directed Paltrow's attention to Soiu's first visit to Santa Monica in May of 1999. "Did that affect the way you saw things?" he asked.

"It escalated my fear to a whole different dimension," she replied, "because in my mind he went from a person who had some kind of unhealthy or unreasonable attachment to me to somebody who would make all the plans and the effort to leave his home in Columbus and fly all the way to the house in Santa Monica, let alone the fact that he really terrified my mother. So those two things in conjunction with each other really stepped up my level of fear."

Brewer asked what she feared might happen.

"I felt that if he had known where I was," Paltrow said, "he would come to me, and it was just chance that I wasn't in Santa Monica those two times that he came, because I'm there so often.

"I just felt a real threat because I felt like I was dealing with somebody who wasn't responding to the laws of the country. I felt like he could be on any street corner, and it was just very threatening to my sense of well-being and safety."

"Given the nature of this person's conduct, what is it you fear he might do if he came in contact with you?"

"Well, the sexual nature of the stuff really made me fear the most for my safety, because I thought, *If I'm in the same place with him, then he would rape me or that he would hurt me.*"

Paltrow testified that this fear of Soiu was constant, and infected every sphere of her existence. When a strange man walked too near in New York City she worried that he might be Dante. In Cleveland to appear at a hemophilia benefit, she heard that Soiu had been stopped at the door. In Williamstown, when she did summer stock, she felt especially vulnerable. "I had to bring security with me," she told the court, "which was embarrassing. It was this little town, and I was scared. Then I was doing a play and I thought, *I'm in the same place every night. There's nothing protecting me.* I was really worried for my safety."

* * *

JUDGE O'NEILL GAVE Soiu the weekend to think over his plea some more. My other trial had concluded and I was back in the picture. I conferred with Ellie Schneir, who told me that her client was considering waiving the jury and going with a bench trial on the underlying charge of stalking. On Monday morning, December 11, the judge explained to Soiu what that entailed.

"Before going any further," he said, "I wanted to run that by you, and see what your feeling is and what you want to do because I don't want to keep doing this every day. I don't want you to keep changing your mind. We're either going to do one thing or the other."

Dante answered that he thought it would be best to have *both* the jury and Judge O'Neill review the evidence. After O'Neill explained how that was not possible, Soiu said, "I think I would like to have a jury look at it."

"Dante," his attorney interjected, "you understand that we're not going to keep recessing this case. We're not going to keep discussing it. We're doing it."

She gestured to the pile of our physical evidence in the courtroom. "Those are the boxes of all the documents and physical evidence," she said. "You know what I mean by physical evidence, the pictures and stuff that are going to be presented to the jury. If it starts making you feel uncomfortable and upset, I'm not going to stop the proceedings every twenty minutes to go and tell the judge that you've changed your mind again and that you want to plead. You need at some point to make a command decision and decide to go one way or the other..."

Soiu addressed Judge O'Neill, a physically imposing jurist with a full beard and magisterial bearing.

"Are you a big movie person?" he asked.

"No," Judge O'Neill answered.

"Do you attend a lot of movies? A lot of my thoughts come from movies."

"I've seen a lot of movies," said the judge. "I watch a lot of TV and a lot of HBO. I'll listen to your insights and inspirations."

"That," said Soiu, "is where a lot of my inspirations come from."

At last he decided not to plead guilty but agreed to dismiss the jury and proceed with a bench trial. Once again, Judge O'Neill explained to him at length what that entailed. Then the jury was excused. Ellie Schneir stipulated to the testimony presented at the preliminary hearing, the admission of all our exhibits, plus Gwyneth's testimony and a couple more items that comprised my case. And so the People rested. I felt we had given Judge O'Neill plenty to ponder, and was confident he'd see things our way.

All that was left, then, was the defense case, which would consist of a single witness, the accused.

The defense also had a single issue—intent.

"When you sent those things to Miss Paltrow," Schneir asked, "did you have any intent to either scare her or threaten her?"

"No," Dante answered. "No way. In fact, there's a golden rule about that in the Bible. You're never to harm a woman, never. Anybody who ever harms women—God strikes them down."

Schneir asked why he had come from Columbus to Santa Monica. Soiu replied that he'd received an "inspiration that said, 'If you don't come, this relationship is never going to materialize. In fact, it's going to go down the tubes. In fact, it will become like poison.' "

He added that he'd regretted ignoring inspirations in the past. While in college, an inspiration had told him, "You must go downstairs and see the girl downstairs now." He didn't, "and just then the girl threw herself through the window in her nightclothes because somebody was going to stab her."

Another time, when he was working as a security guard, the inspiration told him to walk to the street corner and make a phone call. He did, and was able to prevent a car wreck as a result, he testified.

Soiu said his inspiration for visiting Gwyneth Paltrow was wholly benign. "My intent," he said, "was just to stop by and say, 'Hi,' and introduce myself and have her really get to know—see me, know me, feel me. This is the real me that you can talk to and if you had any—I don't know—apprehension, real knowledge about me. This is where it is. You can talk to me right now."

He offered an interesting motive for sending her the sex toys. "Well," he said, "the object is that if a person is a movie star, my idea is they always had to be kept up. One of the big things in therapy—love therapy—is people want to stay calm, and they want to stay in a pleasure mode."

He digressed briefly into the life of Norman Cousins, the late editor of the *Saturday Review*, who wrote extensively on the therapeutic impact of positive emotions on human health.

"If you can get a person's hormones working," he continued, "they'll feel on a high all the time. Therefore, they don't need any drugs to stay high and they won't need a lot of vitamins."

According to Soiu, he had not intended to return to the Paltrow house on May 13, 2000. He claimed on the witness stand that he'd left a note with his telephone number at the hotel, informing the Paltrows that if they wanted to see him, they should just call. To his delight, he testified, that is just what happened. He was invited out to the house to spend fifteen or twenty minutes with Gwyneth before he headed home for Columbus. She would even give him some autographs.

Instead, Dennis Bridwell arrested him; Dante said on the stand that he thought he'd been set up.

"Was it your intent to scare her?" Schneir asked.

"Oh, no. No," he answered.

"When you sent any of the things—the sexual things, the toys, anything—did you ever have the intent to scare Miss Paltrow?"

"No. Never, never. Anything I sent her was to either help her or help her in her career. The sex toys—I got rid of them because that was a faux pas."

"When you wrote her letters from jail, what was your intent in that?"

"That was to explain why I came out and why I had saw her in the first place, how I eventually came out and was planning to leave. I was going to give a whole explanation of it on paper because I used to be auditor from the state of Ohio, and if you ever wanted to do anything real, you have to document it. So

I'm a person who believes in documentation. If I'm going to do something, I've got to document it."

"When you wrote her letters from the jail, was it ever your intent to scare her?"

"Oh, no. Never. Never. In fact, if you ever read the letter, you'll find there's nothing scary in it. All my letters like the one you just showed me there and the one with musical tunes in it—there's nothing scary in it. Nothing."

With that, Ellie passed the witness to me.

THERE'S A WIDESPREAD misconception that insane people are also stupid. This is not necessarily true, though they may do seemingly stupid and illogical things. As Soiu's character emerged from his testimony under cross-examination, it was clear to me that he was definitely not stupid. He was clever, quick, and cunning.

One of the first exhibits I showed him was *Sexual Body Talk*, a paperback by Susan Quilliam, a self-described relationship psychologist and "Agony Aunt" columnist in Britain. The book purports to explain "the body language of attraction from first glance to sexual happiness," and includes photos of several positions for lovemaking. Soiu had sent *Sexual Body Talk* to Gwyneth, and wrote above a page of these pictures, "Which do you like best, beloved?"

Dante said the book came from his Dr. Love library, which included the *Kama Sutra*, *The Joy of Sex*, and numerous other volumes on sexual topics that he frequently quoted in his Internet advice messages. Holding the book in my hand as I approached the stand, and intently thinking how I was going to nail him with this piece of evidence, I heard but did not register when he said, "Everybody has sexual body talk. Even when you're walking up here, you have sexual body talk."

When I got to the stand, I noticed the clerk of the court had his head buried in his hands, laughing. I wondered why. I looked around and saw my cocounsel, Michael Brewer, twisted in his chair so as to hide the fact that he was laughing, too. Ellie Schneir was kind enough to be cool. She had no expression on her face at all.

What the heck's going on? I thought as I began my

questions. I wouldn't find out until I'd completed my cross-examination. To this day, Michael enjoys ribbing me about my "sexual body talk."

I asked Soiu if he was not aware, after speaking with Blythe Danner, that her daughter was disturbed by this type of material arriving in the mail from a stranger.

"I wouldn't really know from her mother if she was disturbed from this stuff," he answered. "I just know that she told me all the stuff I was sending her was thrown in a big trash heap."

"Didn't her mother specifically tell you that you were frightening her family and frightening Gwyneth Paltrow when you went to her house on May 28?"

"No," he said, "she didn't tell me that."

"So if she told that to the police or she testified to that, she would be lying?"

"She never told me that."

It was difficult to determine if Soiu was deliberately lying or had simply edited the meeting with Danner in his head to conform with his delusion. Under oath, he remembered they had "a nice chitchat" at the Paltrows' front gate.

Then I caught him in an obvious lie.

Soiu testified that after his encounter with Blythe Danner in May of 1999, he had only continued to send Gwyneth sexual items "for a short time," no more than a month or so. He claimed that he had only sent her some lingerie and perfume at Christmas, and candy and flowers maybe once a week. I confronted him with the Venus Penis and the vibro balls, both of which had been sent in late 1999. I impeached his testimony, and got him to admit that they were indeed sexual items and that he had, in fact, sent them to Paltrow. The next point was fear.

Soiu had so far danced away from the fact that he was causing Gwyneth and her family fear, a key component of his crime. I picked up our Exhibit 34, an e-mail dated June 30, 1999, the day after Tom Ingram's first visit to him. "This," I said, "is your e-mail that starts off, 'SUBJECT: I will stop all e-mail to you if it causes you fear.'"

"Yes," he admitted, adding, "I always asked, 'Tell me,

write me, or send me something.' And I'd wait and I wouldn't get anything."

I showed him Exhibit 35, another e-mail. "In looking at that e-mail," I said, "you acknowledge that the FBI had come to you?"

"Okay," he said, but instead of answering, he skittered off-topic again, addressing specific points he'd made in the e-mail.

Judge O'Neill cut him off, and I read the e-mail's headline aloud: "You or mom do not want me to contact or write."

"Here's what it says." ——

"Is that a yes or a no?"

Again, Soiu dodged the question, mulling aloud over sections of his e-mail and saying to Paltrow, "Everything is forgiven, and I forgive you."

I decided to pursue the opening.

"What do you forgive her for?"

"For either just not having the availability of getting any of my stuff or reading any of it."

"And not responding to you?"

"Yeah. I got the idea that I was just saying this stuff out in outer space and she wasn't listening to it at all."

"And again, this was very frustrating to you that she was not responding to you?"

"Frustrating. I would say that it was getting tedious."

"It was getting tedious. So you continued to send her items, sexual items."

"I was patient. I'm very patient. Long-suffering would be a better word."

We turned to the curse business.

"What did you say about a curse on her parents?" I asked.

"Well, I just happened to quote that out of the Bible. That means there's not really a curse on them. I'm not cursing them either."

"But," I replied, "that God would curse them if they interfered with your plans, is that correct?"

"No. Would God curse them if they interfered with my plans? Actually, I thought they had their own plans."

Our Exhibit 5 was a letter he wrote on April 5, 1999, about

a week after his very first communication. His subject was sin and Gwyneth's need to repent.

"I thought she was in this relationship with this guy Dave and that guy Brad and another guy Ben. She was in all these relationships. So I said, 'Look, if you're going to go around with all Tom, Dick, and Harry, I can forgive you for all that. Just come out of that because to me you're with sin. So you have to come out of that and repent doing that stuff and marry me.'"

"You weren't happy with these relationships that she was having with Brad and all these other people, is that correct?"

"You read about it in the tabloids that she's doing this and this and that and that."

"How did you react to that?"

"I had to take that with sort of a grain of salt, because here is a woman I'm sparing a lot of love for, and she's doing this, this, and that and that. So I had to get into a state of mind to forgive this woman of all her—forgive her. Any relationship you must have a true basis of forgiveness."

"So unless Paltrow gave up her boyfriends she'd be living in a state of sin?"

"I didn't say she had to give them up. I said she's in a state of sin by running around with every Tom, Dick, and Harry. I said, 'Of course if you ever want to get some true advice, listen to Dr. Laura, and you'll get some true advice.'"

"And you disapproved of this, of her running around with every Tom, Dick, and Harry?"

"I listened to Dr. Laura, and I thought that would be good advice for anybody. If you run around with every Tom, Dick, and Harry, that gives you a lot of problems."

"But when you wrote this letter, you weren't married to her. You hadn't gone through a ceremony, is that correct?"

"I thought that since she's running around with all these Toms, Dicks, and Harrys, something had to be wrong with her."

"But she was cheating on you?"

"I didn't say she was cheating on me. She had a lot of problems."

"That you could solve?"

"Oh yeah."

I showed Dante Exhibit 28, a periodical called *Amateur Erotica*, which he sent Paltrow on November 19, 1999.

"This is one of the best types of material," he said, "because it's nonaggressive, nonviolent."

"It is sexual in nature, is that correct?"

"Yes. Sex is not necessarily violent."

"And you had said that you had stopped sending her sexual—"

He interrupted me. "What was the date?"

"November 19 of 1999."

He again said that *Amateur Erotica* was a quality publication, "and no violence whatsoever."

"I'm not talking about violence," I replied. "I'm talking about hard-core pornography."

"Hard-core stuff," he said, "is all that whips and beat-'em-up type stuff."

"The bottom line," I said, "is you knew that it was bothering her. You yourself said that you had stopped all that stuff after the FBI spoke to you, and yet you continued to send her items like this magazine and items like that Venus Penis and those vibro balls."

Rather than answer the question directly, Soiu again defended his choice of love gifts—"that's best quality," he said—including the Venus Penis. "There's nothing aggressive about that," he insisted. "In fact, when you're at the store, more women go to those stores than men do. In fact, those were recommended by the women who were there."

Dante admitted for the record that Gwyneth never once wrote to him or spoke to him or knocked on his door. However, he added, "If you're psychic, you really don't need that."

Finally we took up the *Better Sex* video series he sent her. Soiu explained that it was "put out by some doctors and Ph.D.s" and "was advertised in all the magazines," and that was why he sent the series to Paltrow.

"You were aware that by sending them these videos you 'freaked them out,' based on your own writing?" I said, showing him one of the letters he had sent.

"Of course," he answered. "I don't know if they were really freaked out. I just put that comment on there. Maybe they thought I was a deviant. I don't know."

Ellie Schneir rose again, this time to ask, "Your Honor, could the court direct my client not to talk when there's not a question pending?"

Judge O'Neill obliged her and admonished Dante to restrict himself to answering the question at hand. That was fine with me.

"I have nothing further," I said.

Ellie had no redirect. The defense and the prosecution rested. The court clerk wheeled the evidence—two shopping baskets filled with pornography and sex toys—into the judge's chamber for him to review.

THREE DAYS LATER, on December 14, 2000, Judge O'Neill returned his verdict.

"From all the evidence that was presented," he said, "I come to the conclusion—I think it's inescapable—that the defendant will stop at nothing to realize his sexual desires for the victim. Despite the pleas from the victim's mother, the constant warnings from the police, nothing will stop the defendant. He has continued pursuit of the victim by his actions, and it was done with the intent to place her in reasonable fear for her safety—and I come to no other conclusion from this evidence—for her safety and the safety of her family."

Therefore, the judge found Soiu guilty of stalking Gwyneth Paltrow as charged. The California Court of Appeal agreed with Judge O'Neill. Soiu's attorney later appealed the guilty verdict, claiming there was insufficient evidence to establish that Soiu had the intent to cause Paltrow fear. In its opinion, the Court of Appeal held that "the element of intent is rarely susceptible of direct proof and must usually be inferred from all the facts and circumstances disclosed by the evidence." The court based its opinion on the fact that Soiu had continued his unwanted pursuit of Paltrow for more than eighteen months, despite being warned by Paltrow's mother and the FBI that he should discontinue his contact with Paltrow and her family because they were fearful; Soiu's "desires to engage in various sexual acts, including violent ones"; his expressed belief that Paltrow was a sinner and bad things would happen to her for resisting their union; and his sending "numerous packages containing various sexual implements which progressively became violent."

After finding Soiu guilty of felony stalking, Judge O'Neill began the second part of the trial—the determination of whether or not Dante was not guilty by reason of insanity. Just prior to trial, after much hesitation and many changes of mind, Soiu had also entered a second plea of not guilty by reason of insanity, or NGI for short. (It is a quirk of California law that the defendant must personally plead NGI, not his or her attorney. To me, it's a matter of common sense that the presumably insane person is hardly in the best position to judge whether he or she, in fact, is insane.)

Ellie Schneir had reports from four experts, including Reid Meloy, who all agreed that her client was legally insane. I did not necessarily agree, however. I think I could have convincingly shown that Soiu knew right from wrong, which is the M'Naghten test. If I did, however, I'd lose by winning, because the defendant would face a maximum prison sentence of three years, and actual release much earlier than that. If he was found NGI, he could potentially spend the rest of his life in a locked-down mental facility. A successful plea of NGI in California means incarceration in a facility for the insane. Hearings are periodically held to review the case. You may get well and eventually be set free. Or you could be locked up for the rest of your life. As a rule, defendants do not plead NGI in California unless they are standing trial for a felony such as homicide for which a guilty verdict may mean a very long sentence.

At the sanity hearing, we had the right to call expert witnesses to testify that Dante was not legally insane. We also had the right to have the defense bring in its four experts who had formed the opinion that Dante was insane. Instead, I chose to stipulate to the defense's expert reports, as it was in everyone's best interest that Dante be confined to a locked-down psychiatric facility. Based on our stipulation, Judge O'Neill made his final ruling, finding Dante to be legally insane. "Therefore," O'Neill concluded, "I will commit the defendant to the California Department of Mental Health for placement in a state hospital pursuant to Penal Code section 1026, and confined for the maximum of three years absent further findings."

After he served the three years, Soiu was evaluated and declared a continuing danger to the community. Subsequent evaluations came to the same conclusion, and he remained in the hospital for several additional years. However, in late 2007, Dante demanded a jury trial on the issue of whether or not he was still a danger to the community.

During the two-week trial in early 2008, four mental health professionals testified that Soiu was still delusional, would probably not take his medications if released on an outpatient basis, and, in all likelihood, would resume stalking. But they differed on the key question whether he would be a danger to the community.

One expert believed Soiu was no danger, whether or not he took his meds. Another opined that there could be unintended harm if Dante started stalking again. He might not mean to hurt a victim, but would do so anyway. Still another expert believed that although Soiu so far had not hurt anyone, he could be quite dangerous if provoked into a rage by another rejection.

Prosecutor Terrence Terauchi asked Gwyneth to testify, but unfortunately her schedule did not permit it. According to Terauchi, Dante himself testified that "he was no longer interested in pursuing Paltrow. He'd given it his best shot and it was over." Blythe Danner was still willing to testify, but because of the numerous last-minute continuances she was unable to fly to Los Angeles when the trial started.

The jury voted to release Soiu from the locked-down facility and allow him to return to Ohio in his brother's care, where he has been placed in an outpatient program. After the trial, several jurors told Terauchi that they might have decided differently had Gwyneth Paltrow, Blythe Danner, or a representative of the family testified to their fear of Soiu.

TEN

MARIE POYNTON CAUGHT very few breaks in life. The fifth of six children in the family of Robert McGowan, a Pasadena tree surgeon, both her parents were alcoholics. Marie's younger brother, Raymond, was institutionalized with severe psychiatric disorders from boyhood. Another brother, Eugene, committed suicide. According to her older sister, Sarah (also known as Sally) Barra, most of the McGowan kids bailed out of the household as early as possible.

In 1981, when she was twenty-seven, Marie was living with Sarah and their mother in an apartment in San Gabriel, just south of Pasadena, where she supported herself cleaning houses and helping Sarah with her catering business. Their mother attended adult education classes, and one night she came home with a pleasant man named Richard Poynton, who she'd met at school. She introduced Richard to Marie. They began dating, and married two years later in December of 1983. "He could be quite charming," Sarah recalls, "but Mother was the only person in the family who ever liked him. Everyone else knew this guy was a jerk. We tolerated him for Marie's sake."

The new Mrs. Poynton knew her husband had had a previous wife. She didn't know that he'd had two, however, and that one had borne his child. She also didn't know that, like his father, Richard had done prison time, or that much of his stint as an Army medic had been spent in the stockade for various offenses, such as going AWOL or impersonating an officer.

Her husband tried to dodge the AWOL charge by claiming that he had "blacked out" and awoken several days later far away from his barracks. Several Army psychologists noted in his record that they didn't believe him, that Poynton, in fact, was malingering—that is, faking his symptoms. He was finally given a general release from the military.

Trying to dodge responsibility for his actions was a lifelong avocation for Richard Poynton.

Richard and Marie's first child was born in 1985. His brother arrived in 1989. Later, the boys' father would move the family almost fifty miles north to Palmdale, where Marie was told not to call her sisters, Sarah Barra and Patty Sandston, or any other member of the family. "He was very controlling," says Sarah. "He obviously wanted to get her away from us."

Marie hid a lot of Richard's behavior. When he started hitting her in front of the boys, she made light of it, laughing that Richard had just spanked her. Sarah remembers discussing the situation with their big brother, Bill. "We've got to get Marie away from him," Bill said at the time.

THE PHYSICAL ABUSE began in the early 1990s, not long after the Poyntons purchased a housecleaning service called Rainbow Cleaners. Richard took an active role in the company for a time, but stopped joining the Rainbow work crews after several customers complained about him. He later took up long-distance trucking, until he claimed that he hurt his back in an accident in Texas.

Sarah remembers that from then on her brother-in-law generally filled his days watching television. About 1996, he also began a long-term affair with Monica O'Hare.* She and her

_____

*Denotes pseudonym

husband were neighbors and friends of the Poyntons, and Marie was soon aware that Richard was cheating on her with O'Hare.

One night in 1997, Richard threw Marie over their living room couch. She grabbed the cordless phone and ran down the street in her nightgown, calling for help from friends—a married couple—as she fled. The husband came to rescue her in his car. Poynton tailgated them as they drove along, repeatedly bumping their car with his.

He set fire to many of Marie's personal belongings and gave away others, including her jewelry.

His wife was granted a temporary restraining order on May 14, 1997, but it did no good. Poynton at first tried to refuse service of the restraining order. When the deputies showed up, along with Marie's sister Sarah and her husband, Don, Richard locked the front door and began shouting and cursing at the officers before they finally persuaded him to accept the document.

Then he ignored it. Marie repeatedly called to report that he was violating the order, but the local police did not respond. According to Sarah, they even ignored her report that Poynton had stolen her car. Marie finally gave up on expecting help or protection from law enforcement.

THE PATTERN OF chronic abuse shifted in late 1998 after Marie found the courage to raise the subject of divorce. To her initial joy and relief, Richard agreed to the idea in early December, but then he only stepped up the violence. On Christmas Day, Poynton threatened to kill his wife, and told her their sons would be better off dead than with her.

"She was terribly afraid," Sarah testified. "She said, 'He says we have to go to Las Vegas tomorrow. I don't want to go. I'm afraid he might kill us and dump us in the desert.' I told her, 'Just refuse to go and tell him the boys can't go either. He can't physically pick you up and put you in the car.'"

On December 28, Patty and Sarah took their sister to the emergency room at Huntington Memorial Hospital. "She just couldn't stop shaking," Sarah told the court. "She couldn't stop crying. She just kept saying, 'He's not going to let us live! He's not going to leave us alone. He's not going to give me a divorce. He's going to kill me. He's going to kill my kids!'"

Doctors at Huntington Memorial prescribed sedatives for Marie. She spent the night with Sarah and Don at their house in South Pasadena. When she telephoned Poynton, he threatened to take the boys from her and called her "a mental case."

The next day, Patty and Sarah accompanied Marie to the courthouse, where she was granted her second temporary restraining order in two years. It was served that evening by Los Angeles County deputies.

"Four weeks ago," Marie Poynton declared in the application's "Description of Conduct" section, "we agreed to divorce. The next day he said he wouldn't divorce me—he would do something better than that. He said he would kill me. He threatened to kill my sister—'I will have your sister toasted for two hundred dollars. You will be sorry you met me. I know how to make a pipe bomb.' During the past four weeks he has threatened me constantly, not allowing my family to call and speak with me. He doesn't threaten me in front of the children, but waits until I am in the garage or away from the children."

In a handwritten addendum, Marie continued: "My husband on December 21, 1998, pushed me in the garage and said he'll have the kids this time next year cause I'll be dead."

The court ordered Poynton to stay one hundred yards away from Marie and their sons, as well as the family house, their school, and her workplace. Even a telephone call to Marie would violate the order.

Richard Poynton kept a personal journal, later seized as evidence by investigators, filled with notes for a scheduled January 21, 1999, hearing on the restraining order. "1. I do not consent to the restraining order requested for the following reasons," he wrote. "A. There has been no domestic violence of any sort, no police reports, police call-outs. Petitioner is fabricating story to keep me out of my lawful owned home and away from our children. 2. I do not consent to be excluded from our residence. A. It is my dream house. B. It has created financial difficulties. C. Their is no reason to exclude me from my house. D. Medical problems."

By far the strangest entry in the journal was the final one. "And in closing," Poynton wrote, "this person named Marie Poynton had a fantasy of having sex with a male prostitute several years ago. I finally gave in so she had this male prostitute come over and she had unprotected sex with him with the children in the house, on three separate occasions, and last year told me that she thought she had AIDS."

He intensified his campaign of terror. Correctly assuming that no piece of paper, no matter how official looking, was going to deter her husband, Marie took her sons to stay with Aunt Sarah and Uncle Don. On January 2, Poynton telephoned his wife at the Barra house. Terrified, she told her sister how he said he was calling from a phone booth at the baseball diamond across the street, and that he had been following her—stalking her—for the past three days

Had Marie reported the calls and threats to the authorities, her husband could have been arrested and prosecuted for aggravated felony stalking. At this point, locking up Richard Poynton was probably the only way to stop him.

Yet because experience had taught Marie that the police couldn't protect her, this time she contacted no one in law enforcement, even though she was long since certain that Richard really would kill her if he could, along with her family. Instead, she told Sarah that there was no place to hide from Richard. "I may as well just take the boys and go back home," she said. "He's going to find me no matter where I am." She also worried that she was further endangering Sarah's life by staying with her.

So Marie Poynton returned home with her sons on January 3. In her final gesture of self-defense, she had the home telephone number changed to an unlisted one.

As soon as Poynton discovered the switch, he began calling Patty and Sarah, demanding that they give him Marie's new number. Both adamantly refused.

On Monday, January 11, Patty took Marie to a paralegal, who would begin preparing divorce papers for her.

Richard kept telephoning Marie's sisters, each time ratcheting up the invective.

In the early hours of Friday, January 15, 1999, he apparently decided it was time to make good on his threats. At 2:15 A.M., he telephoned Patty at her apartment in Glendora, called her a "cum-sucking bitch," and hung up.

He continued calling every half hour or so. Patty ignored the ringing telephone. Then at about 5:30 that morning, as she was talking to Marie over the phone, her call-waiting beep alerted her that someone was trying to reach her.

"Hold on," she said. "It's another call. It's probably him."

It was.

"Get up, bitch!" he said. "You tell your fucking bitch sister that I'm going to kill her. I'm going to kill you and that other bitch sister. You people will be sorry you ever met me!"

"You're a real pig," Patty answered, then hung up and resumed her conversation with Marie. As Patty later recounted to me in court, "I got back to my sister, and she said, 'Was it him?' I did not tell my sister of his threat to her, just to myself. I didn't want her to get all upset again. She had been upset enough.

"She said, 'Watch yourself Patty, please. I beg of you to please watch yourself.' "

"I said, 'All right, dear. I will.' "

UNDER QUESTIONING, RICHARD Poynton would recall that he did not sleep that night. He also claimed that he hadn't eaten for three days. He said he drove around for hours in a battered red 1982 Honda Civic for which he'd recently paid five hundred dollars, rehearsing Marie's murder in his mind. As executed, his plan—which he later claimed had received input from Monica O'Hare, the woman with whom he'd been having an affair—would require a gun and a knife, plus a disguise. It also was a singularly stupid scheme—long on sadistic plotting, short on smarts.

That Friday morning, Marie took the boys to school, then finished up her housecleaning jobs early, by noon. At about 12:30, she stopped by to ask for her sister's help in making out a bank deposit and figuring out what she owed to the women in her cleaning crews.

Sarah had volunteered to file Marie's divorce papers for her that day. But since Marie had already finished her day's work, she decided to take them downtown herself.

"I think I'll take those papers," she said.

"Are you sure you want to do this?" Sarah asked.

"Yeah," Marie replied. "I have to do this."

She returned at just before two that afternoon, and walked

in waving her papers. "It was like saying, 'See! I did it!'" Sarah recalls. It would be her last glimpse of her younger sister alive.

POYNTON HAD SHADOWED Marie throughout the morning. Since he'd just purchased the old Civic, Marie did not recognize the vehicle, or her husband in his disguise. Knowing that she would eventually return north to Palmdale via Highway 2 in La Canada and then the twisty, four-lane Angeles Crest Highway through the high-country of the Angeles National Forest, he drove ahead in his beat-up Honda and lay in wait for her 1996 Saturn to come along the highway.

She drove past him just before three o'clock, and he pulled in behind her. Poynton knew that Marie had developed a deep, anxious fear of traffic accidents ever since she'd been involved in one some years before. He now intended to exploit that fear.

At a downgrade where the highway skirted the western rim of Devils Canyon, he caught up with her and swerved the Honda into his wife's Saturn. A few feet to the right a steep, twenty-foot gully stretched down toward the canyon, where Poynton clearly hoped his terrified wife would plunge to her death.

Instead, Marie somehow maintained control of her car and slowed to a stop on the gravelly shoulder. She had gotten out and was walking onto the highway when Eddie Partridge and his friend, Dave Prescher, came around the corner in the opposite direction in their vehicle. As Partridge later described in court, he saw Marie on the roadway, clearly disoriented and visibly distraught. He also saw her car parked on the shoulder, and a great billow of dust spreading into the air from the roadside about fifty yards behind her.

"I came to a complete stop in the street," he testified, "and I asked her what was wrong. She was upset. She was not crying or delirious, but she was upset. She was flustered. She said, 'I think someone just drove off the canyon. I think they tried to knock me into the canyon. Look at my car.'"

Partridge did, and clearly saw scrapes along the Saturn's driver's side, damage consistent with the sort of intentional collision that Marie Poynton described.

"Are you okay?" Partridge recalled asking her. "She said she thought she was. I told her to stand off the street by her car and I would drive down to see if there was anybody in the gully, go see if anyone was hurt, if I could help in any way."

In the meantime, Eric and Marcia Malm, along with their son, came up the road in their blue van. The Malms, who had been out celebrating their son's twelfth birthday, saw Marie standing by her car and pulled over to offer their assistance. Eric Malm would remember Marie as hysterical. She told him what had occurred, and that she had just gotten a restraining order against her husband, who was crazy. She didn't know if he, or someone he knew, was responsible.

Eddie Partridge slowly pulled his car left across the two northbound lanes, Prescher seated next to him, then stopped on the shoulder, where he got out to go investigate the dust cloud on foot. Just then he saw a man he identified in court as Richard Poynton slowly emerge from the cloud at the wheel of his faded red Honda. Poynton, who had nearly killed himself instead of his wife, pulled to a stop perhaps twenty feet away.

Dave Prescher got out of Partridge's car, lit a cigarette, and sat down on the hood. Poynton, who was in dark jeans, an Army jacket, and a gray, soft-brimmed hat pulled down low over his eyes, exited the Honda and approached Partridge.

"Did you see anyone go into the gully?" Partridge asked. "There's a lady up the road who said that somebody might have driven into the gully."

"Yeah," Prescher added. "Some chick up the road said some asshole tried to run her off the road."

Poynton at first was silent.

"Hey, I didn't do nothin'," he finally said. "I didn't do anything." Then he turned back toward the Honda, gesturing as he did so. "Look at the car," he said with some agitation. "There's no damage on my car!"

Partridge would remember the vehicle, in fact, was covered in dents.

"Why don't you come up and talk to her and straighten this out?" Prescher then asked.

"Absolutely," Poynton replied. "I'll go up and talk to her." He drove north along the shoulder to where Marie was talking with the Malms and parked in front of their cars. Partridge, who at this point wasn't sure what role, if any, Poynton had played in the incident, told Prescher to jot down the Honda's license number just in case.

Mr. and Mrs. Malm by now were standing near their van; their son remained inside the vehicle. Marcia Malm remarked to herself that the man in the Honda really "zoomed" up to them, and then for some reason didn't get out at once. He kept "fiddling" with something, as she put it, which she also found odd.

Eddie Partridge by now had completed a U-turn and pulled up alongside Marie's car. Marie walked over and leaned in the passenger-side window.

"Hi," she said. "Is this him?"

"Yeah," Partridge answered. "He said he'll come up and talk to you."

"Okay," Marie replied, obviously still unaware that it had been Richard who'd nearly run her into the canyon, and now was seated in his car, not twenty feet away. There was no reason she would've—the car was unknown to her, and Poynton was disguised by a large hat he'd pulled down to his eyes.

"I guess I'm a witness," Partridge added. "Let me give you my name and number."

She began to write down his information, joking about whether he was related to the Partridge family on TV, when Poynton at last climbed out of his car.

"Did you bring your insurance papers with you?" Mr. Malm asked Richard.

"Yep," Poynton replied as he walked by, his collar up and the hat pulled low over his eyes. Eric Malm didn't notice the handgun in Poynton's right hand.

His wife did.

"Oh my God! He's got a gun!" she screamed.

Eddie Partridge looked through his windshield to see Poynton walking briskly toward Marie, carrying a gun in his right hand and a long-bladed knife in his left.

"You fucking bitch!" he said as he neared her. Marie at last recognized her peril and tried to step backward as Poynton hit her twice in the face with the gun. Then with Partridge,

Prescher, and the Malm family (including their twelve-year-old son) all looking on, transfixed with horror, he began slashing at Marie with the knife.

"My God! He's going to kill her!" Dave Prescher shouted.

"She was laying on the ground in the fetal position," Partridge testified. "She was, like, trying to protect herself. She was moving around, fighting, and she had her knees drawn up to her chest, and she had her hands up, trying to cover her face. And the defendant was standing behind her facing me, and he was just stabbing her."

The attack lasted no more than fifteen to twenty seconds. When he was through, Poynton stood up from Marie's motionless body, walked to her Saturn, got in, and drove away. The handgun (actually a pellet gun) had served its purpose. None of the witnesses had risked intervening in the bloody assault. In fact, Partridge and the Malms then drove away from the scene in fear. Partridge testified that he'd feel forever guilty for not trying to stop Poynton.

Neither he nor Prescher nor the Malms had cell phones, so Partridge and Prescher headed south down the highway to a little market/café where they called 911 and told the people inside of the killing that had just occurred. Then they returned to the scene, where the lifeless Marie Poynton lay on her stomach, surrounded by a pool of her blood. The Malms had come back as well, in the company of Don Longwood, a uniformed Parks employee. Together, they all waited for the authorities to arrive. It was then about three o'clock in the afternoon on January 15, 1999.

RICHARD POYNTON WOULD later offer multiple, and contradictory, explanations for murdering his wife that day, all of them somehow casting himself as a victim in the affair, which is typical among stalkers. Their crimes are always someone else's fault—if not the victim's, then the victim's family or friends. Not until the very end would Poynton concede what his true intentions and plans had been all along.

What we know with certainty is that Poynton drove his dead wife's car north, and about three miles from the murder scene he discarded the floppy gray hat, which was recovered in the roadway a few hours later by Captain Larry Hill of the U.S. Forest Service.

Poynton continued north to Lancaster, a town near Palmdale where he'd been living in a trailer house. On a desolate dirt trail off the highway, he discarded the pellet gun, knife, knife sheath, and Marie's purse, including its contents. Then he continued on to Bakersfield, where he arrived at about five o'clock, just as the first reports of the murder were being broadcast. He ditched Marie's Saturn about four blocks from the bus station and boarded a Greyhound for Las Vegas.

En route he reconsidered—Las Vegas, he thought, would likely be saturated with news accounts of the murder. So he switched buses at Barstow and headed east to (then) tiny Laughlin, Nevada, where he assumed that news traveled slower and therefore with less emphasis. He figured that he might be able to hide out there a while longer.

Poynton, who had not changed out of the blood-splattered clothes he'd worn to kill Marie, climbed off the bus in Laughlin at about 2:00 A.M. on January 16, 1999. He bought a new hat—"so I could disguise myself a little bit"—and gambled until it was nearly dawn. He couldn't take a room, he said, because he didn't want to show ID that would give him away. He also spoke by telephone with Monica O'Hare, who told him his picture was all over the news and that surrender was probably his best option. On her advice, he eventually turned himself in to the security staff at the Riverside Casino in Laughlin.

"I'm NOT A killer," Poynton told the casino security detail in a videotaped interview right after confessing to them that he'd just murdered his wife.

"What happened is, she got a restraining order for the second time in two years, in which she said I was not to come near—I love my kids dearly—and she wouldn't even let me talk to them on the phone or call my son to wish him happy birthday on his birthday. And her sister was calling me all the time, calling me names, and stuff, and I just went off yesterday."

He explained that the crime occurred on the road.

"I pulled up alongside her, smashed into her car to get her to stop. She, uh, stopped. She didn't recognize me."

"Uh-huh."

"She stopped. Some other people stopped. And I, uh, got out of the car with—I had a hat on."

"Uh-huh."

"And I just walked up to her and started stabbing her."

A security man asked if Marie was armed.

"She didn't attack me," Poynton replied. "I'm not claiming that."

"The people that stopped, they saw you do that?"

"Yeah."

"Did they try to stop you?"

"No."

"Say anything to you?"

"No."

"They didn't?"

"They ran off."

Poynton refocused the discussion on himself.

"Something inside of me snapped yesterday, you know?" he said. "I have never hurt a human being in my life. I was a medic in the Army."

"Just one—"

"I just snapped."

"Just one incident too many?"

"Yeah. That was it. I was lonely. I miss my kids."

The security officers said little except to punctuate Poynton's remarks with "yeahs" and "uh-huhs" and the occasional question that betrayed their skepticism at his story.

"I didn't care about the divorce," he went on. "But she got a restraining order, and she said I was physically, emotionally, and mentally abusive to her. I wasn't."

"Uh-huh?"

"I had never laid a hand on her 'til yesterday."

"Well, what did you intend when you stopped her?"

"I wanted to talk to her. I wanted to try to convince her that I need to be in the kids' life, too."

"I don't understand. Why would you take a knife with you for that?"

"Huh?"

"Why would you take a knife?"

"Cause I have a knife. I already had the knife."

"Oh?"

"It wasn't—"

"Okay. Okay."

"Can I have a drink of water?"

AT 3:15 THAT afternoon, Los Angeles County Sheriff's Department homicide detectives Bobby Taylor and Delores Perales conducted a second interview with Poynton at the Laughlin jail. Both investigators had been at the crime scene on the Angeles Crest Highway until eleven the night before.

This time, Poynton elaborated a slightly different version of the previous afternoon's events. "I have a friend who has sort of started talking to me," he told Taylor and Perales. "She thought there were reasons that I need to take Marie out."

"A friend?"

This would be the first of several instances where Poynton tried to implicate Monica O'Hare in his wife's murder. Mrs. O'Hare adamantly denied any role in the crime. Detectives Taylor and Perales would look hard for any evidence to corroborate Poynton's allegations, but never found any.

"Yeah," Poynton said, "and this friend would come up with ideas such as, 'Why don't you knock her off the road with your car and push her down a drainage ditch?' Stuff like that. You know, even when I grabbed Marie I didn't want to hurt her. Uh, I still loved her. I never really . . . in my whole entire life . . . never hurt a thing. I was a medic. I never put violence toward anything.

"But I was just so full of rage. She got out of the car. She looked at me. She didn't know who I was . . . I was sort of disguised with a hat on. I was sort of slumped over. I walked over to her and then I looked up at her and she said, 'Richard,' like nothing had happened, you know. I said 'Bitch.' I said, 'How can you do this? How can you do this?' Because she knows I really love the kids. And I just got a knife and I just—then I just blanked out."

"Blanking out" was a familiar excuse for Richard Poynton, at least as far back as his legal problems while in the Army.

He'd soon lose track of his narrative, however, and describe how he murdered his wife in crystalline detail.

"I hit her over the top of the head with the gun twice," Poynton told the detectives.

"Did she start to back up or run from you?"

"No, no she didn't. She didn't seem to. She said something. I forget what she said, and then I just took the knife and I just started stabbing her."

"Do you know how many times you stabbed her?"

"No, I don't."

"Do you know where you stabbed her?"

"I think I stabbed her here—"

"That being her left shoulder—"

"—and then I think I got her right here—"

"Center chest."

"—and I think I got her down here."

"Lower right abdomen."

"Then I think I got her across the neck a little bit, and then I think maybe once in the back somewhere up here in the shoulder blade. Does that sound familiar?"

"What did the people do that were standing there?"

"They were just in shock."

"Did they stay around or what?"

"Nah. The person who was driving the van started taking off in the van going down the hill."

"Okay."

"The two guys in the car thought, I guess, that I was coming after them. That's when they headed the other way toward the market."

"What happened after it was over?"

"I hopped in Marie's car and took out of there."

Poynton told the sheriff's detectives that he would not fight extradition back to California, that he wanted to plead guilty, and that he'd ask for the death penalty for killing Marie. He also told them, as he had the casino security officers, that he'd planned to commit suicide immediately after the murder. His first plan, he said, was suicide by cop. "I was going to pretend that gun was a real gun," he explained, "and make them shoot me."

Then he settled on an overdose of Vicodin, the popular prescription medication he was taking for back pain. Poynton told Taylor and Perales that he had forty-one tablets of Vicodin, 750 milligrams each, with him. He stopped and picked up a six-pack of beer to help wash them down.

"I drank all the beer and I ate all the pills," he claimed.

"And nothing happened to you?"

"Nah."

"You didn't get sleepy or anything?"

"I got sick."

"Oh."

"You didn't throw up or anything?"

"Yes."

"Oh, you threw up?"

"All over the place."

POYNTON AT FIRST lied to Detective Taylor, telling him he'd gotten rid of the murder weapon and other evidence in the desert between Palmdale and Bakersfield. Then on February 2, when Taylor arrived back in Laughlin to escort his prisoner by air to California, Poynton offered to show him exactly where he dumped the evidence in Lancaster.

He explained that Taylor had been honest with him, and that he wanted to return the favor. Moreover, there were pictures of Marie with their sons in her wallet. He said that he didn't want just anyone discovering them.

Deputy and suspect flew together to Los Angeles International Airport, then drove in a sheriff's black-and-white patrol car to Lancaster, where Poynton led Taylor directly to the gun, knife, sheath, and purse, which lay undisturbed along the remote dirt track where he'd dumped them.

The prisoner was booked at the sheriff's office in Lancaster. Bail was set at one million dollars. At his arraignment on February 24, 1999, Poynton, contrary to what he'd told the detectives, pleaded not guilty to murder (including the use of a deadly weapon, the knife) and stalking. His preliminary hearing was set for Monday, April 19.

THE CHARGES HAD been filed by a prosecutor in Glendale, who contacted me a short while later to discuss the case. He knew

I was experienced at stalking prosecutions, and that the stalking charge would be a key element in the Poynton case. In a straight murder case, the state is limited in the sorts of details it can introduce about the victim and the defendant, as well as the circumstances prior to the crime. The stalking charge meant we could get into years of Poynton's behavior to establish the patterns of conduct necessary to prove stalking. When my colleague in Glendale suggested I take over the case, I agreed to do so.

Since there was no question that Poynton had killed his wife, there would be just two major issues to resolve: Would we seek the death penalty, and how would the defense try to explain away the crime?

The earliest (and unsurprising) hint of their strategy came in a telephone call from Richard Poynton's older sister, Charlene Williamson. She told me, confidentially, that on a visit to her brother in jail he had been cavalier about his legal predicament, reassuring their mother that all would be well. "Don't worry about it," he said, "I'm going to get off on an insanity defense."

I HAD TRIED several murder cases in my career but had never before sought the death penalty. As a prosecutor, I'm naturally tough on crime. But my social views and politics are fairly liberal, and I was less than a hundred percent certain about taking someone's life under any circumstance. On a more practical level, our office sets the bar high when it comes to considering the death sentence.

In general, death is reserved for cases where there are multiple victims, where the accused has a long, violent criminal history, or where the victim is a police officer, judge, prosecutor, or some other member of the criminal justice system. The bottom line is to show why committing *this* homicide merited execution, when the great majority of murder convictions led to life in prison.

Also, in order for a homicide to rise to the level of a death penalty case, the crime must include what we call a special circumstance. Often, the special circumstance is a felony committed in the course of the homicide, such as rape or arson or robbery. Other catchall special circumstances include the use of torture, poisoning, or lying in wait.

Lying in wait is just another form of stalking. However, it doesn't only mean hiding in ambush. It also covers concealment of purpose. When Richard Poynton resorted to a disguise—which he freely admitted—he was creating his own special circumstance.

Yet another critical element in the case was victim impact. Historically, victim impact was not legally determinative in arguing a death penalty; a prosecutor could raise the issue but not rely on it. However, under a recent California Supreme Court ruling, victim impact could now be raised as a main issue.

In Marie Poynton's case, there was first the impact of her husband's abundant cruelty preceding the homicide: the assaults and the threats to harm not only Marie but also their sons and her sisters. Then there was the brutality of the murder itself. According to the autopsy, Mrs. Poynton was covered with defensive wounds from trying to fend off his attack. Her right wrist was nearly severed. In her right hand she still held the pen she'd been using to take down Eddie Partridge's information.

Marie's murder devastated her fourteen-year-old and nine-year-old sons. Both were overcome with shock and grief. The fourteen-year-old tried to run away and, for a time, planned to commit suicide. Their aunt Sarah would require repeated hospitalization in the aftermath of Marie's murder for severe asthma attacks.

The witnesses were traumatized as well. They had all watched the horrific scene play out in its entirety, and all still carried its indelible memory. In particular I felt for the Malms' young son, who will remember every year that on his twelfth birthday he watched a woman be hacked to death.

According to office practice, no decision on whether to ask for the death penalty is made until after the preliminary hearing, when the assigned prosecutor assesses the evidence and the witnesses, plus aggravating and mitigating circumstances and other factors, and prepares and submits a detailed written report and recommendations for consideration by a committee of senior prosecutors. The defense attorney is also invited to join the process by submitting written arguments of his or her own to the special circumstance committee.

There are four main factors the prosecutor must address:

1. The protection of society: Will imposition of the death penalty in this case make the world safer?
2. Will the death penalty help deter others from committing similar homicides?
3. Does the punishment fit the crime?
4. Is there any hope of rehabilitating the killer?

I submitted my report. In July, while I was in court for a pretrial hearing, I was notified that the committee had decided to pursue the death penalty. As Mr. Poynton now faced the death penalty, bail was denied as well.

I remember chills went through my body when I received the call. I had an overwhelming feeling of responsibility to Marie's family, and yet realized that if I did my job right, the man seated at the defense table would one day be executed as a result of my efforts. Loathsome as I found Richard Poynton, it was sobering to take his life into my hands.

The defendant—who made repeated outbursts throughout the hearings, as well as in front of the jury during his trial—made no response at all when I announced in open court that the people would seek the death penalty. He was still wearing his no-big-deal expression. He seemed to believe he was invulnerable.

WE FINALLY STARTED picking a jury in late January of 2001, more than two years after Marie's murder. Two days into the trial, I received four boxes of Poynton's medical and psychiatric records, along with doctors' reports, dating all the way back to his time in the Army and later in prison. I assumed the defense hoped, or expected, that with the heavy time demands of the trial—I prosecuted the case as we prosecute all cases, alone; there was no second chair—I would not have time to plow through the thousands of pages. I was determined, however, to digest every scrap and to annotate what I'd read for quick reference. I would not be taken by surprise, and certainly not by their star witness, a forensic psychologist.

Michael Brewer, my colleague who helped prosecute Dante Soiu, remembered hiring this psychologist as a defense witness when he was with the public defender's office. Brewer had a valuable piece of advice for me. "Just let her blabber," he suggested. "She'll eventually hang herself."

That didn't mean I wouldn't take her testimony very seriously. Her key finding, that Poynton had suffered an extremely rare episode of what is called a dissociative fugue—that is, he'd blacked out—at the moment he killed Marie, could have exonerated him of legal culpability if the jury bought it. This was not the insanity defense that the defendant had confidently bragged about to his sister and mother months before. It was the unconscious defense, and it was necessary for me to destroy it utterly.

From the moment that Franklin Peters, Poynton's trial attorney, put the forensic psychologist on the stand for the first of her four straight days of direct testimony, she was clearly prepared to make social as well as legal excuses for the accused. She described a hellish boyhood of abuse by his father and mother, as well as bitter conflict with his older sister, Charlene Williamson. She described in detail an instance where Charlene hurled a pair of pliers at her little brother, which became embedded in his head.

Charlene, whom I called as a rebuttal witness, begged to differ. She told the court that their father was absent so much of the time—either behind bars or chasing skirts—that he wasn't around enough to be consistently abusive. Her mother, she said, struck Richard exactly twice, both times after he was well into his teens. The pliers incident had indeed occurred, Charlene agreed, but the tool did not get stuck in her brother's head. And yes, they did fight as children. But the set-tos usually began with Richard slugging her. Because she was faster than he, it was simple to run away from him.

The psychologist also demonized Marie Poynton, characterizing the dead woman as a horrible mother and the source of most of Poynton's problems. Only because his wife had refused to have sex with him, the witness asserted, had Poynton turned to Monica O'Hare for companionship.

Her clinical diagnoses were inconsistent as well. She reported that Poynton was suicidal, schizophrenic, and bipolar.

In my cross-examination, I forced her to concede that despite her diagnoses, she had not actually conducted any of the standard tests commonly used to help ratify such conclusions. When the psychologist claimed that the entire Poynton family suffered from bipolar disorder, I asked her if she'd reviewed any of their medical or psychiatric records besides the defendant's. She admitted that she hadn't.

According to the psychologist, Poynton had followed Marie around that day because he wanted to talk to her about their sons. But he just couldn't find the courage to step out of his car and approach her. He couldn't face her.

It was just a coincidence, the psychologist testified, that the accused was parked along the roadway as she drove by on her way home. And the only reason he rammed her car was so they could talk.

In the defense expert's version of the story, Poynton brought the knife to commit suicide if Marie turned down his request to see the boys. When he got out of the car, his intent was still only to talk to her, but that was the point at which he blacked out, and he did not regain his memory until he had driven away and thrown his hat out the window.

What occurred, the psychologist claimed, was that Poynton's mind reverted in that moment to an incident when he was a four-year-old child, trying to protect himself from his evil older sister, Charlene. He was fighting Charlene with his fists out on Angeles Crest, not realizing that he had the knife in his hand and in fact was murdering his wife, she testified.

When I later asked her why Poynton had thrown away his hat if he did not remember committing murder, she had no answer.

My evident skepticism as I questioned the psychologist seemed to get under the defendant's skin. At one point in court Poynton called me a "lying creepy bitch" and defended the psychologist against my assault on her credibility. "You have no right to talk to this doctor the way you have been talking to her," he yelled. "You know why? Because this doctor knows more, a lot more, than you will ever know about me."

A short while later, Judge Tricia Ann Bigelow, who was also trying her first capital case, ordered Poynton removed from the courtroom. This would happen several more times over the course of the trial.

I was also interested in exploring the range of research that underpinned the psychologist's conclusions and diagnoses. In all, she'd billed in excess of seventeen thousand dollars for three hundred hours of work. Among her interviewees, she listed Poynton, his mother, his stepfather, and his sister, Charlene.

Originally, the defense's expert claimed she interviewed Poynton's mother and sister in December at the offices of the defendant's attorneys. Only after I showed her the invoice she submitted did she correct herself and agree that the alleged interviews had taken place a month earlier.

Charlene Williamson said she herself was never interviewed, though her stepfather was. And according to Charlene, only her mother had spoken with the psychologist that day in November, and then just briefly and never again. Charlene also explained that Mrs. Poynton is deaf and has only a rudimentary mastery of sign language. In the boxes of documents belatedly provided me by the defense, I found what appeared to be a note that the psychologist wrote to Poynton's mother during their short interview. "You have to help me," it reads. "You have to help Richard."

The psychologist at first claimed to have taken notes during the sessions, but then said that she had shredded them. Later she remembered that she hadn't actually taken notes after all. The situation had been too "chaotic," she explained.

When I first looked up "dissociative fugue" in the American Psychiatric Association's *DSM IV*—the APA's official manual of mental disorders—I noted with keen interest that malingerers frequently try to fake the symptoms of dissociative fugue—claiming they blacked out—to weasel out of personal responsibility for crimes and other objectionable behavior.

Echoes of Richard Poynton's military past practically jumped from the page. When I asked the defense psychologist if she was aware of this phenomenon, she said she was.

There's a well-established test called the Minnesota Multi-Phasic Inventory (MMPI), which is often used in combination with other strategies to flag malingerers and liars. She had not given the test to Poynton, however. And her rationale for not doing so was that the MMPI does not work with non-Caucasian, non-English-speaking subjects who had not completed a traditional course of education. She also added that the test was not appropriate for incarcerated subjects.

Uncertain if I'd heard her correctly, I got the psychologist to agree that Richard Poynton *was* an English-speaking Caucasian who had finished high school.

Then I asked, "The MMPI is used by other mental health professionals in the jail population, is that not correct?"

"Yes," she replied, then added that the psychologist who'd trained her was, in fact, using the MMPI on inmates in the jail psychiatric ward as we spoke. I decided to let that testimony speak for itself.

My hope throughout her testimony was that Michael Brewer was correct and that the weight of her unlikely explanations for Richard Poynton's behavior, together with the strange inconsistencies in her testimony, would finally lead the jurors to disbelieve her altogether. In the end, they needed to see that fancy labels and tortured logic aside, Poynton was nothing more complicated than a vicious criminal, a point that he himself would ultimately make in front of them.

In the boxes I'd received from the defense, I had also noticed a report from Dr. Joseph Ortega, the supervising psychiatrist at the jail psychiatric ward, who had examined Poynton and agreed with one of his colleagues, another psychiatrist, that the prisoner was trying to manipulate the staff into placing him on the psychiatric ward. Ortega would testify that Poynton originally came to his attention for banging his head against the wall and his cell bars, as well as being combative with the deputies.

"He is not mentally disordered," Ortega said on the stand, "but personality disordered. I think I labeled him a sociopath."

"What exactly is a sociopath?" I asked.

"A sociopath," the psychiatrist answered, "is a person with antisocial personality disorder. It is not a mental disorder, such as schizophrenia or bipolar."

Ortega said that he also believed Poynton was malingering, and based that belief in part on Poynton's threat to commit suicide if he was sent to general population, as well as the accused's stated intention to tell the authorities at general population he'd kill himself if he was not returned to the psychiatric ward. "For me," testified Ortega, "it demonstrated malingering."

He added: "I identified Mr. Poynton as the type of gentleman we try to keep out of the psychiatric ward."

On cross-examination, Poynton's defense attorney, Franklin Peters, who knew that his client was nonetheless still being held in the psychiatric ward, asked Ortega if this was so. The psychiatrist said yes. Peters, however, did not ask *why* the defendant remained on the ward.

That would be my pleasure. It was the one question everyone in the courtroom was dying to have answered.

"Because," Dr. Ortega explained, "one of the other doctors had a forensic fellow who wanted to work with a true sociopath."

BESIDES HIS VERBAL assaults on me, the common theme of Poynton's repeated courtroom tantrums was his desire to be convicted and executed. On several occasions he openly dared the jury to put him to death.

The panel for the most part looked on and listened impassively during these episodes, patiently waiting their turn to be heard. That opportunity came on February 27, 2001. After just ninety minutes of deliberation, the jurors returned guilty verdicts on all counts. Judge Bigelow set the start of the penalty phase for March 5.

Any mystery as to how the jurors would vote was effectively erased in the course of this two-day mini-trial when the defendant, who had not previously testified, told the room, under oath:

"The murder of my wife was a premeditated act. I had help. Somebody helped me plan it. And we went to great lengths discussing it. We even actually dug a grave to bury her in. It sort of fell apart on the fifteenth, didn't go according to plan.

"I was supposed to grab her and take her out and kill her and bury her. I'm not afraid of telling you that. It's the truth. I have no reason to lie about it."

This time the jury met for four hours before unanimously agreeing to grant Richard Poynton his wish. All that was left was for Judge Bigelow to review and ratify their determination. For this, she set one final court date, April 9, 2001.

Poynton's older son, then sixteen, was in the courtroom that morning as Judge Bigelow began reading her findings.

"First, I find that the first degree murder of Marie Poynton was an intentional killing," the judge pronounced, "personally committed by the defendant, Mr. Richard Poynton, who personally used a knife to fatally stab his wife, Marie Poynton, thirteen times."

As she spoke, the killer, seated at the defense table, began to nod as if in agreement with Bigelow.

"I further find that the murder was premeditated, deliberate, willful, and committed with malice aforethought."

Poynton kept nodding.

"If these findings such be required . . ."

"Stop nodding your head, you fucking idiot!" came an enraged voice from the back of the courtroom. It was his son, and as he spoke, he made straight for the defense table.

The father turned to confront his son, as bailiffs moved in to prevent the boy from vaulting the low barrier behind the defense table. It appeared as if he were going to physically attack his father, who squared like a brawler as the boy approached.

"You want to have at me?" he snarled. "Come on!"

Judge Bigelow rapped the proceedings into recess, ordered the defendant removed, and called out to the bailiffs who were trying to subdue the teenage boy. "Don't hurt the boy!" she said. "Please don't hurt him!" as the struggling youth was carried from the courtroom.

I was stunned by the incident and, like the judge, deeply concerned about the teenager. I knew from his aunts how fresh the pain of his mother's murder remained and how hard everyone was trying to help him work through his anger and loss. Obviously, his father's antics had triggered something very deep. My heart went out to the boy.

Once order was restored—the boy did not return to the courtroom—the judge resumed. She called Poynton's behavior "bone-chilling, vicious, and callous," and dismissed the psychologist's testimony as "inherently unbelievable by simple resort to common sense and in light of a review of the facts of this case." Never before or after have I heard a judge summarily dismiss professional testimony in this way. Judge Bigelow also pointedly noted that the defendant himself had refuted the defense by his personal testimony during the penalty phase.

Then the judge allowed Marie's sisters, Sarah and Patty, to speak, after admonishing them both to address her, not the defendant.

"I believe that the correct verdict was reached," Sarah said, "and I think only when Mr. Poynton is executed that I will be able to sleep peacefully, knowing that there is no opportunity for him to escape from jail or prison and come and kill any other people, including his children."

"Oh, please," Poynton scoffed.

"Mr. Poynton," said the judge, "you're going to need to remain quiet."

"There's no evidence of that," he persisted.

"You are going to need to remain quiet," Bigelow repeated. "Go ahead," she said to Sarah, who concluded with a request that she and the boys be notified of any future change in Poynton's status or whereabouts.

Patty confined herself to two sentences. "I, too, feel he has gotten what he deserves," she said. "He has shattered his children's lives and my life terribly, and I hope he burns in the fires of hell when he leaves this earth."

Next was Poynton's turn.

"First of all," he said, "I want to apologize to my children. I know this has been a traumatic experience for them, but in all war there's casualty. Marie was the first. I'm the second.

"I'm willing to pay that price for whatever I did. I'm not worried about losing my life, Your Honor.

"To my ex-sisters-in-law—hey, sorry. You know, you declared war. One down on each side. What can I say? That's how it goes. When you declare war, there's no winners."

He went on in the same vein for a short while longer, promising to successfully appeal—"I will come back, Your

Honor," he vowed—then sat down, leaving it to Judge Bigelow to conclude the day's grim business.

"Richard James Poynton, it is the judgment and sentence of this court," she said, "that you should be sentenced to death and that said penalty should be inflicted upon you within the walls of the state prison at San Quentin, California, in the manner prescribed by law, and at a time to be set by this court in the warrant of execution."

POYNTON ARRIVED AT San Quentin a short time later to begin what will undoubtedly be a long process leading to his eventual execution. On January 9, 2002, he sent a letter to his former sisters-in-law.

"Dear Sally and Patty," he typed, "I am very comfortable, with my color tv, radio, typewriter, electric razor, and all the store I want. Enclosed is a price list of all the things we can buy, and along with that a thirty pound package from home every ninety days. How sweet it is. And you thought I would be hurting for the comforts of home. I'm in a one-man cell and get to go outside every day, playing pinochle, chess, basketball, and in general having fun."

The letter concluded, "Don't forget the third anniversary of January 15 coming up, as I won't. What a good day that was. I will never regret that day or my actions. Good-bye, Richard."

ELEVEN

By 2002, I was transferred to our Van Nuys office, where I was assigned to the Victim Impact Program, handling stalking and domestic abuse cases. I continued to lecture and write about stalking, as well as prosecute felony trials, such as the disturbing case involving Janice Sugita.

To Diana Martin,* Janice Sugita was at first irresistibly clever and charming. Only later did she also turn deadly.

They met in 1996 at a Hollywood film lab, where Diana, forty-four, drove the delivery van and Janice, thirty-six, was a newly hired technician.

Sugita had undeniable flair, from her auburn-dyed hair to the sleek red '85 Jaguar XJS she drove. She told a lot of obvious whoppers—that her family was very rich, that she'd attended USC law school, that she was a graduate of the Los Angeles Police Academy, that she'd sat on the Coca-Cola Company board of directors—but she was also bright, personable, very capable, and, to Diana, quite attractive. Within

---

a few months, they became lovers. Martin moved out of the Sherman Oaks house she co-owned with Mimi Watson,* her partner of twenty-three years, and into her own place.

Then Diana began to have second thoughts. Unlike Mimi, Janice was possessive, suspicious, and intensely jealous, even of a male friend of Diana's from work. She had a sinister side, as well.

Martin was surprised one day to discover a very large black handgun in one of Janice's closets. She made no mention of it to Sugita, but wondered what its purpose might be. The gun was way too big for self-protection alone.

There was also the "Diana M" that Janice had tattooed just above her groin. It embarrassed Martin, who asked Sugita to have it removed. She refused, and instead embellished it with camels and a desert scene. Janice sometimes called Diana "my desert rose."

By the spring of 1998, Martin and Watson had decided to get back together. Breaking the news to Sugita was not easy.

She cried, and complained that Diana had never given her a chance in their relationship. The split was full of rancor and ill will. Sugita told Lou Marsalis, a friend at work, that Diana was only interested in Mimi because of the house they owned together.

According to Martin, she and Janice did not see or speak to each other except once—at an AIDS benefit—until well into 1999, when Janice called one day to report that her mother had died, in London. Sugita said the body was being flown to Hawaii, where her mother would be buried with Janice's grandmother in the family plot.

Sugita, counting on Diana's natural trust and empathy, had fabricated the story as a wedge back into her former lover's life, and it worked. They lunched together a couple of weeks later, and began to exchange phone calls every now and again. Occasionally, Diana and Mimi and Janice would all meet for a meal, and sometimes the three of them golfed together on weekends. The tone of these get-togethers was generally positive; Watson had no fear of Sugita rekindling her affair with Martin. But Janice's peculiarity always lingered just below the surface. "I picked the wrong one," she told Mimi at one point. "I should have picked you. I'm sorry for interrupting your lives."

"It was like she was trying to add herself to the relationship," Mimi remembers.

Janice continued to spin tales. She told Diana and Mimi of fabulous houses her family owned in the best neighborhoods of San Marino and Pacific Palisades. She bragged of investing in a Hollywood nightclub called the Sunset Room.

She sometimes hinted at a sinister past, too. She said that "Jenny," a previous girlfriend, had been killed in a car wreck. Then Sugita changed that story and said that Jenny had likely been killed by the government after Janice had committed a series of errors on a clandestine assignment that, of course, she couldn't discuss.

In February of 2000, Mimi and Diana made plans to spend three days with some French friends at Borrego Springs in the desert. When Janice learned of the trip—and that she wasn't invited—she announced a gala fortieth birthday party for herself at a friend's house in Beverly Hills on the date of their departure. Immediately following the party, Sugita said, she was leaving by Concorde for a two-day trip to France. After Watson and Martin returned from the desert, they discovered in their mailbox a postcard from Janice with a clearly fake French stamp and postage affixed to it.

Janice was beginning to wear on their nerves.

The first hint that she might be capable of violence came in January of 2002. Sugita announced that she was throwing yet another gala; this time at the big house she allegedly owned in Pacific Palisades. For weeks, she called Diana nearly every night to discuss her plans for the January party: the food, the wine, the flowers, everything.

Then, late on the day before the big event, Janice appeared at Diana and Mimi's front door carrying a large duffel and backpack. It was a surreal moment. Janice announced that she'd come to say good-bye for good. She'd soon be going away on a secret mission for the federal government and would not be coming back. Also, unfortunately, Diana and Mimi could not come to her gala the following night because other federal agents would be there.

As Martin later testified in court, "You know, we didn't believe her. And we said, 'Could you show us any kind of identification?'

"She said, 'No, federal agents do not carry identification. But I can show you something they have issued us.'"

"What did she show you?" I asked.

"She pulled out a large gun," said Diana, who recognized the firearm as the same one she'd seen in Janice's closet four years earlier. Sugita held the gun up for Martin and Watson to see, told them it was a Glock, and said she was a dead shot with it in case they ever needed someone "taken out."

"What was your reaction?" I asked.

"Our reaction was, 'Okay, that's fine. You can put that back in and leave our home.'"

"Were you upset?"

"Yes, we were."

THE EPISODE WITH the gun introduced a new element into Diana's relationship with Janice—fear.

A few days later, Diana found a card affixed to the Windstar she drove at work. "They are watching you," it read. She recognized the handwriting as Janice's.

Later in the week, Sugita called her on the company cell phone that Martin carried on her delivery rounds.

"Hi," she said.

Diana was alarmed at once. "Why are you calling?" she asked.

"I just wanted to say good-bye. I'm still leaving and I just wanted to say good-bye."

Martin cut the conversation short. "Good-bye," she said, "and please don't call me again."

Weeks and then months passed with no further communications from Janice. Diana and Mimi began to relax. It seemed that the disturbing Ms. Sugita may actually have meant it when she made her farewells in January. They certainly hoped so.

Janice Sugita, however, was far from finished with Diana Martin.

Diana next heard from Janice in August of 2002. "She started calling me again, saying, 'I would like to see you. I miss you. I miss talking to you.'"

Diana called it a "desperate kind of calling" that she did not welcome.

"I don't want anything to do with you," she told Sugita. "You are not supposed to be calling me."

A week or so later, she encountered Sugita at the Fashion Square mall in Sherman Oaks, where she had gone to return a purchase. Although Janice acted as if it was a purely random encounter, Diana knew better.

She testified that Sugita said she wanted to explain all about her secret work for the government. Also that "she could tell me exactly where I've been for the last four months; any day, any given time."

Janice took Diana out to her Jaguar in the parking lot.

"Pick a date," she said. "I can tell you exactly where you've been."

Diana chose the previous day.

Sugita produced a small laptop computer and punched some buttons on it. A few minutes later her cell phone rang.

"She took the call," Martin recalled, "read off a bunch of numbers and letters, code numbers, and then she proceeded to tell me what they were saying to her on the phone." Chillingly, what Sugita was reciting was exactly what Diana had done on the previous day.

"I went golfing with a cousin of mine. She told me exactly what golf course I went to. She told me exactly how I went, down which streets. She told me exactly what I was wearing, what the person I was golfing with was wearing... What time we finished, where we went after that. What time we left the restaurant. Which way I went home. All the way to that," Martin remembers.

"I figured she was tailing me, following me, stalking me. I was nervous and concerned."

A couple of days later, as Mimi Watson walked into the front yard to collect their morning newspaper, she found a single nine-millimeter round glistening in the sun on their porch. She prudently saved the bullet, which was the correct caliber for use in the Glock that Mimi and Diana later described to us.

The following week, Janice called Diana on her work cell phone to say that she was deeply depressed and had decided to commit suicide. She asked if Martin could meet her at the Beverly Garland Hotel in Studio City as soon as possible.

Accustomed as she was by now to Janice's histrionics, Diana was nevertheless moved.

"Did you meet her?" I asked.

"She was crying and she was desperate and pathetic and I did," Martin answered.

They met in the hotel parking lot, then went together to Janice's room.

"She unloaded a bunch of her possessions," Diana testified, "her clothes and her personal things, radios, pictures, cards, and asked me to get rid of this stuff for her."

Janice also showed Diana two wrapped packages in her trunk. She said they were fiftieth-birthday presents for Martin, even though the date had passed four months earlier.

"I don't want any gifts—*please*," she told Sugita.

Diana remembered her main purpose that day was to persuade Janice not to kill herself. She said she hoped her former lover would reconsider "and try to talk to somebody and get some help." Then they parted, once again supposedly for the last time, and Martin went home. The next day, she and Watson got rid of Sugita's belongings. By now, neither of them expected they'd ever get rid of Sugita herself.

Janice surfaced once more about ten days later. Diana was working the three to eleven-thirty shift on Friday, August 30, 2002, when Sugita called her at about four that afternoon. She announced that she had decided against suicide. Instead, she was moving to Palm Springs with some friends. Diana thought she sounded happy, upbeat.

"I'd like to say good-bye to you," she said. "Could we meet up?"

Martin at first said she was very busy and didn't think she'd have time.

"You must have five minutes of your life to stop and say good-bye to me," Janice pressed her, petulantly.

The conversation went back and forth in this way for another few minutes before Diana at last gave in, as she usually did. Martin said she'd see Sugita on her nine o'clock break. At Janice's suggestion, they agreed to meet in front of a church on Whipple Street, a quiet residential lane off Cahuenga Boulevard in North Hollywood, not far from the photo lab.

Diana telephoned Mimi with the news that Janice had not

killed herself after all, and in fact was planning a move to Palm Springs. She also told Watson that she was to meet with Janice that evening to say farewell, again.

Mimi, far more skeptical of Sugita's motives than Diana, had difficulty believing what her partner was saying. "Why?" she asked. "Why are you meeting with her?" Diana could only say that Janice had been very insistent.

She arrived in the Windstar at the appointed time, and noted at once that Whipple Street was very dark. There were no streetlamps. Martin didn't notice any pedestrian traffic, either. In her rearview mirror, she saw Janice in her Jag pull up behind the van almost at once. They both exited their vehicles and met between them.

"We greeted each other," Diana testified. "I said, 'Hello.' She said, 'Hello,' in a nervous sort of way. She said to me, 'I know you don't have a lot of time. I have a couple of things for you.'

"I said, 'I thought we were just here to say good-bye, and you are on your way out of town?'

"'Well, yeah,' Janice answered, 'but I want to give you this stuff.'"

Martin testified that Sugita retrieved at least two large, long boxes from the passenger seat of her car—Diana recognized them as the same gift boxes she'd seen in Janice's trunk at the Beverly Garland Hotel—and started to put them into the back of the Windstar.

Diana protested.

"I said I didn't want the items," she remembered. "What are these?"

As before at the hotel, Sugita explained that they were birthday presents.

"I don't want this stuff," Diana said.

"You don't have to open it here," Janice answered. "You can just take it. I've had it for a while."

They argued over the boxes until Martin finally gave in once again, said okay, and closed the back of the minivan.

"I know you have to get going," said Janice. "So I don't want to take up any more of your time."

"Okay," Diana replied. "I'll see you. I'll talk to you, I'm sure. You are always calling me. Good luck in Palm Springs."

As she climbed back into the driver's seat, grateful that the encounter had been brief, she heard Janice call out, "Wait! Wait! I have one more thing for you."

Diana watched her approach, carrying yet another box. This one was about twenty inches long, Martin later guessed. It was tied with black ribbon and a black bow.

She'd also remember that Sugita cradled the package in an awkward way. Her left hand was resting on top of the box. Her right hand, which was concealed, seemed to be holding it from behind.

"I have this one last gift to give you for your fiftieth birthday," Janice said.

"I don't want anything for my fiftieth," Diana answered. "I don't want what you've put in the back of the van, either. What is this?"

"Oh," Sugita said, "this is something very special for your birthday and it has to ride up front with you."

She pushed the box to within about a foot of Diana, then deliberately brushed two small objects—a sachet and a little round disk—off the top with her left hand. They fell onto the floorboard in front of Martin.

"Oh, could you get that for me?" Janice asked. "I dropped something."

As Diana was leaning forward to pick them up there came a flash and a deafening explosion in her left ear.

What was that? she thought, momentarily stunned.

"I didn't shoot you! I didn't shoot you!" Janice cried.

Diana put her hand under her shirt. It came back covered in blood.

"You shot me!" she exclaimed. "What did you shoot me for?"

"I didn't shoot you!" Sugita yelled. "It was a red paint ball!"

Although she was scared and panicked, Martin remained remarkably lucid, which may have saved her life. She opened the van door, pushing aside Sugita, who hurriedly dropped the gift box and kicked it under the van.

Suddenly it was clear to her what had happened. Janice must have been holding the gun with her right hand, inside the box, as she shoved it through the window. Sugita had brushed the sachet and disk onto the floorboard in order to get a clear shot as Martin reached down for them.

As Diana stood by the door, collecting her wits, Janice reached into the van to retrieve the sachet and disk from the floor. She also grabbed Martin's keys from the ignition.

"Oh, no!" Diana cried. "I'm injured. I've got to get to the hospital. Give me the keys!"

"No! No! You can't have the keys!" said Sugita. "The police will be involved!"

Diana raised her shirt to show Janice the gaping hole in her chest.

"You shot me in the chest!" she said.

"No, it was a paint ball," Sugita insisted again. "I didn't shoot you."

Janice then offered to drive Diana to the hospital herself. Martin understandably refused.

"I figured she wanted to finish me off," she explained in court.

They struggled for the keys until Diana was able to slug Janice hard in the face and take them from her. As she stumbled back to the driver's seat, she heard Sugita talking to herself.

"I have to get the stuff out of the back," she was saying. "I have to get the stuff out of the back of the van that I put in there."

Martin dropped the vehicle into drive and hit the gas. She glimpsed Sugita throwing the boxes out onto the ground as she drove away.

Her first thought was of Mimi at home, about four miles to the west. Had Janice already visited their house? Diana groped around the seat in search of her cell phone to call Mimi, but couldn't find it in the darkness.

When she pulled up, Diana could see that Mimi had the lights on and the TV going. "Mimi, open the door!" Martin yelled from outside.

"What happened?" Watson asked, coming to the door.

"Janice fuckin' shot me!"

Mimi, a trained health-care worker, took Diana into the bathroom, conducted a brief examination of her wounds, and then rushed her partner the short distance to the emergency room at Providence–St. Joseph's Hospital in Burbank.

There, Dr. Peter Obligato, the ER physician, discovered that the single bullet from Janice's covert gun had ripped into Martin's left breast, then exited and re-entered her body to bury itself in two fragments within the soft tissue below her right breast. Dr. Obligato would testify that "surprisingly" no vital organs were hit. Diana would survive, luckily, because the large-caliber slug had missed her heart by just an inch.

MIMI DROVE DIANA home from Providence–St. Joseph's after 2 A.M. on Saturday morning, August 31. Before they left the hospital, patrol officers interviewed Martin, who recounted the crime and identified Janice Sugita as her assailant. At the time, she described Sugita as an "ex-friend."

The patrol officer's report, with "ATTEMPTED MURDER" typed across the top line, as a matter of routine came to the attention of Detective Alex Vargas, with whom I'd worked numerous cases, including Lamont Mitchell in 1998 and Marlon Pagtakhan just the year before. Alex had since left the TMU and was then assigned to the Crimes Against Persons team out of LAPD's North Hollywood Division.

Based on the bare details available in the report, Vargas questioned whether the victim was telling the truth about her past relationship with the suspect. "I could see there was more to the story than what she first told the officers," he remembers. Vargas then visited Diana at home, where she admitted that Janice Sugita had been her lover six years earlier.

The detective never doubted that Diana had been shot as she described. When he visited the crime scene later that morning, he found blood on the street exactly where Diana said she had parked, as well as evidence that someone had tried to wash away the blood with water.

His paramount concern then was to find Janice Sugita before she decided to finish the job, a possibility that naturally terrified Diana and Mimi. "Basically, we were racing the clock," he says. "We knew we had a dangerous person on our hands, a lady who would risk it all to kill her ex-lover."

Until the suspect was under arrest, all police working in

the area of Diana and Mimi's Sherman Oaks residence were advised to treat any call from that address as a Code Three— respond with lights and sirens. Vargas also gave the women the numbers necessary to reach him at any time of the day or night, and told them to never hesitate to call.

He had several possible addresses to check in his search for Sugita; none yielded any leads. Janice's mother, very much alive, was cooperative, according to Vargas; unfortunately, she had no idea where her daughter might be.

His suspect first surfaced a few nights later, on Tuesday, September 3. Lou Marsalis, Janice's friend from the photo lab, was driving home from work that night when he received a call from Sugita on his cell phone. Marsalis so far knew nothing of the Friday night incident on Whipple Street.

She told him that "a terrible, terrible accident," had occurred. Sugita was already sketching in her defense.

"A car accident?" Marsalis asked.

She wouldn't say.

Janice sounded "really, really bad" to Lou, who said she spoke in a tone of voice he'd never heard before. "I thought I should talk to her," he later testified.

They agreed to meet where they often did, at a Starbucks near the intersection of Ventura and Laurel Canyon boulevards in Studio City. Ten minutes later, Marsalis saw Sugita standing on the sidewalk on Ventura. Her Jaguar was parked well behind the coffeehouse.

"She looked horrible," he remembers. Janice's signature outfit was Levis, a Hawaiian shirt or polo shirt, and black shoes. This night she wore hiking boots, a sweatshirt, baggy jeans, and dark glasses. She got into Lou's Mercedes and he pulled into the parking lot.

They each lit a cigarette and started to talk.

"I'm going to go away," Sugita said.

"Why?" he asked.

"I can't tell you."

"Why?"

"You can't tell. Promise not to tell?"

"Okay, I swear."

"I accidentally shot Diana."

"What?"

"It was an accident."

"How'd that happen?"

"I was feeling depressed. I was handing her my gun when it went off."

"How's Diana?" Marsalis asked, trying to comprehend what he was hearing.

"I don't know," Janice answered.

Lou was incredulous. "Didn't you take her to the hospital?" he asked.

"She didn't want me to."

"Where's the gun?"

"I don't know. I picked it up and threw it."

"Where?"

"I don't know."

"Did you call her?"

"No."

"How come?"

"I don't know what she'd say."

"Why?" Lou asked. "What difference does that make? There should be only one story."

Sugita changed the subject. She told Marsalis that she was worried that the more she told him the more problems he might have.

I asked him about that on the stand.

"I told her whatever somebody else does can't get me into trouble," he testified. "I have to get myself into trouble."

"Was that the conversation pretty much?" I asked.

"That's pretty much the gist of it. You know, she'd said that if she called Diana, she thought Diana would hang up on her. I thought, *Well, you know, you did shoot her.* I told her that she needed to get a lawyer and call the police. And she said okay."

Marsalis reported the conversation to Alex Vargas the next day. Sugita, who had learned from the people Vargas had contacted that he was looking for her, telephoned the detective on September 6 at his office. She would only tell Vargas that she'd been involved in an accident and that she needed to consult an attorney.

On September 8, acting on a tip, Vargas—along with three other detectives and two patrol officers—converged on an apartment complex in Universal City near the Hollywood Freeway. The landlady showed them to the unit Janice had rented. Her red Jaguar was parked outside.

Repeated knocks on the door, which was locked from the inside, went unanswered. When the officers forced the chain lock open, they expected to find their suspect barricaded in the apartment or possibly dead. Instead, she was gone, having apparently departed via a window. Vargas impounded the Jaguar and kept on searching for Sugita.

"We just couldn't find her," he says.

Weeks passed, until finally an attorney representing Janice Sugita telephoned and arranged to surrender her client at nine o'clock on the morning of September 24, nearly four weeks after the shooting. Alex Vargas was there to meet them. He found Sugita polite and cooperative but unwilling to discuss any matter of substance. After he read Janice her Miranda rights, she refused to waive them and was taken straight to a cell.

The detective was disappointed.

"That would have been an interesting interview," he said.

WE WENT TO trial in April of 2003 in front of Judge Michael R. Hoff in Van Nuys. Janice Sugita waived a jury trial.

She'd been in jail for more than six months, but incarceration had hardly dimmed the grandiosity that is commonly seen among stalkers. Every day, when Janice was brought into court from the lockup, looking tiny in her jail uniform, she'd calmly survey the courtroom to see who was there. Her demeanor was both arrogant and defiant. She seemed smugly confidant that with her superior intelligence she would beat the charges against her.

She kept very busy at the defense table, taking more notes than even her lawyer, Gerard L. Garcia-Brown. She also kept engaging him in conversation, which seemed to annoy Garcia-Brown as he tried to keep focused on the witnesses and their testimony. Sugita's obvious message to the court was that she was in charge.

She contended when she took the stand that the shooting was an accident. According to Sugita, she had suffered periodic episodes of deep depression in the summer of 2002. Diana Martin, concerned that she might use the gun to kill herself, had asked Janice to give the firearm to her for safe-keeping. As Diana testified, they did meet on Whipple Street on the night of August 30, 2002. But Janice's sole intent had been to hand over the weapon, she said, as well as give Diana a few birthday presents. They also had planned for her to ride for a while that night with Martin as she made her delivery rounds.

Their affair, Sugita testified, had been Diana's doing. Martin was tired of Mimi Watson. "She told me that she had been unhappy for years," Janice said. "That it just wasn't working out, and they separated."

Diana had initiated their relationship and had pursued her, ardently, not the other way around. If there was a victim in this affair, it was she, not Martin. Janice seemed intent on playing to Judge Hoff's sympathies. If she had been a better liar with a better memory, she might have gotten away with it. I could not wait to cross-examine her.

The courtroom was surprisingly full for a bench trial. A group of Diana and Mimi's friends—none of whom were potential witnesses—sat in the courtroom throughout the trial. All were familiar with Janice. During breaks we'd chat, and they often offered me very useful tidbits of information to help guide me.

For example, Sugita testified under direct examination that she'd purchased her handgun one day in January of 1995, after visiting her grandmother's grave in East Los Angeles. Afterward, she said, she happened on a yard sale where, quite by chance, she saw the handgun and bought it—for self-protection—for seventy dollars.

I think she threw in the cemetery story for the judge's benefit. Trouble was, it never happened. Diana and Mimi's friends told me that Janice's grandmother was still alive in 1995. When she did die, later, she was cremated and her ashes were sent to Hawaii.

I began my questioning at a little past eleven in the morning. I first wanted her to repeat the lie.

"You said that you had purchased your gun in 1995, is that correct?" I asked.

"That's correct," she replied.

And where did she buy it?

"I had swung by a florist to visit my grandmother's grave," Sugita said. "So it's in the East Los Angeles area."

At a little past two, just as I was concluding my cross-examination, I sprung my little trap.

"Now you previously had mentioned something about your grandmother," I said. "Isn't it a fact that she died in 1998?"

"She had passed away, yes," Sugita answered.

"In 1998?"

"Yes."

"And her body was shipped back to Hawaii, correct?"

"Her ashes."

I stole a look at Judge Hoff. He got it.

BECAUSE OF A defense motion, all witnesses and potential witnesses were excluded from the courtroom, which meant that Diana Martin, Mimi Watson, and Lou Marsalis had to wait outside. What was more, I was barred from discussing with them the testimony of other witnesses or the defendant. It was frustrating for all three, particularly Lou.

The whole intent of my cross-examination was to dismantle Sugita's preposterous contentions, point by point. According to her, Diana's decision to go back to Mimi in 1998 was simple, self-serving pragmatism: She wanted to live in the house again. Janice also testified that Diana assured her there was no physical relationship with Mimi, and that she believed her. In fact, she said, Diana continued to pursue her romantically right up to the time of the shooting.

Under my cross, she admitted knowing that Martin and Watson shared the same bedroom in the house, and that they'd shared a room on each of the two trips they'd taken together with her to Las Vegas.

"So," I asked, "it was very difficult not to realize that they had more than a platonic relationship, isn't that correct?"

"Not fully," Sugita replied. "I mean, they had a very long-term relationship. I understood that. There's a certain familiarity and comfort zone you have in that. You can be very good friends. I've known people to do that. They have very good relationships. They are very close. You want to assume that they're having an intimate relationship, which they are not."

"But you believed that they were from what you observed?" I asked. "You saw them being affectionate together, putting their arms around each other when you'd go to Vegas, when you'd go play golf. You saw signs of affection?"

"More of a friendly affection. It wasn't like they were all very demonstrative publicly at all."

Incredulity somehow slipped into my voice.

"You are a very intelligent woman," I said. "You didn't *really* believe that there was no sexual contact between Mimi and Diana after she went back to Mimi, did you?"

"Well, I believed Diana's words," she answered.

My next topic was a love note Janice paid to have appear in *Lesbian News*, a local monthly, in the summer of 2002. "My desert rose," it read, "you are the greatest of all my desires. Most beautiful I have beheld, the gift of treasured memories and the pride and joy within my heart. Thank you for my once in a lifetime. Peace be with our souls."

Added to the bottom was a brief line—"Love always be with you"—written in Croatian.

I asked Sugita why. She explained that Diana's mother was part Croatian. She also said she'd placed the ad at about the time of her meeting with Martin at the Beverly Garland Hotel.

Again, I waited to the end of my cross-examination to complete the thought.

"Diana never put any ads in the *Lesbian News* for you, did she?"

"No."

On to the tattoo.

"When did you first put your tattoo on your body?"

"August 31, 1997," she said.

"And when you first had the tattoo put there, what was on the tattoo?"

"Initially it was just her name and a rose, the beginning of a rose."

"And where did you have the tattoo placed?"

"It's like the right hip area above the pelvic bone."

"In the front?"

"Yes."

I then led Janice through the several additions she'd made to the Diana tattoo; two camels (one with a rider) and a Saharan sandscape executed to resemble a female figure. She denied that Diana had ever asked her to remove the tattoo, but also conceded that Martin had never been tattooed *for her*.

Then we turned to the night of the shooting. Sugita testified that she had seen Diana regularly since May of 2002—"Quite a number of times, actually"—and that on the night of the thirtieth she brought with her five boxes for Martin, four presents and a fifth box that contained her gun.

"So you waited three months until August 30 to give her her present?" I asked.

Janice answered that the packages contained multiple gifts she'd acquired for Diana both before and after her birthday. She also claimed that Martin gave her a love letter that night, which she still had but had not yet produced because, "I hadn't thought about it. I was thinking this case primarily surrounded the incident." The alleged letter never did surface.

After Sugita described how her gun, in a closed box, somehow spontaneously discharged with what she called a "bomp!" sound, driving a bullet into Diana's upper chest, I asked her what had happened next.

"I had to place the box down to investigate."

"And where did you put the box down?"

"I had put it on the floor—the floor of the vehicle, that's right—that's the easiest accessible location at that point."

I pounced once again. "Now isn't it a fact that when you spoke with Lou Marsalis, you had told him you had thrown the gun?"

"No," she replied. "I believe he said, 'What happened?' And I said it was in a container. He asked me, 'How did it happen?' I says, 'I don't know how it happened. It was in a container. It was in a box, in a carton.'

"He says, 'Well, where is it?'

"And I believe he took it that I had thrown it down on the floor to investigate what had happened, not in the context of thrown in the air."

This was preposterous.

"You heard Lou Marsalis's testimony," I said. "He said you specifically told him when he said, 'What did you do with the gun?' you told him, 'I threw it.'"

"I believe," Janice said, "he might have misunderstood what I had said."

"And Lou is a very good friend of yours, correct?"

"Well, he's a good friend. Yes."

Sugita denied that she and Martin had struggled that night.

"How long did Diana stay at the location before she drove off?" I asked.

"Quite some time, actually," she replied, and said that Martin had helped her remove the gift packages from the back of the Windstar. She also remembered insisting on taking Diana to the hospital, "because I was so concerned about her condition."

"So Diana was bleeding," I said. "You saw the blood at the time? That is correct?"

"Yes, that's correct."

"And you were concerned about her getting to the hospital. Is that correct?"

"That is correct."

"And yet you stood there and let her unload the boxes from the car?"

"Actually," Sugita said, "not to my consent. I initially said, 'Who cares? Let's go!' She originally consented and then changed her mind immediately and said, 'No. No, you are not supposed to be here. I don't want anyone to know that you were here.'"

According to Janice, she didn't argue or protest when Diana insisted that the boxes had to be moved back to her car, as well. Sugita said she tried to do it alone, but needed Martin's help to open the Windstar's rear door.

I pointed out to her that when Lou Marsalis asked if she'd been in touch with Diana since the shooting, "You noted that you hadn't because you didn't know what story she would tell. Is that correct?"

"I was under that impression at the time, yes," she replied.

"That was after Diana took the boxes out of the car to help

you, didn't want anyone to know, and that was how she left you. Is that correct?"

"Yes."

Then I addressed a final inconsistency in her testimony.

"You said you didn't know if she was going on vacation with Mimi. Is that correct? You testified to that yesterday."

"I didn't say I didn't know. We didn't discuss it. I had not asked her."

"And didn't you also testify after that yesterday that the reason you didn't call Diana at home was that you knew she was on vacation with Mimi?"

The question flustered Janice. "She addressed the issue of concern," she answered nonsensically. "At that point in time, I guess she had mentioned or had worked out with Mimi that she would not be—or she had not been calling me or she had not been speaking with me."

I asked Judge Hoff to strike this answer as not responsive. He did.

"If you could answer the question?" I asked. "You testified that you did not know if she was going on vacation with Mimi, correct?"

"Correct. I had not asked her."

"And then you testified a little while after that that the reason you didn't call Diana was that you *knew* that she was on vacation with Mimi."

"No," Sugita said. "I said I believe that I knew she would be at home. As far as going on vacation with—that to me pertains more to going on a vacation like a getaway. That's the context that I take that as."

JANICE'S FORGETFULNESS MADE it easy for me. By the time we were finished that afternoon, Judge Hoff seemed totally disgusted with the defendant. He found her guilty on all counts, and sentenced Sugita to twenty years in prison. Under the terms of the sentence, she must serve at least 85 percent of her term, which means she'll remain in prison at least until the year 2020, when she'll be sixty years of age.

Her victims feel neither forgiveness nor forgetfulness

toward Janice Sugita. "I hate her because she made a fool out of me and Diana," says Mimi Watson.

Whenever I see them, Diana always asks me to double-check that Sugita is still behind bars, testimony to the permanent scars that all stalkers leave on their victims. "I'll always remember this would-be murderess I brought into my life," she says with bitterness.

TWELVE

ALTHOUGH I CONTINUED to prosecute stalkers well into the new millennium—among them Marlon Pagtakhan, Richard Poynton, Dante Soiu, and Janice Sugita—I found myself increasingly in demand both outside the courtroom and outside Los Angeles. In the decade or so since we first rewrote the California stalking law, dozens of other states, as well as several foreign countries, had updated their own statutes and had of course come to me for consultation.

We also faced new issues in California. In 2002, I needed to make another change to the stalking law. The original 1991 stalking law required both that the victim suffer substantial emotional distress as a result of the stalker's conduct and that she or he be placed in fear by the conduct. When I rewrote the law in 1994, I did not change the language regarding "substantial emotional distress." In 1999, this omission came back to haunt us with a newly published case, *In Re Ewing. Ewing* held that, "Severe emotional distress means highly unpleasant mental suffering or anguish from socially unacceptable conduct, which entails such intense, enduring, and nontrivial emotional distress that no reasonable person in a civilized society should be expected to endure it." Defense attorneys had a field day with this language. In the past, we had been able to demonstrate that a victim had suffered "substantial emotional distress" and "was placed in fear," as the law put it, by looking at the victim's actions and from her or his testimony on the stand. *In Re Ewing* raised the bar considerably. I began receiving dozens of phone calls from prosecutors within my office and all over the state of California, asking for my help in overcoming the *Ewing* issue.

Under *Ewing*, the victim had to practically seek psychiatric care to pass the Court of Appeals test. Since a lot of people who are being stalked do not have the money or inclination to see a psychiatrist, this had become a real problem for us.

I researched the law and determined there was no need to keep the words "substantial emotional distress" in the stalking statute. It was redundant because the statute already called for the victim to be in reasonable fear. Now the question was how to get rid of the troublesome language.

The answer was to enlist State Senator Sheila Kuehl from Santa Monica, a strong feminist (and, incidentally, a onetime child star, best known for her TV portrayal of Zelda Gilroy on the old series *The Many Loves of Dobie Gillis*). Kuehl had contacted me on an unrelated issue, and I used the opportunity to propose that she sponsor a bill that would excise the "substantial emotional distress" clause altogether, thereby neutralizing the court's opinion in *Ewing*. She agreed that the language had to be eliminated, and brought a bill to the legislature eliminating the troublesome words. The bill sailed through both houses of the legislature. Once again, success in Sacramento.

I FOUND THAT official disbelief and denial still complicated the job of enacting intelligent stalking legislation in other countries, just as it had in California in 1993. Law enforcement activists had been unsuccessful in trying to pass a stalking law in Great Britain. As a pair of visiting English detectives explained the situation to me, the House of Commons had listened to law enforcement and voted for a stalking law. But the House of Lords, apparently loath to concede that England was afflicted with stalkers just like everywhere else, had balked. Not until 1997 did Parliament finally pass its first stalking law.

The Germans took even longer. Although by 2004 countries as various as Switzerland, Great Britain, and Japan had firmly established criminal penalties for stalking, Germany had only a civil law. If a person in Germany was under threat or being stalked, his or her only remedy was to hire a lawyer to file a civil action against the offender. If the verdict was guilty, the penalty was a fine (which was paid to the court, not the victim). If the defendant reoffended, the victim's only recourse was again to hire a lawyer and sue once more. If found guilty a second time, the defendant merely paid a larger fine.

Two of the leaders in the movement to criminalize stalking in Germany were Stephan Rusch, the police chief of Bremen, and a young civil lawyer named Volkmar von Pechstaedt. Volkmar had read of my efforts to change the California stalking laws, and was instrumental in bringing me to the town of Kassel in November of 2005 to participate in Germany's very first symposium on stalking. Attendees included police officials from around the country, representatives from victims' rights groups, lawyers, and officials from Chancellor Gerhard Schroeder's coalition government, plus members of the competing coalition, led by Angela Merkel, which would take over in December of 2005, when Merkel became Germany's first female chancellor.

Following my speech at the symposium, which was assembled in the Kassel town hall, Schroeder's Minister of Justice rose to denounce the idea of criminalizing stalking. He said Germany already had too many criminal laws. With that, Chief Rausch grabbed an audience microphone and started a shouting match with the minister. It felt like my first trip to Sacramento all over again.

In the end, someone from Merkel's camp took the podium to assure everyone that Germany would criminalize stalking under the new government. A strong criminal stalking law was finally passed in March of 2007.

* * *

POLITICIANS ARE HARDLY the only people who need help in grasping the dynamics of stalking and its prevention. In the summer of 2006, I participated in a committee of lawyers, prosecutors, and victim advocates brought together by the American Bar Association (ABA) to promulgate practice standards for lawyers assisting victims in protection-order cases. While this may sound like a very narrow slice of law, we addressed issues of key importance.

One was attorney preparedness.

It is not unusual for a well-meaning lawyer to volunteer legal assistance to victims of stalking or domestic violence. However, such an attorney—whose main practice might be corporate law or civil litigation or even admiralty law—needs to be careful not to exacerbate a client's problems out of ignorance.

Take restraining orders. The pro bono lawyer might not have the time to adequately explore details of the case at hand. Without that full knowledge, he or she can be taken off guard in court by a savvy opponent who opposes the order on the argument that the victim is lying or exaggerating. If the offender prevails, it only adds to the stalker's sense of power and entitlement.

Or the victim's lawyer might agree to the issuance of a mutual restraining order, thinking that at least the victim is afforded legal protection. Who cares if the offender receives equal protection? Well, the stalker does, keenly. In his mind, the issuance of an undeserved mutual restraining order is a victory, a vindication of his behavior and encouragement to persist in his stalking.

The committee ranged over a number of other topics, too, such as understanding the role of culture in these cases, or language, immigration status, age, personal background—even a victim's possible physical or other disabilities. The standards we proposed to ensure that stalking victims receive the most effective counsel possible were adopted by the ABA in August of 2007.

I BEGAN TO accept more and more personal speaking invitations. I delivered my anti-stalking lecture in every state except

Hawaii, and frequently appear on television as an expert commentator, especially when a celebrity or otherwise notable case occurs.

I worked hard to network my knowledge and experience within the worldwide law enforcement community. From 1997 to 2004, for example, I was honored to work with the U.S. Secret Service training program that educates senior law enforcement officials from all over the country and Canada as to the complexities of threat and stalking investigations.

Close coordination with police and security services of all types characterized my stalking prosecutions from the day that Doug Raymond first brought the Susan Dyer case to my attention in early 1992. That same year I was among the first presenters at the opening conference of the Association of Threat Assessment Professionals (ATAP), an organization started by LAPD's newly established Threat Management Unit.

ATAP brings together detectives, lawyers, psychiatrists, and anyone else in law enforcement or the private sector with a professional interest in the developing field of threats and stalking, with an emphasis on networking and education. There are now more than eight hundred members nationwide. Between 1999 and 2004, I was president of ATAP's Los Angeles chapter.

I also joined the American Society for Industrial Security (ASIS), a huge organization with many thousands of members focused on violence and terrorism in the workplace. I addressed its 1999 international convention in Las Vegas, which drew an attendance of 17,000.

Shortly thereafter I created the Los Angeles Stalking Task Force, a group of local, state, and federal prosecutors; law enforcement officers; and probation and parole agents—no private security people because of confidentiality issues— who met every month or so to discuss developments in stalking laws and cases we were working, as well as to analyze new cases. It was gratifying to see so many disparate agencies working together for a common purpose.

ON THE PERSONAL front, my oldest son, Doug, currently holds a very senior job with major responsibilities at New York's

Metropolitan Transit Authority. He is also married now, and has made me a grandmother twice over. We are both at peace. Doug realizes how much I've always loved him, and I'm eternally gratefully for the chance to finally show my son that love. My second son, Sean, has graduated law school, passing the California bar exam on the first try, and is working for a very prestigious Los Angeles law firm. He is the perfect lawyer—brilliant and compassionate. Shannon, my baby girl, is completing her college degree, majoring in both film studies and political science, so she may be following in either my artistic or my legal footsteps. These three young adults are my proudest accomplishments and my true legacy.

FOR ALL THE progress I can report since my very first stalking case in 1992, there has also been one unfortunate constant in my life: Susan Dyer.

After she slipped off her ankle bracelet and popped up in Santa Monica during the Spielberg trial in 1998, she was returned to custody for a year. But just because Susan was locked up did not mean that she would give up. She continued to write angry letters to me, to the district attorney's office, to members of the SWAT team who arrested her, and even to Jane Smith's mother, accusing us all of railroading her.

In September of 1999, as her second release date neared, I received a second Tarasoff letter. A staff psychologist at the Central California Women's Facility in Chowchilla warned me that Dyer "has communicated to me by her behavior, manner, and psychological state that she could be a serious threat of violence against you." The letter continued: "The inmate communicated this threat against you in interviews held in early August. When directly questioned about violent behavior, inmate Dyer denies any such intention, but it is my professional opinion it is highly likely that she will act out violently."

Instead of releasing her that time, the Department of Corrections placed Susan in a locked-down mental facility. She demanded a jury trial on her commitment. Two years later, in 2001, a jury somehow determined that she was no longer a danger, and she was released back into the community.

Dyer continued to allege perjury by Jane Smith and others at her 1992 trial. "My life has been completely destroyed by this dishonest and cruel ex-girlfriend and corrupt police involved in the case," she wrote my office in December of 2001. "I want this resolved and a financial settlement to compensate for the nine long, painful years that I was falsely imprisoned. I want to get on with my life and I want the individuals punished for the perjury that they committed to bring about my intentional wrongful conviction."

Susan returned to some of her old habits, as well.

In 2002, the LA County Sheriff's Department was called in to investigate a series of bizarre phone calls that had been left on the answering machine of a Santa Monica advertising firm. Dozens of messages, often rambling and filled with obscenities, appeared on the message machine every night. The caller, who identified herself as "Susan," evidently mistook the ad agency's number for Jane's work phone.

At the same time, Jane's mother was in a state of terror because Susan had been sneaking up to her porch in the middle of the night and taping harassing letters to the front door.

Los Angeles Sheriff's Department investigator Rick Pfaff and his partner, Rod Wagner, of the sheriff's Major Crimes Division were assigned to this new case. I had worked with both men for many years, and they were well-schooled on Susan and her long story.

Rick, a veteran of at least seventy-five high-profile stalking cases, typically tried to establish a relationship with stalking suspects, the better to understand their motives and intentions. In the Dyer case, he contacted her at the number recorded on the ad agency's machine. Rick said that he was working for Judge Smith—who'd also received a considerable amount of mail from Susan—and that he wanted to meet with her in order to sort out her many allegations for the judge.

Aware of her history with weapons, Pfaff suggested they meet in the downstairs cafeteria of the criminal courts building, where Dyer would have to pass through a metal detector. They spoke together in the cafeteria for perhaps forty-five minutes, during which time Rick remembers Susan going through several distinct mood swings. *We have a serious problem here,* he thought as they talked, *and it was not solved in prison.*

Dyer eventually caught on that the sheriff's investigator was more interested in finding out about her than about her complaints, and so she bolted. An eight-person surveillance team trailed her to Santa Monica, where she disappeared into the campus of Santa Monica City College. They later determined that she was then living in a homeless shelter.

On a subsequent visit to Jane Smith's mother—whom Dyer continued to harass—Pfaff and Wagner noticed Susan drive by the house in a distinctive, burnt-orange Mercedes. They gave chase in their police car, but Dyer lost them.

She went below the radar until 2004, then reemerged on my website, www.stalkingalert.com, posting messages to me under "H8crimevictim" and "perjuryisfelony." "Jane is a pathological liar," Susan wrote me on October 20. "I was seduced by Jane Smith and she told the stalker stories so no one would find out about our relationship."

Further down the long note, Dyer added, "I have a box full of evidence that the pathetic public defender never collected for a case she never planned on defending in the first place. It's time you take responsibility for the crimes your witnesses committed against me."

In a November 28 posting, Susan denied that she ever lived beneath Jane's house, and claimed her work records proved it. "I guess," she wrote, "you didn't learn 'Investigations 101' at USC." The mention of my alma mater wasn't lost on me. Susan, a diligent stalker, was letting me know that she did her homework.

On December 3 she complained in capital letters of both abuse and bias. "I COULDN'T TESTIFY AFTER 6 MONTHS OF TORTURE AND I AM A SHY PERSON ANYWAY. I WAS DEPRIVED OF MY RIGHT TO REASONABLE BAIL, RIGHT TO A SPEEDY TRIAL, AND YOU GOT THE COOPERATION OF PUBLIC PRETENDER DEFENDERS OFFICE IN VIOLATING MY RIGHTS. I WAS DEPRIVED OF CLEAN WATER, EDIBLE FOOD, WARM CLOTHING, SLEEP, MEDICAL ATTENTION, SHOWERS, PHONE

CALLS, ETC. THEN YOU BRING ME OUT IN AN IN-
COMPETENT CONDITION WITH MY FACIAL HAIR
UNBLEACHED AND UNTRIMMED AND THEN HO-
MOPHOBIC LIE AFTER LIE TO A JURY OF STRAIGHT
PEOPLE."

December 8: "I know you monitor the computers I use
and all your little talks about stalking that appear in the local
papers, etc. Let's go on any show you desire and talk about
the relationship and the case. This case was a big secret at the
trial because the police and Jane didn't want their perjury per-
formances publicized."

Shortly thereafter, Dyer dropped out of sight again, although
I kept receiving letters, e-mails, and the occasional obscenity-
laced telephone call from her. I was, in short, being stalked.
Worried that the stream of invective might presage a serious
attempt at actual harm, I turned to our bureau of investigation.

One of our investigators tracked Susan to Alaska, where
she had registered for a driver's license, and then on to Madi-
son, Wisconsin, where she was working for a railroad company. The investigator also came to my house and suggested
certain security measures, which I immediately had installed.
The angry e-mails and phone calls never let up.

In June of 2005, my office received an e-mail from a
woman who'd served time with Dyer in California. Her purpose in writing was to warn us that Susan might soon be on
her way back to Los Angeles, intent on doing me harm.

"I'm writing because she is CRAZY," the woman informed
us. "Susan and I are friends, or we were—I do not think I
can continue contact with her because her obsession with Ms.
Saunders and her victim is frightening. I know she is still trying to pursue a legal remedy to what she considers the injus-
tice she suffered, but when this continually fails I'm afraid
she will completely snap and return to CA to pursue another
form of 'justice.'

"Susan is a good person who is very sick. She needs hospitalization and medicine. If she could be medicated it is possible she could clear her mind for long enough to get beyond
the past, take responsibility, and move forward. I am writing
to let you know this because I hope you can help her if and

when she returns to LA County. I care about Susan, but I don't want her to hurt anyone, including herself."

Dyer's friend was not exaggerating Susan's mental condition. On Monday, September 19, 2005, I learned that Dyer was in custody in Wisconsin. She had been seen lying in a ditch, and the local police were summoned. When they responded, Susan jumped up and ran to her car, screaming that people were out to kill her. A high-speed car chase ensued. When officers finally cornered her, Dyer threw a blanket over her head and body. As they approached her on foot, she pretended to have a gun under the blanket, evidently hoping the police would shoot her, committing suicide by cop.

She was placed in a locked-down mental facility for three weeks, then released. A short while later, she started sending me e-mails that we traced to a computer located in Santa Monica. My investigator determined that Susan was now back in town, living out of her car, less than fifteen miles from my workplace.

The following July, I was on a Mediterranean cruise with my family when I received an e-mail from my assistant, Marie Johnson. "Susan's been shot by the police in Palmdale," it read.

"Is she dead?" I immediately e-mailed in reply.

"Unfortunately, no," Marie answered.

As soon as we reached port, I called Marie. She told me that a local newspaper reported that Dyer had stolen two guns from her brother's house in Santa Monica and gone to Palmdale city hall, where she began threatening several city employees with the guns.

When the police arrived, Susan turned the guns on one of them and was about to fire when the officer, for his own safety, shot her two or three times. She fell to her knees. As the officer and his partner approached, she jumped to her feet and leveled her guns again at them. The second officer emptied his shotgun at her.

Somehow Dyer survived the shootout, and was returned once again to the psychiatric hospital. This time, upon her release from the hospital, she was immediately taken into custody by the police. Five felony charges, including two strikes, were filed against her.

Susan faces prosecution that will nearly certainly send her to prison into her late old age, with no chance of parole. Although twenty-five years as a prosecutor have taught me never to say never, it appears at last that this long, painful, and frightening saga is at an end.

COMBATING STALKERS: A PUBLIC POLICY BLUEPRINT

ACROSS A QUARTER century of prosecuting criminals, I've had an inside view of how the system works (and doesn't work), particularly when it comes to stalking cases. Based on that experience, here's my agenda for building on the great progress we've made in bringing stalkers to justice.

Laws

Although all states and the District of Columbia now have stalking laws on their books, there's widespread room for improvement. In some states, for example, stalking remains a misdemeanor unless a restraining order is violated, a weapon is used, or the stalker inflicts great bodily injury on the victim. If that were true in California, most of the offenders in this book would have spent little or no time behind bars for their crimes.

Sentencing is also an area of concern. In California, I lobbied successfully to have the maximum sentence for stalking increased from three to five years, but in my opinion that is still not long enough.

I discovered in Sacramento that the major resistance to lengthening prison terms for stalkers was centered in the appropriations or finance committees, where I was told that the added costs of prison construction and additional personnel necessary to administer longer sentences were viewed as prohibitively high.

The issue as I see it is money versus lives, and the money argument unfortunately seems to be winning. Obviously, the way to turn this reasoning around is for law enforcement, victim advocacy groups, and anyone else interested in safer communities to make their feelings known, especially in election years.

Training and Education

I recently conferred with a small-town Colorado police investigator on a cyber-stalking case. He told me he was looking forward to closing the matter so he could dump all the specialized material he'd gathered, "because we'll never have another one of these to handle again."

Unfortunately, this sort of misunderstanding about stalking and stalkers continues to circulate in law enforcement agencies and in the judicial system. The frequency, nature, hallmarks, and dynamics of the crime need to be taught at every police academy, judges' college, and prosecutors' training program. The best stalking laws in the world are of little use unless those in the justice system have a command of the issues.

The Media

I have a love-hate relationship with the news and entertainment media. Cameras in the courtroom, for example, are a bad idea. They add a counterproductive element to the difficult task of putting on a fair trial. In the case of celebrity stalkers, the added attention often plays to the defendant's narcissistic need for notoriety. Robert Hoskins, for example, was arraigned on TV over my objections. When he returned to jail that night, his fellow inmates greeted him with cheers as "The Material Man," which became his nickname of pride among them.

Yet the press can also be a powerful tool for educating the public about stalking, and what individuals can do to protect themselves. My television appearances always generate lots of calls and e-mails from both victims and law enforcement officials requesting information and advice. I find that many victims lack even a basic understanding of their options, and are often tearfully grateful to learn that there are ways of fighting back.

It would be great if TV would spread this useful news on its own, perhaps through public service ads. Not many people know that Congress has made January "Stalking Awareness Month," in part because the press does very little to explore stalking as a topic of national concern.

On the entertainment side, we need to stop glorifying stalkers as was done in pictures such as *The Graduate* and *The Cable Guy*. In each film, the hero—a stalker—ignores a victim's repeated demands to be left alone, and in the end triumphs due to persistence and an unwillingness to take "no" for an answer.

While such a theme may seem harmless, it's the wrong message to send those people who need to understand that there are boundaries that they should not cross, and better not cross, lest they create serious trouble for everyone, including themselves.

Finally, I propose that we rein in the paparazzi, or "stalkerazzi," as I call them. Although the vast majority of us will never have a problem with hordes of cameramen stalking us, trying to take our photos, this behavior does present a serious and spreading threat beyond the harassment of celebrity victims.

Probably the best-known example was the 1997 death of England's Princess Diana in a Paris car crash as she was being chased by paparazzi. As these photographers have grown even bolder, they present a danger to everyone around them.

They are particularly reckless behind the wheel. One increasingly common tactic is to actually ram a target's car in the hopes of cornering the celebrity victim and capturing a valuable photo of the star or celebrity expressing anger or fear.

This sort of behavior goes well beyond anything protected by the First Amendment.

Right now in California, a paparazzo pays only a civil penalty of up to fifty thousand dollars if convicted of harassing a victim. That is no deterrent when the right photo will fetch five times that much.

There are plenty of photographers willing to risk their own and other people's safety for such a reward. I think it is inevitable that a carload of paparazzi in chase of some victim will one day miss a turn, or jump a curb, and kill or injure innocent people, all for a picture.

So, since 2005, I have proposed that this behavior be considered criminal conduct, not merely a civil offense. First offenders, if convicted, would face a year in jail. Upon completing their sentence, a restraining order would be issued, as California prosecutors now can for stalkers under my law. If the stalkerazzo reoffends, I propose the sentence be increased to two to five years in state prison.

With such a law in place, I think we'd find our streets and other public places suddenly much safer.

Victims

Many changes are still needed to improve victims' support and protection, and these improvements will require adequate funding. Although celebrities, a small minority of those who are stalked, can often afford the necessary measures to make themselves and their families safer, ordinary citizens, who make up the great bulk of the victims, do not usually have the resources.

Often something as simple as a cell phone, on which to dial 911 when a stalker menaces, is beyond a victim's financial reach. A basic home security system, costing several hundred dollars, is even less of a possibility for many of them.

They need psychological counseling, too, as do members of their families, to help them cope with the trauma of victimization. Support groups for stalking victims are very helpful but also quite rare. Relocation funding is difficult to secure.

Peaches Thompson was a vivid example of this. California does maintain a fund for helping victims of crime such

as Peaches, but the money's usually spent by the middle of
each budget year. It required months of telephoning and filing
paperwork to numerous agencies before I found the money
to move Peaches and her kids so they'd be safe from Shujaa
Silver.

The Criminal Justice System

I strongly believe that all law enforcement jurisdictions should
establish a threat management unit such as the groundbreak-
ing one set up by the LAPD in the early 1990s. Counties and
cities should create some form of a specialized stalking unit
such as STAT in their prosecutor's office.

Whatever way the team is assembled, the key organizational component must be vertical prosecution, in which a
single prosecutor stays with the case from the very beginning
to the very end.

In most offices, two, three, or more prosecutors may enter
and leave a criminal case before it is decided. Such a system
may be adequate for some types of crimes, but not for stalking, where a command of the entire case, not just parts of it,
is vital. For one thing, stalking typically entails multiple incidents occurring over time and in various settings, and involves
numerous witnesses and pieces of evidence. Pulling together
a stalking prosecution requires command of much detail. It's
like assembling a puzzle. One missing piece can cost you the
case.

There is also the victim to consider. He or she should not
have to relive the details of the case over and over as each new
prosecutor enters the picture. Furthermore, stalking cases
rarely end for good with a conviction and incarceration of the
offender. As we've seen, stalkers often continue their harassment even from prison. Victims know this, and look to prosecutors not to desert them at the end of the trial. A prosecutor
who is familiar with the case needs to follow up and make
sure that the reoffending stalker suffers the consequences.

In one of my cases, the defendant was convicted of solicit-
ing the murder of his wife. He and his girlfriend had stalked
the victim for months before he made his final move. Fortunately, his wife survived. She was thrilled when I convinced

the jury and judge to send her husband to prison for nine years.

I kept in contact with the victim because we both knew that he would eventually be released and would seek revenge. When that time arrived, I checked to make sure that he was placed on high-risk parole, with a condition of parole that he not go within five hundred yards of his ex-wife's home or business. He also was supposed to be paroled more than thirty-five miles away from his wife's last-known address.

But there was a glitch. He was assigned instead to a parole office located in the town next to the one where his wife lived. This parole officer had obviously not read his file. Then we found out that the defendant had gotten a job located five minutes away from his ex-wife's house. The parole officer did not return any of our calls.

So I called a friend of mine, a highly placed parole administrator in Sacramento. Within a week, the parole officer was replaced, and the defendant was told to quit his job and move to the town of Antelope Valley, well beyond the thirty-five-mile limit. While we will never know for sure, both I and the victim believe this intervention likely saved her life.

WHAT YOU SHOULD KNOW ABOUT STALKING

What Is Stalking?

"Stalking" is a legal term that is defined by statute.* All fifty states, the District of Columbia, and the federal government have some form of stalking law, some better than others. In fifteen states, including California, conviction of a first offense of stalking can be prosecuted as a felony. The rest of the states require a second conviction of stalking or aggravating circumstances, such as use of a weapon, violation of a protective order, or the age of the victim, before felony stalking can be charged.

Over one million women and close to four hundred thousand men are stalked annually in the United States. One in twelve women and one in forty-five men will be stalked in their lifetimes.† Although the media in the United States focus primarily on high-profile, celebrity-stalking cases, such as those

---

*Please check your state's penal code to determine the elements required in your jurisdiction. Go to: www.ncvc.org/src/main.aspx?db10=dash home

†Tjaden and Theonnes, "Stalking in America."

involving Madonna or Steven Spielberg, statistics show that the majority of stalking cases involve domestic violence.*

Generally, a prosecutor must prove three elements to establish the crime of stalking:

1. Repeated unwanted conduct

Most states require only two or more acts of following or harassment. For example, in California an ex-husband called his wife and discovered that she had a male guest visiting. He started to scream and yell obscenities at her over the phone. She slammed the phone down. Twenty minutes later, the ex-husband showed up outside the house, banging and kicking at the front door. When his ex-wife refused to open the door (I wonder why), he walked to the side of the house and tried to climb a trellis to the second-story balcony. He failed to reach the second level, but continued yelling threats and curses. Within fifteen minutes, he was back in front of the door, threatening to kill his ex-wife, and was still there a half hour later when the police arrived and arrested him for stalking. The entire incident occurred over less than four hours, on the same day. The Court of Appeal upheld his conviction of stalking, stating that the initial phone call, banging on the door, trying to gain access to the second story of the house, and his return to the front of the house each constituted separate acts for purposes of proving two or more acts of harassment. The courts have rejected stalking charges when the conduct consists of someone following a person down a freeway on only one occasion or making a single phone call.

2. A credible threat of violence or injury

The threat can be direct or indirect. For example, a direct threat would be, "I'm coming to kill you." An indirect threat can be conveyed to a victim through the stalker's conduct, such as leaving a love note on the victim's car—with a .38-caliber bullet as a paperweight. When William Cloward left a bullet on his ex-wife's car after he vandalized it, he was sending her a message that it was not only her car that was in jeopardy.

---

*Tjaden and Theonnes, "Extent, Nature, and Consequences of Intimate Partner Violence."

In domestic violence cases, the threat could be a word or phrase used by an ex-husband or boyfriend that has a sinister meaning known to only the victim, such as a phone message that states, "I would love to take you on another trip to Las Vegas." On its face, this language appears harmless. But the victim was terrified, because when she had previously gone to Las Vegas with the stalker, he had beaten her so badly that she'd been hospitalized for several days.*

The implied threat can also be sexual, if the stalker sends the victim pornography, explicit sexual messages, sex objects, or graphic e-mails. In several cases, stalking victims have received pornographic pictures on which their stalkers have written, "This is me, and this is you," leaving victims terrified that their stalkers intend to rape them.

In many states the threat can be directed against either the victim or the victim's immediate family. The threat does not have to be made in person, but can be conveyed by mail, telephone (including voice messages), text messages, e-mail, fax, third parties, Internet chat rooms, or sites such as YouTube or MySpace. Generally, threats regarding child custody, civil suits, or release of embarrassing information about the victim do not constitute stalking.†

3. The stalker knew or should have known that the credible threat would place the victim in reasonable fear

The third and final element that prosecutors need to establish is both the stalker's and his intended victim's state of mind. We need to show that the stalker intended to place the victim in fear for her safety or the safety of her family. We also need to show that the victim was actually scared by the stalker's conduct, and that this fear is objectively and subjectively "reasonable."

---

*80 percent of women who are stalked by former husbands are physically assaulted by that partner and 30 percent are sexually assaulted by that partner. Center for Policy Research, *Stalking in America*, July 1997.

†However, depending on the laws of your state, this type of conduct could result in the prosecution of other types of crimes, such as extortion.

The stalker's intent to place the victim in fear can be shown through his conduct, such as continuing the behavior after being informed of the victim's fear via a restraining order; being told by the victim that he or she is afraid and wants the stalking to stop; or receiving a warning from a law enforcement officer, the court, or another third party that the victim is in fear because of the stalker's behavior. Dante Soiu and Marlon Pagtakhan were put on notice by law enforcement that their unwanted conduct was frightening the victims. When they later claimed ignorance of their victims' fear, the previous warnings were used to impeach their testimony.

The victim's conduct toward the stalker can also serve as notice that the victim is afraid. Actions to take include hanging up the phone every time the stalker calls; avoiding all contact with the stalker; screaming or running/driving away from the stalker when encountered; filing complaints against the stalker with law enforcement, supervisors at work, human resource officers, or school authorities; or obtaining a protective order against the stalker.

Not only do prosecutors need to show that the victim is fearful, but we need to prove that the fear is *reasonable*. As a prosecutor, whenever I reviewed the suitability of filing stalking charges, one of my primary considerations was, "Would an ordinary person, listening to the evidence, be thinking, 'If this was happening to me, or a loved one, I'd be afraid'?" In other words, would an average person, neither overly thin- nor thick-skinned, have a rational reason to believe that the stalker was going to harm them or a loved one? This is an objective standard.

We must also establish that the victims themselves are actually in subjective fear of their stalker. It is not enough for victims to merely say, "I am afraid"; they must be willing to explain to a judge and/or jury *why* they are afraid. In other words, what specifically was it about the stalking conduct that made them believe they or their family members were in physical danger?

Establishing the element of fear is not difficult if the correct questions are asked by law enforcement or prosecutors. We do not have to show that a victim sought out mental health services or is currently on medication. We only need to show that the stalker's conduct has severely impacted the victim's life. This can be illustrated by changes in sleep patterns, such as repeated nightmares or inability to fall or stay asleep because of fear that the stalker has broken into the house, or changes in the victim's daily routine, such as not allowing her children to walk to school alone, nervously looking around every time she leaves the house, isolating herself from friends and family, changing her phone number, moving from her residence, leaving her job, or limiting her social activities. Keep in mind that we do not have to show that the stalker has shown up with a knife, gun, or bomb, or even that he possesses a weapon. Stalking is a crime of *mental* terrorism, one that insidiously destroys the victim's world.

Categories of Stalking

Typically, the relationship between stalker and victim can be divided into four categories:

1. Intimate Relationship
The stalker and victim have had an intimate past relationship, such as husband and wife or boyfriend and girlfriend. It encompasses situations in which the victim and the stalker are or were married, dated, lived together, have a child together, or are related. This is the most dangerous form of stalking, statistically leading to the highest incidence of murder, assault, and rape. The stalker is enraged and his ego is bruised because his "property" has left him. The stalker is seeking to reestablish power and control over the victim through the use of fear. This type of stalking is not fueled by "love" but by anger and rejection. Richard Poynton and William Cloward are prime examples of the explosiveness of stalking arising out of intimate relationship violence.

2. Non-intimate Relationships
This category involves stalkers who are known to the victim, but where there has been no prior intimate relationship between the two. The stalker either desires to start a relationship with the victim but is ignored, or has some real or imagined grievance.

This type of stalker can be a casual acquaintance, a neighbor, a person the victim dated briefly or whom the victim turned down for a date, a security guard, a mailman, a store owner, or someone from the gym. This category also includes campus stalking situations, in which the victim is stalked by a fellow student, a professor, someone working on campus, or an outsider coming onto the campus seeking out the victim, as well as workplace stalking, in which a coworker, supervisor, customer, vendor, or repairman abnormally focuses on a person in a business setting.

3. Erotomania

This is a delusional disorder in which the stalker believes either that there is a love relationship between himself and the victim, or that if the victim would only get to know him, that person would fall in love with the stalker. In the majority of these cases, the victim does not know the stalker. This type of stalking is most prevalent in celebrity-stalking cases (i.e., Dante Soiu, Jonathan Norman). Occasionally, as in the Rebecca Schaeffer case, the erotomania can turn deadly if the stalker believes he is being rejected or betrayed. Robert Bardo, Schaeffer's murderer, started out as a fan who felt betrayed when he saw her acting in a movie love scene. He came to Los Angeles for the sole purpose of killing her so that he could "save her innocence." Third parties, such as Gwyneth Paltrow's mother, can also be drawn into the line of fire, when the erotomanic stalker believes that person is an obstacle between him and his desire.

4. False Victimization

This occurs when an alleged victim invents the stalking situation. It occurs in less than 2–3 percent of all stalking cases. The alleged victim may be seeking attention, revenge, or avoidance of a troubling situation. In the mid-nineties, a schoolteacher from New England was stalked, and her stalker went to prison for several years. When he was released, threatening unsigned letters began appearing on her desk inside the classroom. Threats were also spray-painted on the outside of the school and on the teacher's home. Obviously, suspicion fell on the newly released stalker. However, he had a solid alibi that he was hundreds of miles away when these threats were made. The FBI and local police became involved in looking for the suspect. After a thorough investigation, suspicion turned on the teacher. When she was confronted, she broke down crying and admitted that she had written the letters to herself and spray-painted the school and her home. She told the detectives that she was so frightened that the stalker had been released from prison and might start to stalk her again, that she created this scenario hoping that he would be arrested and put back in prison. Generally, these types of cases are easy to spot, as a red flag goes up when there's no corroborating evidence or witnesses to any of the events claimed by the victim. With that said, the majority of stalking cases are very real, despite bizarre scenarios or victims who are so traumatized that they behave in a manner that might appear to others to be inappropriate.

Cooperation with Law Enforcement

It takes teams consisting of law enforcement, prosecutors, and the victims themselves to successfully put together viable stalking cases. The investigation of these types of criminal cases are often work-intensive; the stalking incidents may take place over a period of time ranging from a couple of months to several years, as opposed to a burglary or robbery charge in which the criminal act takes place in a matter of minutes. Each incident needs to be documented. A proper stalking investigation may involve numerous witnesses, locations, and pieces of evidence. Whether it is at home, in the community, at work, or at school, the help of law enforcement is necessary to defeat a stalker. And in order for the police, prosecutors, and courts to best help victims, victims must first help them. They are in the best position to give the police the information they need to put the case together successfully.

What to Do If You Are Being Stalked

1. The moment you believe you are being stalked, immediately notify your local police department. Continue to notify the police after each subsequent occurrence so that you establish a

paper trail if charges are later filed. If the officer at the desk or on the phone refuses to take a report, ask to speak to a supervisor and/or request that he or she at least take a field report. Obtain and write down the name and badge number of the person who is taking the report, the date that the report was made, and any identifying number on the report. When you are interviewed by the police, be as thorough as possible. Don't let them rush you. Make sure they are taking down notes as you give them the information.

2. Explain to the detective when the harassment first started. If you were in a relationship with the stalker, did the stalking behavior begin during the relationship, after it had ended, or both? When and why did you leave the relationship?

3. If the suspect made a threat, what were the *exact* words used? What did those words mean to you? Often the words used by the stalker need to be taken in context of the parties' previous relationship. For example, a stalker might leave a message, "Why don't we take another trip to the mountains." On the surface, these words don't appear threatening, but they would be if the victim associated "the mountains" with a particularly brutal or frightening previous experience. Let the police know why the stalker's words or conduct are so personally frightening to you.

4. Document the "when," "where," and "hows" of the stalking conduct. Keep a log documenting date, time, and place of each occurrence, including phone calls, letters, e-mails, faxes, text messages, sightings of the stalker, following incidents, receipt of packages, and suspect showing up in front of your house, school, or work. Turn a copy of this log over to the police, but always keep a copy for yourself.

5. Was anyone else present who observed the stalker or overheard his threats? Witnesses are important. Write down the names of any persons, such as neighbors, friends, coworkers, security guards, classmates, family members, mailmen, or delivery persons, who were present during each occurrence.

Give the police the names, phone numbers, and address of the witnesses. Give the witnesses a "heads-up" that the police will be contacting them. Tell them to cooperate with the police; their testimony is very important.

6. When was the last time the suspect met with or tried to contact you, directly or through a third party? Have you initiated any contact with the suspect since the stalking began? Don't be embarrassed if you have, but let the officer know so that we won't have any surprises later on.

7. If you believe that the stalker will physically harm you or other people, explain why. Has he harmed you in the past? Has she been violent toward or made threats against your family members, pets, or friends?

8. Describe a typical day before the stalking conduct started, and a typical day since the stalking began. In other words, what changes have occurred in your life that illustrate your fear and the impact the stalking conduct has had on your life? As a prosecutor, I have to prove that the stalker's conduct and/or words fall outside of First Amendment protection. The only way I can do that is by showing that he or she is engaging in criminal conduct by intentionally trying to terrorize you.

9. If you have obtained a restraining order, note who served it and when, and give a certified copy of the restraining order, and the affidavit you filled out at the time you applied for the restraining order, to the police. Tell the police if there are any other types of court orders in effect or ongoing court proceedings, such as in child custody or divorce matters. Let them know why you originally obtained the restraining order and if you had obtained previous restraining orders against the suspect. Has the stalker violated the order on prior occasions? Was he prosecuted for the violation? If so, note when and where. You are the most important source of information to alert the police if the stalking previously took place in different cities or states. Often the police do not have the resources to know if previous reports have been made in a different jurisdiction.

Make sure to let the officer know if:

- There has been a history of violence between you and the suspect.

- You have any physical evidence, such as phone messages, letters, photographs, e-mails, or medical reports. Turn these items over to the police.

- To your knowledge, the stalker owns any guns or other weapons. (This is also for the officer's safety.)

- The suspect has a history of mental illness and/or drug or alcohol abuse.

- The suspect has been arrested on other occasions. If so, what were the charges? Was the suspect convicted? Be completely honest with the police and prosecutor. *You* cannot shock or embarrass us. However, it will be embarrassing if there is something we don't know and the defense attorney springs it on us at trial.

Reassure the police and prosecutor that you will continue to cooperate fully with them—and mean it.

Be Responsible for Your Own Safety

At Home or in the Community

1. Ask friends and relatives to not give out your information. If someone requests information about you from them, they should tell you immediately. Ask them to get that person's information and you will contact that person if you so desire.

2. Do not destroy, delete, or throw away evidence, such as voice messages, e-mails, letters, or packages:

a. Voice messages: Do not delete them from your system. Find a tape recorder, put the message on speakerphone, and record the message. There is no expectation of a privacy violation if the stalker is stupid enough to leave the message on your voice mail. Often, it's not what is said by the stalker but the *way* it is said that creates the victim's fear.

b. Text messages: Do not delete. Take a photo of the message or phone number if it appears on your screen.

c. E-mails: Do not delete. Keep in your "saved" file. Print out hard copies.

d. Letters: Do not throw away. Place in sealed plastic food bags. Handle on the edges if possible. It doesn't happen often, but occasionally we can get a viable fingerprint from a letter or package.

e. Packages: (See "d" above.) If you are not expecting a package or if the package doesn't have a return address from someone you know, don't open it. Turn it over immediately to the police or your security department.

f. Instant messenger: Take a picture of the screen. These types of messages cannot be saved.

3. Cooperate with law enforcement. In many cases, the problem will not "go away by itself" and could escalate to violence.

4. Do not feel sorry for or make excuses for the stalker. Stalkers are very good at making the victim believe that the victim is being overly sensitive or is to blame for the stalker's conduct. Stalkers rarely, if ever, take responsibility for their own conduct—it's always someone else's fault. Richard Poynton's chilling words to the court at the time of his sentencing, in which he blamed his wife's death on the "war" she and her sisters had started against him, fully illustrates the psychopathy of these criminals. Thomas Agee's frightening voice mails and letters vilifying his victims and blaming them for bringing his threats on themselves further illustrate the stalker's total lack of remorse.

5. Have no contact with the stalker. If you mistakenly pick up the phone and he is on the other end, or she encounters you on the street, say *once*, in no uncertain terms, that you do not want anything to do with him or her. Then hang up the phone or leave immediately. Do not respond to e-mails, letters, text messages, or telephone calls. If the stalker tries to approach you, walk quickly away in the opposite direction. Run and yell if necessary.

6. Do not agree to meet the stalker, even if he promises to leave you alone if you see him one last time. If you do, you could be in physical danger. Janice Sugita lured her victim to a dark and deserted street and came within an inch of killing her. Agreeing to meet with your stalker also empowers him to believe that he can make you do whatever he wishes. We're brought up to be polite, and stalkers capitalize on that. A stalker will call or send a message: "Meet me on the corner or have coffee with me and I'll never bother you again." The victim agrees, thinking this will resolve the problem. But it only reinforces the stalker's mind-set that he or she can control the victim.

7. Never open the door to him—tell him if he doesn't leave, you will call the police. If he doesn't leave, *call the police*.

8. If you are in a car and see him following you, drive to the nearest police station or fire station. Call 911 immediately if he is following you in his car, trying to block your car, or driving erratically. Do not drive home. If you see a police car on the street, honk your horn to get the officer's attention.

9. If there are court orders granting child visitation or joint custody rights, arrange to have the children picked up and dropped off at a neutral party's home or at the local police station. Do not allow the stalker to come to your house or apartment. Do not allow him to manipulate the terms of the custody agreement. If he's calling you a dozen times a day, allegedly to check up on the children's welfare, document the times and frequency of the calls and bring it to the court's

attention. Similarly, if he is repeatedly calling you late at night or becomes verbally abusive, notify the police. Don't let him use the children as an excuse to harass you.

10. Never go alone to any court hearing. Take a friend or family member with you. Your lawyer cannot be with you all the time. If the suspect attempts to approach or talk to you, notify the bailiff immediately.

11. Obtain a restraining order, but be aware that it can be a double-edged sword. On the one hand, it's a tool for law enforcement and the victim. Without it, a stalker can sit across from you at work or school. A restraining order allows police to arrest a stalker on the spot. It also puts the stalker on notice that the victim is afraid, which is a crucial element needed in prosecuting a stalker. The stalker can no longer claim, "I didn't know she didn't want me around."

However, a restraining order is not a magic wand that will make the stalker go away. It is an excellent tool for law enforcement and prosecutors. But many stalkers just consider it an annoying piece of paper and will ignore it. It may also make a stalker angry and violent. Keep in mind that after Richard Poynton murdered his wife, he left behind in his car a copy of the restraining order that she had obtained against him. The final decision whether or not to obtain a restraining order is up to you.

12. Alert your neighbors, friends, and coworkers that you are being stalked. They are extra eyes and ears for your protection. They can warn you if they notice strangers or unfamiliar cars in the neighborhood or at work. In domestic stalking, they might recognize the stalker and warn you if they see him or her. Third parties make excellent witnesses for the prosecution, should the case go to trial.

13. Take a self-defense class. It will not only help you to defend yourself but will empower you and mitigate the feeling of loss of control over your life. If your children are old enough, enroll them in self-defense classes also.

14. Be vigilant about your privacy. For example, have a post office box address printed on your personal checks instead of your home address. Don't give out any personal information, including phone numbers and e-mail address, unless absolutely necessary.

In some states, such as California, if you have a valid police report or restraining order in effect, the state will grant you confidentiality in your voting and/or driving records. Be aware that magazines, catalogs, online shopping sites, and even some banks will sell their subscription lists to third parties, no questions asked.

15. Get a dog—preferably a very loud one. I am not kidding! Dogs have better hearing than humans and can detect someone lurking around your house before you notice anything. If you hear your dog barking, pay attention. Also, a dog deters a stalker because it is human nature to be afraid or more cautious around an aggressive animal.

On the other hand, it is not uncommon in stalking cases for the stalker to commit pet abuse because he knows that it will devastate the victim. He wants to send the message that he is so ruthless that if he can do this to a helpless animal, imagine what he can do to you. If you do have an animal, take extra precautions for its safety, such as keeping it inside the house.

16. Keep a disposable camera at hand in your purse or by your window. If you see your stalker, cautiously take pictures of him. Try not to let him see you taking the pictures.

17. Always carry your cell phone, even on short errands or while using the restroom at work, at school, or in a restaurant. Program the telephone number of your local police department or the detective in charge of your case into your phone. If your children are old enough, provide them with cell phones programmed with your work and home number, 911, and an emergency contact for a trusted relative or family friend.

18. Notify your child's school about the situation and, if possible, give personnel a picture of the stalker and an emergency number where you can be reached.

19. Do not put your child's name on his or her backpack where it can be seen. Do not dress your child in clothing that has his or her name or initials on the outside.

20. Show your children a picture of your stalker or give them a good description of him. Tell them that if they see this person not to talk to him, allow him inside the house, or get close to him. Tell them to run to the first responsible person they see and know, such as a teacher or a neighbor, and report the sighting.

21. Make sure your children understand not to talk to or give personal information to strangers. Establish a code word with your children that will be used in case of emergency. Reinforce the fact that you will never send someone to them who doesn't know the code word. Give the code word to a trusted relative or friend whom you can call if you are in trouble and cannot speak freely.

22. If the stalker leaves threatening, obscene, or other types of intimidating messages on your phone, do not disconnect it. Leave the voice mail on. Don't erase the messages. Do not answer that phone. If possible, get a second phone and only answer that phone. Give that number only to a select number of trusted people.

23. Change your daily routine often. Take different routes to work or school, and change the hours you drive to school, work, or appointments. Don't allow your children to walk to school alone or even with one other friend.

24. Change the locks on all your doors. Put in dead-bolt locks. Install a security system with a panic alarm that goes directly to the police or fire department. Some security systems come with a portable keypad with a panic alarm in case the stalker confronts you in front of your house or as you are getting into your car at home.

25. Trim all trees and bushes around your house so there is no place for the stalker to hide. Don't leave out ladders or

other objects in your yard that the stalker can use to climb into your house.

26. Install a motion-detector light in the front and back of your house.

27. Have an escape plan in place at home and at work. Keep an extra set of keys, a credit card, medication, and cash in one place and keep it close to you at all times in case you have to "run for it." Rehearse your escape plan with your children so they will know what to do in an emergency.

28. Have an unlisted and unpublished telephone number.

Protect Yourself in the Workplace

1. Stalkers know that the easiest place to find their victims is usually at work, because it is much easier for a stalking victim to change his or her home address or phone number than it is to change jobs. Tell your supervisor, Human Resources Department, and trusted coworkers if you are being stalked.

2. Request a parking space close to the door of your office building and ask for an escort to and from your car. A parking lot can be a very solitary and dangerous place.

3. Let the receptionist, security guard, and other people in your office know about your problem so that they don't inadvertently give the stalker information as to your whereabouts or schedule. Your coworkers provide extra eyes and ears around you. Keep a picture of the stalker posted in the front office and at the security desk.

4. If possible, stagger or change your working hours or location to make it more unpredictable. In domestic violence stalking cases, the stalker will often cause disruption in the workplace in an attempt to get the victim fired or have her quit her job because the job represents independence and he wants to regain control and power over her.

5. Have someone screen your calls. Make sure that person doesn't inadvertently give out information about you, such as, "Oh, she just left for lunch at the corner deli. She'll be back by 1:30."

6. Inquire as to whether your Human Resources Department has specialized programs to help employees who are victims of domestic violence and/or stalking. Many larger companies have policies that allow you time to go to court to obtain a restraining order or to testify in a case. Often, they may provide a support person to accompany you to court or provide counseling services. In some states, if the situation is affecting the workplace, the company can obtain a "workplace violence" restraining order that would cover you at work and at home, and also protect your coworkers. It is obtained in the name of the company rather than under your name, so it could deflect some of the stalker's anger away from you.

7. If the stalker is a coworker, report the conduct immediately to your Human Resources Department. If there isn't a Human Resources Department, report it to your supervisor. If your stalker is your supervisor, report it to the next higher level. Request to be transferred to either a different shift or a different location. Document not only the stalker's conduct but the date, time, place, and name of the person to whom you made the report.

8. Don't be embarrassed to let people know that someone is stalking you. It is not your fault. Remember, under OSHA regulations, an employer has a legal duty to provide a safe workplace.

Protect Yourself on Campus
1. Document and report the stalking to your campus police immediately. Give them a description of the stalker and his name, if known.

2. Never remain in a classroom, library, or lab by yourself.

3. If you are out on campus at night, always call the campus police or community service officers for an escort back

to your dorm or car. Most campuses have escort services available twenty-four hours a day. Don't hesitate to call for an escort, even if you've had a drink or two. This is when you are most vulnerable and most in need of assistance. They can call a cab for you if necessary to drive you to your apartment if it is off campus.

4. Make sure the outside doors to your dorm and your dorm room are locked. If you have a roommate, tell her about your situation and impress on her the importance of keeping your door locked and not allowing strangers into your room.

5. If the stalker enrolls in your classes or follows you into a classroom, don't confront him but immediately notify the professor or teacher's assistant. If necessary, report it to the school administration. Let them know if you've filed previous reports with the campus police about the stalker.

6. Tell the administration, your friends, advisors, and trusted professors if you are being stalked. Give them a description of your stalker.

7. Do not give anyone your class schedule; do not post it on any websites.

8. Tell your friends not to give your personal information to strangers or casual acquaintances without your permission.

9. Date rape drugs are becoming more prevalent. Never leave your drink unattended at a party, local bar, or restaurant. Never accept a drink from a stranger.

Protect Yourself from Cyber-stalking*

Cyber-stalkers collect data that they use to locate and terrorize you and the people you care about. A cyber-stalker will spend hours scouring the Internet looking for any byte of information that leads them to their next "fix" of information about you. They

---

*With many thanks to Catherine Monson.

will spend hours looking at image sites for photos, blogs for information about your schedule, and people search sites to find your address and telephone number. Information is everywhere. Be aware that in this technological age, if someone really wants to find you, they can. But you can make it more difficult for them.

Stalkers endanger not only you but the people around you. All the precautions that you take to keep yourself safe online should be taken by the people you associate with. The term "Neighborhood Watch" now incorporates not only those neighbors that you physically live next to but your online neighborhood as well.

1. Do not give out your e-mail address to casual acquaintances or strangers.

2. Get a P.O. box and use it for all your correspondence. Use it when online shopping, when signing up for e-mail accounts, for subscriptions, on your checks, and as a return address. If possible, have all package deliveries sent to your office address.

3. Do not use your real name or date of birth as your online screen name or user ID.

4. Set up multiple e-mail accounts. For example, one for ordering items/giving to people online, one for family and close friends, and another that you can use for acquaintances or people that you don't know that well. Providers such as Gmail or Hotmail allow you to set up multiple free e-mail accounts.

5. Never give your username or password to someone else. Ex-partners or friends that turn into stalkers don't just happen in the movies. Identity theft by a stalker isn't make-believe.

6. Periodically check your credit on sites such as Experian (www.experian.com), Equifax (www.equifax.com), and Transunion (www.transunion.com). These sites may show if someone is using your personal information to apply for credit cards or loans.

7. If you bank online, access your accounts—including checking, savings, and bank-issued credit cards—on a daily basis and look for unauthorized charges or withdrawals. Notify your bank immediately if there are charges or withdrawals that you have not authorized.

8. Keep your personal information off the Internet. Do not publish personal information on Internet sites such as YouTube or MySpace or in chat rooms. It is best to avoid these sites completely. Do not post where you live; your telephone number; your legal name; what type/color/model of car you drive; the names of your spouse, children or pets; where you visit on specific times (I go to dinner every night at____); or pictures of yourself or people that you associate with. If possible, don't let the company that you work for post pictures of you on its website either.

9. Search your name online on various "find someone" websites. If you find your information is listed, notify the company to take your information off their site immediately.

10. Keep copies of all the e-mails you send and receive. Log AIM chats, IRC, et cetera. You never know when you will need to retrieve these communications to establish a course of conduct.

11. Do not use your company/business e-mail account for personal e-mail interactions or shopping online. Not only can you get into trouble with your employer, but many company e-mails contain footers with the location and phone number of where you work. You don't want your stalker to show up at your workplace.

12. Keep a log of every contact you have had with the stalker and after you tell him to stop. Record every instance of contact in your log. This includes e-mails, attempts to IM you, caller ID logs, voice mail, et cetera. When logging Internet communications, include the IP (Internet provider) of the e-mail, IRC contact, et cetera, in your log. Keep every item that you are logging.

13. Save anything that the stalker does online that involves you. For instance, if he blogs about you on his blog page, save that page with what he said on it.

14. Do not close the e-mail account the stalker is attempting to contact you through. Discontinue using it for your other interactions, but allow the e-mail account to stay open to collect any additional attempts at contact the stalker makes.

15. Change all your passwords frequently, including your computer password, your online banking account password, and all your e-mail account passwords. Change to an individual password that you have never used before. Use five letters and at least two numbers in each new password.

16. Report any threats to your Internet provider and the stalker's provider. Most Internet providers have special departments that will investigate inappropriate use of their site.

17. Do not respond to the stalker's e-mails. Do not be drawn into the stalker's attempts to instant message you. If you are in a chat room (which you shouldn't be in in the first place) and the stalker signs on, sign out immediately.

18. Keep your spyware and virus protection up to date. Perform scans frequently.

Commonly Asked Questions about Stalking

Are certain types of people more likely to be stalkers?

People think stalkers have a particular look or profile, such as transients like Robert Hoskins. But anyone can be a stalker, and anyone can be a stalking victim. You can't tell by appearance alone. Although the majority of stalkers are male, there are female stalkers who are just as devious and dangerous. Stalkers can be any age, race, religion, or occupation, rich or poor. In one of my cases, the stalker was a seventy-two-year-old businessman without any previous criminal history. He not only stalked his ex-wife but blew up her motor home and truck with homemade pipe bombs. At trial he tried to portray himself as just an addled old man, but the jury didn't buy it and he was convicted and sent to prison for twelve years. When I told the victim that she no longer had anything to fear, as he would not be released from prison until he was at least eighty years old, she mournfully told me, "That's good, but this man is so mean and evil, he'll probably live to be a hundred years old. And as long as he's alive, he will want to kill me."

Are celebrities more vulnerable to stalking?

It's the opposite actually, but you hear and read more about the celebrity-stalking cases. The media doesn't seem interested in focusing on stalking cases that don't involve famous people. The majority of stalking cases involve average, everyday people, and most are related to cases of domestic violence against women. Studies have been done showing that the majority of women who leave an abusive relationship will be stalked by their former partner. A separate study showed that over 30 percent of women stalked by an intimate after a relationship ended were also stalked during the relationship by the same person.

What should people understand about stalkers?

It's hard to say why some people stalk or develop their fixations. There is no real profile of a stalker. A stalker can be anyone from a crazed transient to a Supreme Court judge. Anything can trigger them. The one thing that all stalkers have in common is that they are driven by obsession, revenge, ego, rejection, or a desire for notoriety. Also, stalkers never think their crimes are their fault. They blame the victim. They even blame the police. They never take responsibility. Stalkers don't get rehabilitated. They often come out of jail or prison more determined than ever. If a stalker does go away, often it's only because they've fixated on a new victim.

Has the Internet made it harder to prosecute stalkers?

Not at all. Law enforcement is becoming much more sophisticated in investigating these types of crimes. However, the problem is the amount of personal information a stalker can easily find about anyone from the Internet. And we are seeing more and more cyber-stalking cases. Before, it would take a stalker a lot of time to send a letter—writing, addressing, and stamping it, then having to take it to the post office. Not any more. All the stalker has to do is write the e-mail and click "send." In Marlon Pagtakhan's case, he flooded Paramount Studios with so many e-mails that it caused its Internet system to crash. Cyber-stalking cases can be especially frightening to the victim because often the identity of the person sending the messages is unknown.

What has changed in the way stalkers are prosecuted?

Plenty. The justice system is just beginning to understand that people are dying because of stalking, and that stalkers are dangerous criminals, not just "pests." In 1990, when California was the first place in the world to enact a stalking law, the law was very weak. Stalking was a misdemeanor unless there was a restraining order in place, which did nothing for the victims because many were too afraid to obtain one. State legislators complained that it would cost too much money to provide more prison space to house stalkers! It took another three years of lobbying to strengthen the law. Among other changes, we were able to get a first-time stalking classified as a felony even if the victim did not have a restraining order. Today, every state, the District of Columbia, and the federal government have some form of stalking law. Canada, Great Britain, Japan, Austria, and now Germany all have criminal stalking laws also.

RESOURCE AND READING LIST

Websites

www.dhs.gov/dhspublic: Latest Homeland Security news, alerts, and emergency planning information.

www.ilj.org: Institute for Law and Justice.

www.ncjrs.gov/pdffiles1/nij/182369.pdf: Bonnie Fisher et al., U.S. Department of Justice, NCJ 182369, *The Sexual Victimization of College Women* (2000).

www.ncvc.org/src/main.aspx: Stalking Resource Center, *"The National Center for Victims of Crime, Stalking Fact Sheet"*—a downloadable fact sheet.

www.ncvc.org/src/main.aspx?db10=dash_home: National Center for Victims of Crime—stalking laws in your state and other resources.

www.prosecutor.info: Find prosecuting agencies from every state.

www.stalkingalert.com: Updated information and articles about stalking and stalking laws.

www.usacops.com: National Law Enforcement Site: Search for state and county police departments, sheriffs' departments, and other law enforcement agencies.

Books and Periodicals

Lim, Kim C., John Rioux, and Ellen Ridley. *Impact of Domestic Violence Offenders on Occupational Safety and Health: A Pilot Study*, 2004: http:www.state.me.us/labor/laborstats/publications/dyreports/domesticoffenders report.pdf.

Meloy, J. Reid, et al. *The Psychology of Stalking: Clinical and Forensic Perspectives*. New York: Academic Press, 1998.

———. *Public Figure Stalking, Threats, and Attacks: The State of the Science*. New York: Oxford University Press, 2008.

Mohandie, Kris, J. Reid Meloy, Mila Green McGowan, and Jenn Williams. "The RECON Typology of Stalking: Reliability and Validity Based upon a Large Sample of North American Stalkers." *Journal of Forensic Sciences* 51 (2006).

Orion, Doreen. *I Know You Really Love Me*. New York: Macmillian, 1997.

Tjaden, Patricia, and Nancy Theonnes. "Extent, Nature, and Consequences of Intimate Partner Violence." Research report. Washington, D.C.: National Institute of Justice, U.S. Department of Justice, 2000.

———. "Stalking in America: Findings from the National Violence Against Women Survey." Research brief. Washington, D.C.: National Institute of Justice, U.S. Department of Justice, 1998.

INDEX